Guided Comprehension
in the
Primary Grades

Maureen McLaughlin
East Stroudsburg University
of Pennsylvania
East Stroudsburg,
Pennsylvania, USA

INTERNATIONAL
**Reading
Association**

800 Barksdale Road, PO Box 8139
Newark, Delaware 19714-8139, USA
www.reading.org

IRA BOARD OF DIRECTORS

Jerry L. Johns, Northern Illinois University, DeKalb, Illinois, President • Lesley Mandel Morrow, Rutgers University, New Brunswick, New Jersey, President-Elect • MaryEllen Vogt, California State University Long Beach, Long Beach, California, Vice President • Rita M. Bean, University of Pittsburgh, Pittsburgh, Pennsylvania • Rebecca L. Olness, Black Diamond, Washington • Doris Walker-Dalhouse, Minnesota State University Moorhead, Moorhead, Minnesota • Patricia L. Anders, University of Arizona, Tucson, Arizona • Timothy V. Rasinski, Kent State University, Kent, Ohio • Ann-Sofie Selin, Cygnaeus School, Åbo, Finland • Cathy Collins Block, Texas Christian University, Fort Worth, Texas • James Flood, San Diego State University, San Diego, California • Victoria J. Risko, Peabody College of Vanderbilt University, Nashville, Tennessee • Alan E. Farstrup, Executive Director

The International Reading Association attempts, through its publications, to provide a forum for a wide spectrum of opinions on reading. This policy permits divergent viewpoints without implying the endorsement of the Association.

Director of Publications   Joan M. Irwin
Editorial Director, Books and Special Projects   Matthew W. Baker
Production Editor   Shannon Benner
Permissions Editor   Janet S. Parrack
Acquisitions and Communications Coordinator   Corinne M. Mooney
Associate Editor, Books and Special Projects   Sara J. Murphy
Assistant Editor   Charlene M. Nichols
Administrative Assistant   Michele Jester
Senior Editorial Assistant   Tyanna L. Collins
Production Department Manager   Iona Sauscermen
Supervisor, Electronic Publishing   Anette Schütz
Senior Electronic Publishing Specialist   Cheryl J. Strum
Electronic Publishing Specialist   R. Lynn Harrison
Proofreader   Elizabeth C. Hunt

Project Editors   Matthew W. Baker and Shannon Benner

Art Credits   Cover Design, Linda Steere
Cover Photos, Leslie Fisher and Linda Brajer; Interior Photos, Leslie Fisher and Karolyn Martin

Copyright 2003 by the International Reading Association, Inc.
All rights reserved. No part of this publication may be reproduced or transmitted in any form or by any means, electronic or mechanical, including photocopy, or any information storage and retrieval system, without permission from the publisher.

Web addresses in this book were correct as of the publication date but may have become inactive or otherwise modified since that time. If you notice a deactivated or changed Web address, please e-mail books@reading.org with the words "Website Update" in the subject line. In your message, specify the Web link, the book title, and the page number on which the link appears.

Library of Congress Cataloging-in-Publication Data
McLaughlin, Maureen.
    Guided comprehension in the primary grades / Maureen McLaughlin.
        p.   cm.
Includes bibliographical references and index.
    ISBN 0-87207-005-0
1. Reading comprehension--Study and teaching (Primary)--United
States--Handbooks, manuals, etc. I. Title.
    LB1525.7 .M35 2003
    372.47--dc21
                                                                    2003004886

For Tom Culliton

CONTENTS

PREFACE

As reading teachers, our ultimate goal is for our students to become good readers—readers who are actively engaged with text and naturally use a repertoire of strategies to facilitate the construction of meaning. We know that comprehension strategies and the skills that underpin them can be taught in the primary grades, yet one of our persistent challenges is finding meaningful ways to teach these essential ideas to our students. Guided Comprehension, a context in which students learn comprehension strategies in a variety of settings using multiple levels of text, provides a viable framework for such instruction.

Guided Comprehension is based on the idea that reading is a thinking process and that the complexity and depth of students' thinking increase as they learn. This means that the repertoires of comprehension strategies that students use to read in the intermediate grades build on and refine the strategies and related skills that they learned in the primary grades. *Guided Comprehension in the Primary Grades* provides a practical framework for such skill and strategy instruction.

The Guided Comprehension Model for the Primary Grades fosters students' transactions with text by integrating direct and guided instruction of comprehension strategies; multiple levels and types of text; and varied, scaffolded opportunities for strategy application. To facilitate the use of the Model in the primary grades, this volume explains what we as teachers can do to help students construct meaning when they read, presents a variety of methods for teaching comprehension strategies in multiple settings, and provides a full range of resources to facilitate the Model's implementation.

Guided Comprehension in the Primary Grades explains the research-based Guided Comprehension Model and how it functions in the primary grades. It describes how to implement the Model, situates it in theme-based contexts, and presents detailed lesson plans to facilitate its use. A wide variety of reproducible resources are also provided and samples of student work are featured throughout the book. The Guided Comprehension Model for the Primary Grades is adapted from the Model that first appeared in *Guided Comprehension: A Teaching Model for Grades 3–8* (McLaughlin & Allen, 2002a) and is designed for use in grades K–3 to parallel primary-grade developmental continuums, state standards, and federal educational emphases.

Part One provides the theoretical framework for Guided Comprehension as well as a detailed explanation of the Model and how it functions. Chapter 1 presents the research-based tenets that underpin Guided Comprehension. The Guided Comprehension Model for the Primary Grades is delineated in Chapter 2. Chapters 3 and 4 offer in-depth information about organizing and managing comprehension centers and routines, including descriptions of a variety of centers and primary-classroom models of routines such as Literature Circles, Reciprocal Teaching, and Cross-Age Reading Experiences. Chapter 5 focuses on practical assessments and using assessment results to make meaningful matches between students and leveled texts. Numerous reproducible blackline masters support these chapters.

In Part Two, Guided Comprehension is situated in four themes: Favorite Author Eric Carle; The Neverending Adventures of Arthur the Aardvark; Animals, Animals; and Dinosaur Discoveries. Each theme-based chapter features multiple primary-level lessons as well as a variety of resources and examples of student work. The lessons, which were developed and taught by primary-grade teachers, are presented through first-person commentaries. Each of these chapters includes the following components:

- theme description
- theme-based plan for Guided Comprehension
- planning forms
- three teacher-designed Guided Comprehension lessons
- teacher-authored lesson commentaries
- samples of student work
- theme-based resources including teaching ideas, related texts, websites, performance extensions across the curriculum, and culminating activities

In Chapter 10, resources for situating Guided Comprehension in additional themes—including The Ocean, Poetry, Transportation, and Weather—are provided. This chapter also features practical forms for planning themes and lessons based on the Guided Comprehension Model.

The appendixes contain a variety of resources for teaching Guided Comprehension. These include a literacy continuum for the primary grades; teaching ideas and booklists focused on phonemic awareness, phonics, fluency, vocabulary, and comprehension—the emphases of the National Reading Panel report (National Institute of Child Health and Human Development [NICHD], 2000) and other recent U.S. government publications and legislation; comprehension-based teaching ideas and blackline masters; resources for organizing and managing comprehension centers and routines; assessment blackline masters; sources of leveled narrative and expository texts; and ideas for making home-school connections.

Guided Comprehension in the Primary Grades is designed to be a focused and easily accessed comprehensive resource for classroom teachers, staff developers, Title I reading specialists, curriculum coordinators, and teacher educators. It contains everything necessary to teach comprehension strategies in the primary grades.

ACKNOWLEDGMENTS

As always, there are many people to thank for making this book possible. I express appreciation to all who contributed to the manuscript's development. I am especially thankful for their enthusiasm for the project, their willingness to be action researchers, and their amazing ability to find humor in tension-filled moments.

I am particularly grateful to the following people:

- Leslie Fisher and the first-grade students of Nixon Elementary School, Roxbury School District, New Jersey
- Leala Baxter and the first-grade students of Allamuchy Elementary School, Allamuchy School District, New Jersey
- Karolyn Martin and the first-grade students of Kennedy Elementary School, Roxbury School District, New Jersey

- Victoria Principe and the second-grade students of Arlington Elementary School, Stroudsburg School District, Pennsylvania

- Stacey Bardonnex and the first-grade students of Arlington Elementary School, Stroudsburg School District, Pennsylvania

- Samantha Shyka and the second- and third-grade students of Athlone School, St. James Assiniboia School Division # 2, Winnipeg, Manitoba, Canada

- Tanya Kubrakovich and the kindergarten students of Athlone School, St. James Assiniboia School Division # 2, Winnipeg, Manitoba, Canada

- other primary-grade teachers and their students who participated in my research study and contributed lessons and student examples to this volume: Jennifer Barrett, Kimberly Burke, Lynn Foerster, Sharon Gilroy, Melissa Gleason, Amy Homeyer, Diane Kaminski, Heather Kretschmer, Tom McLaughlin, Stacey Meckes, Julie Mignosi, Maren Moseley, Paige Nish, Tina Rava, Kerry Safin, Jennifer Sassaman, Michael Sauers, and Melinda Yurick

- graduate assistants Judy Mesko, Jean Sandberg, Molly Brundage, Denise Delp, and Jenna Macciocco, and student assistants Stacey Sharek, Kelly Jo Smith, and Christine Krisovitch

- Mary Roehrenbeck and Francesca Roehrenbeck

- my colleague, Stephanie Romano

- Mary Beth Allen, cocreator of the Guided Comprehension Model and coauthor of *Guided Comprehension: A Teaching Model for Grades 3–8* and *Guided Comprehension in Action: Lessons for Grades 3–8*

- Shannon Benner, IRA production editor

- Matt Baker, IRA editorial director, for his insight, encouragement, and unparalleled editorial expertise

Finally, I thank you for your continued interest in the search for effective ways to curricularize the teaching of reading comprehension strategies. I hope that you find this book to be a valuable resource in enhancing your students' engagement with and understanding of text.

MM

PART ONE

Guided Comprehension: A Teaching Model for the Primary Grades

Focus: A detailed description of the Guided Comprehension Model for the Primary Grades and how the Model functions, including its research base, multiple stages, organization and management, assessment connections, and use of leveled text.

Theoretical Underpinnings: In Chapter 1, 10 research-based tenets demonstrate the Model's emergence from research and current beliefs about best practice.

The Guided Comprehension Model for the Primary Grades: In Chapter 2, the Model is explained and the comprehension strategies and related teaching ideas are presented.

Comprehension Centers: A wide variety of ideas for centers and related center activities are described in Chapter 3. Organizing and managing the comprehension centers is a special emphasis.

Comprehension Routines: Literature Circles, Reciprocal Teaching, and Cross-Age Reading Experiences are explained and teaching models from primary classrooms are presented in Chapter 4.

Assessment and Leveled Texts: In the first part of Chapter 5, the multiple roles of assessment in Guided Comprehension are discussed, connections are made to state assessments, a variety of assessments are described, and the Guided Comprehension Profile is introduced. In the second half of the chapter, the roles of leveled text are discussed, methods of leveling are presented, and the role of assessment in creating student-text matches is delineated.

CHAPTER 1

Reading Comprehension in the Primary Grades

As primary-grade teachers, we want our students to become active, engaged readers. We want them to be motivated to listen to and read a variety of texts and use a repertoire of strategies to construct meaning. We want to hear them giggle when they read Shel Silverstein's poetry and Jon Scieszka's humorous transformations of traditional fairy tales. We want to hear them express their emotions when they read Eve Bunting's *Wednesday Surprise* or *Fly Away Home*. We want to see their looks of amazement as they read Seymour Simon's *Wolves* or Gail Gibbons's *Sea Turtles*. We want to see their faces bursting with pride as they read sentences and stories they have written or share their ideas in discussion. Helping students to become active, strategic readers is a challenging process, but to be successful, one aspect is clear: We need to teach comprehension skills and strategies right from the start. The Guided Comprehension Model for the Primary Grades, a teaching framework in which students learn comprehension skills and strategies in a variety of settings using multiple levels and types of text, provides a viable format for such instruction.

Reading comprehension researchers including Duke and Pearson (2002), Hilden and Pressley (2002), and Pressley (2001) note that reading comprehension strategies can be taught in the primary grades. Pressley (2001) suggests that students begin learning comprehension skills and a few strategies as early as kindergarten. Pearson (2001b) reports that the three most important things we have learned about comprehension in the past 30 years are that (1) students benefit from using comprehension strategies and routines; (2) having opportunities to read, write, and talk matters; and (3) knowledge helps comprehension by providing a starting point—where readers are and what they know.

A variety of other sources support the need to teach comprehension strategies in the primary grades. The Continuum of Children's Development in Early Reading and Writing in *Learning to Read and Write: Developmentally Appropriate Practices for Young Children* (International Reading Association & National Association for the Education of Young Children [IRA & NAEYC], 1998) suggests that students use reading skills and strategies as early as kindergarten (see Appendix A). Continuums that delineate students' achievement of state standards, authored by educational teams such as the Pennsylvania Department of Education and Pennsylvania Association of Intermediate Units' *Early Childhood Learning Continuum Indicators* (Partnership for Educational Excellence Network, 2001), also support students' learning reading comprehension strategies in the primary grades (see http://www.pde.state.pa.us/nclb/lib/nclb/earlychildhoodcontinuum.pdf).

Further, the National Reading Panel (NICHD, 2000) suggests that we focus our teaching on five areas: phonemic awareness, phonics, fluency, vocabulary, and comprehension. U.S. federal documents such as *Put Reading First: The Research Building Blocks for Teaching Children to Read* (Partnership for Reading, 2001) also promote these aspects of literacy as components of good first teaching. Students' understanding of the first four areas contributes to comprehension, so it is only logical to include such aspects of literacy when discussing reading comprehension in the primary grades. And although the National Reading Panel emphases permeate the Guided Comprehension themed lessons, a variety of resources for phonemic awareness, phonics, fluency, and vocabulary—including definitions, practical teaching ideas, and related resources—are included in Appendix B.

In this chapter, Guided Comprehension's natural emergence from current research is delineated. To illustrate this relationship, 10 research-based comprehension tenets are presented. Each is followed by a brief discussion of its relationship to the Guided Comprehension Model for the Primary Grades (see Chapter 2).

TENETS OF READING COMPREHENSION

Studies have shown that multiple factors affect successful reading comprehension. The following research-based tenets describe the current most influential elements (McLaughlin & Allen, 2002a):

- Comprehension is a social constructivist process.
- Balanced literacy is an instructional framework that fosters comprehension.
- Excellent reading teachers influence students' learning.
- Good readers are strategic and take active roles in the reading process.
- Reading should occur in meaningful contexts.
- Students benefit from transacting daily with a variety of texts at multiple levels.
- Vocabulary development and instruction affect reading comprehension.
- Engagement is a key factor in the comprehension process.
- Comprehension strategies and skills can be taught.
- Dynamic assessment informs comprehension instruction.

Although the tenets have strong research underpinnings, they are also designed to inform instruction. In the section that follows, each tenet is discussed and connections are made between theory and practice.

Comprehension Is a Social Constructivist Process

From a constructivist perspective, learning is understood as "a self-regulated process of resolving inner cognitive conflicts that often become apparent through concrete experience, collaborative discourse, and reflection" (Brooks & Brooks, 1993, p. vii). Constructivists believe that learners make sense of their world by connecting what they know and have experienced with what they are learning. They construct meaning through these connections when educators pose relevant problems, structure learning around primary concepts, seek and value students' ideas, and assess students' learning in context (Brooks & Brooks, 1993).

According to Short and Burke (1996), constructivism frees students of fact-driven curricula and encourages them to focus on larger ideas, allows students to reach unique conclusions and reformulate ideas, encourages students to see the world as a complex place with multiple perspectives, and emphasizes that students are responsible for their own learning and should attempt to connect the information they learn to the world around them through inquiry.

Cambourne (2002) notes that constructivism has three core theoretical assumptions:

- What is learned cannot be separated from the context in which it is learned.
- The purposes or goals that the learner brings to the learning situation are central to what is learned.
- Knowledge and meaning are socially constructed through the processes of negotiation, evaluation, and transformation. (p. 26)

Constructivists believe that students construct knowledge by linking what is new to what is already known. In reading, this concept is reflected in schema-based learning development, which purports that learning takes place when new information is integrated with what is already known. The more experience learners have with a particular topic, the easier it is for them to make connections between what they know and what they are learning (Anderson, 1994; Anderson & Pearson, 1984). From a constructivist perspective, comprehension is viewed as

> the construction of meaning of a written or spoken communication through a reciprocal, holistic interchange of ideas between the interpreter and the message in a particular communicative context. Note: The presumption here is that meaning resides in the intentional problem-solving, thinking processes of the interpreter during such an interchange, that the content of meaning is influenced by that person's prior knowledge and experience, and that the message so constructed by the receiver may or may not be congruent with the message sent. (Harris & Hodges, 1995, p. 39)

Vygotsky's principles enhance the constructivist perspective by addressing the social context of learning (Dixon-Krauss, 1996). According to Vygotsky, students should be taught within their zones of proximal development (Forman & Cazden, 1994; Vygotsky, 1934/1978). Instruction within the zone should incorporate both scaffolding and social mediation. As Dixon-Krauss notes when explaining this Vygotskian principle, "It is through social dialogue with adults and/or more capable peers that language concepts are learned" (p. 155). Such social interaction encourages students to think and share their ideas.

Constructivism is manifested in classrooms that are characterized by student-generated ideas, self-selection, creativity, interaction, critical thinking, and personal construction of meaning (McLaughlin, 2000b). In such contexts, authentic literacy tasks assimilate real-world experiences, provide a purpose for learning, and encourage students to take ownership of learning (Hiebert, 1994; Newmann & Wehlage, 1993).

Guided Comprehension connection: The Guided Comprehension Model is based on the view of comprehension as a social constructivist process. This is evinced in the Model in numerous ways including the ultimate goal of students' transaction with text and the value placed on learning in a variety of social settings.

Balanced Literacy Is an Instructional Framework That Fosters Comprehension

Balanced literacy is a curriculum framework that

> gives reading and writing equal status and recognizes the importance of both cognitive and affective dimensions of literacy. It acknowledges the meaning-making involved in the full processes of reading and writing, while recognizing the importance of the strategies and skills used by proficient readers and writers. (Au, Carroll, & Scheu, 1997, p. 4)

Authentic texts, print-rich environments, and opportunities to read, write, and discuss for a variety of purposes characterize balanced literacy classrooms. Pearson (2001) suggests that the model of comprehension instruction supported by current research actually does more than balance these learning opportunities: It connects and integrates them.

In this integrated view, reading, writing, and discussion are all thinking processes focused on the construction of meaning. They are response related and promote students' transactions with texts and others. Both direct and indirect instruction are valued components of balanced literacy. In this context, direct instruction is characterized by the teacher purposefully interacting with students and taking an active role in promoting their acquisition of skills and strategies by explaining, modeling, and guiding (Almasi, 1996; Dahl & Farnan, 1998; Duffy et al., 1987; Roehler & Duffy, 1984). Indirect instruction affords students opportunities to make discoveries without teacher guidance (Au et al., 1997).

Balanced literacy has cognitive, social, and affective dimensions. It promotes higher order thinking, interaction, personal response, and comprehension. Situating teaching and learning within this curriculum framework creates an optimal environment for engagement.

Guided Comprehension connection: Guided Comprehension is naturally situated in the framework of balanced literacy for numerous reasons. These include the following shared beliefs: Reading is a meaning-making process; reading, writing, and discussion are integrated; both cognitive and affective aspects of literacy have value; student ownership of learning is critical; and the explicit teaching of comprehension skills and strategies is essential.

Excellent Reading Teachers Influence Students' Learning

Excellent reading teachers are valued participants in the learning process. As the National Commission on Teaching and America's Future (1997) has reported, the single most important strategy for achieving U.S. education goals is to recruit, prepare, and support excellent teachers for every school.

It is the knowledge of the teacher that makes a difference in student success (IRA, 1999). A knowledgeable teacher is aware of what is working well and what each student needs to be successful, and he or she knows the importance of every student having successful literacy experiences.

The teacher's role in the reading process is to create experiences and environments that introduce, nurture, or extend students' literacy abilities to engage with text. This requires that teachers engage in explicit instruction, modeling, scaffolding, facilitating, and participating (Au & Raphael, 1998).

Both reading researchers and professional organizations have delineated the characteristics of excellent reading teachers (Fountas & Pinnell, 1996; IRA, 2000; Ruddell, 1995). The following characterization of such reading teachers integrates these ideas.

Excellent reading teachers believe that all children can learn. They base their teaching on the needs of the individual learner. They know that motivation and multiple kinds of text are essential elements of teaching and learning. They understand that reading is a social constructivist process that functions best in authentic situations. They teach in print-rich, concept-rich environments.

Such teachers have in-depth knowledge of various aspects of literacy, including reading, writing, and discussion. They teach for a variety of purposes, using diverse methods, materials, and grouping patterns to focus on individual needs, interests, and learning styles. They also know the strategies good readers use, and they can teach students how to use them.

Excellent reading teachers view their teaching as multifaceted and they view themselves as participants in the learning process. They integrate their knowledge of the learning cycle, learning styles, and multiple intelligences into their teaching.

These teachers understand the natural relationship between assessment and instruction, and they assess in multiple ways for a variety of purposes. They use instructional strategies that provide formative feedback to monitor the effectiveness of teaching and student performance. They know that assessment informs both teaching and learning.

Guided Comprehension connection: Teachers who engage in Guided Comprehension are knowledgeable not only about the concept but also about their students. They know that students read at different levels, and they know how to use the Guided Comprehension Model to accommodate each reader's needs. These educators are participants in the reading process. They know how to use a variety of materials in a variety of ways, within a variety of settings. Guided Comprehension provides a context for such teaching.

Good Readers Are Strategic and Take Active Roles in the Reading Process

Numerous reading researchers have reported that much of what we know about comprehension is based on studies of good readers (Askew & Fountas, 1998; Duke & Pearson, 2002; Keene & Zimmermann, 1997; Pearson, 2001a; Pressley, 2000). They describe good readers as active participants in the reading process who have clear goals and constantly monitor the relation between the goals they have set and the text they are reading. Good readers use comprehension strategies to facilitate the construction of meaning. In Guided Comprehension, these strategies include the following: previewing, self-questioning, making connections, visualizing, knowing how words work, monitoring, summarizing, and evaluating. Researchers believe that using a repertoire of such strategies helps students become metacognitive readers (Duke & Pearson, 2002; Keene & Zimmermann, 1997; Palincsar & Brown, 1984; Roehler & Duffy, 1984).

Good readers read from aesthetic or efferent stances and have an awareness of the author's style and purpose (Rosenblatt, 1978, 2002). They read both narrative and expository texts and have ideas about how to figure out unfamiliar words. They use their knowledge of text structure to efficiently and strategically process text. This knowledge develops from experiences with different genres and is correlated with age or time in school (Goldman & Rakestraw, 2000).

These readers spontaneously generate questions at different points in the reading process for a variety of reasons (Keene & Zimmermann, 1997). They know that they use questioning in their everyday lives and that it increases their comprehension. Good readers are problem solvers who have the ability to discover new information for themselves.

Good readers read widely. This provides exposure to various genres and text formats, affords opportunities for strategy use, increases understanding of how words work, provides bases for discussion and meaning negotiation, and accommodates students' interests.

Good readers construct and revise meaning as they read. They monitor their comprehension and know when they are constructing meaning and when they are not. When comprehension breaks down due to lack of background information, difficulty of words, or unfamiliar text structure, good readers know a variety of fix-up strategies to use. These strategies include rereading, changing the pace of reading, using context clues, cross-checking cueing systems, and asking for help. Most important, good readers are able to select the appropriate strategies and to consistently focus on making sense of text and gaining new understandings.

Guided Comprehension connection: Helping students to become active, strategic readers is the ultimate goal of Guided Comprehension, and students fully participate in the process. Students' roles are extensive and include engaging in comprehension as a thinking process and transacting with various levels of text in multiple settings. Students then incorporate the strategies they learn into their existing repertoire and use them as needed.

Reading Should Occur in Meaningful Contexts

Lipson and Wixson (2003) suggest that the context is a broad concept that encompasses instructional environments, settings, resources, and practices. Duke (2001) proposes that we view context as including curriculum, activity, classroom environment, teaching, talk, text, and society.

More specific, literacy-based descriptions of context include ideas offered by Gambrell (1996a), Hiebert (1994), and Pearson (2001a), who suggest that the classroom context is characterized by authentic opportunities to read, write, and discuss. They further note that the instruction of skills and strategies, integration of concept-driven vocabulary, use of multiple genres, and knowledge of various text structures are other contextual components.

Guided Comprehension connection: Guided Comprehension is a context for learning. Its three stages incorporate a variety of settings, resources, approaches, and tasks.

Students Benefit From Transacting Daily With a Variety of Texts at Multiple Levels

Students need to engage daily with multiple levels of texts. When such levels of text are being used, teachers scaffold learning experiences and students receive varying levels of support, depending on the purpose and context of the reading. When text is challenging, students have full teacher support. For example, teachers can share the text through read-aloud. When the text is just right for instruction, students have support as needed, with the teacher prompting/responding when required. Finally, when the text is just right for independent reading, little or no support is needed.

Transacting with a wide variety of genres enhances students' understanding. Experience reading multiple genres provides students with knowledge of numerous text structures and improves their text-driven processing (Goldman & Rakestraw, 2000). Gambrell (2001) notes that transacting with a wide variety of genres—including biography, historical fiction, legends, poetry, and brochures—increases students' reading performance.

Guided Comprehension connection: In Guided Comprehension, students have opportunities to engage with a variety of texts at independent, instructional, and challenging levels on a daily basis.

Vocabulary Development and Instruction Affect Reading Comprehension

Vocabulary instruction, another valued component of balanced literacy, has strong ties to reading comprehension. As the National Reading Panel (NICHD, 2000) notes, "Reading comprehension is a complex, cognitive process that cannot be understood without a clear description of the role that vocabulary development and vocabulary instruction play in the understanding of what has been read" (p. 13). Snow, Burns, and Griffin (1998) support this view, observing, "Learning new concepts and words that encode them is essential to comprehension development" (p. 217).

In their review of the existing research, Blachowicz and Fisher (2000) identify four guidelines for vocabulary instruction. They note that students should (1) be actively engaged in understanding words and related strategies, (2) personalize their vocabulary learning, (3) be immersed in words, and (4) develop their vocabularies through repeated exposures from multiple sources of information.

Baumann and Kameenui (1991) suggest that direct instruction and learning from context should be balanced. The instruction should be meaningful to students, include words from students' reading, and focus on a variety of strategies for determining the meanings of unfamiliar words (Blachowicz & Lee, 1991). Another important aspect of such teaching is making connections between the vocabulary and students' background knowledge.

Vocabulary growth is also influenced by the amount and variety of text students read (Baumann & Kameenui, 1991; Beck & McKeown, 1991; Snow et al., 1998). Teacher read-alouds, which offer students access to a variety of levels of text, contribute to this process (Hiebert, Pearson, Taylor, Richardson, & Paris, 1998).

Guided Comprehension connection: In Guided Comprehension, students are immersed in words. They engage daily with texts at multiple levels in a variety of settings, and they learn words through both direct instruction and use of context. They also learn vocabulary strategies in scaffolded settings that provide numerous opportunities for practice and application, paired and group reading, and teacher read-alouds.

Engagement Is a Key Factor in the Comprehension Process

The engagement perspective on reading integrates cognitive, motivational, and social aspects of reading (Baker, Afflerbach, & Reinking, 1996; Baker & Wigfield, 1999; Guthrie & Alvermann, 1999). Engaged learners achieve because they want to understand, they possess intrinsic motivations for interacting with text, they use cognitive skills to understand, and they share knowledge by talking with teachers and peers (Guthrie & Wigfield, 1997).

Engaged readers transact with print and construct understandings based on connections between prior knowledge and new information. Tierney (1990) describes the process of the mind's eye and suggests readers become part of the story within their minds. Teachers can nurture and extend this by encouraging students to read for authentic purposes and respond in meaningful ways, always focusing on comprehension, personal connections, and reader response. Baker and Wigfield (1999) note that "engaged readers are motivated to read for different purposes, utilize knowledge gained from previous experience to generate new understandings, and participate in meaningful social interactions around reading" (p. 453).

Gambrell (1996a) suggests that "classroom cultures that foster reading motivation are characterized by a teacher who is a reading model, a book-rich classroom environment, opportunities for choice, familiarity with books, and literacy-related incentives that reflect the value of reading" (p. 20). Gambrell, Palmer, Codling, and Mazzoni (1996) note that highly motivated readers read for a wide variety of reasons including curiosity, involvement, social interchange, and emotional satisfaction.

Motivation is described in terms of competence and efficacy beliefs, goals for reading, and social purposes of reading (Baker & Wigfield, 1999). Motivated readers believe they can be successful and are willing to take on the challenge of difficult reading material. They also exhibit intrinsic reasons for reading, such as gaining new knowledge about a topic or enjoying the reading experience. Motivated readers enjoy the social aspects of sharing with others new meanings gained from their reading.

Guided Comprehension connection: The Guided Comprehension Model is based on students' active engagement. Guided Comprehension is a cognitive experience because students think through the reading process, it is motivational because students' interests and opportunities for success are embedded in the Model, and it is social because students interact with teachers and peers on a daily basis.

Comprehension Strategies and Skills Can Be Taught

Durkin's research in the late 1970s reported that little if any comprehension instruction occurred in classrooms. Instead, comprehension questions, often at the literal level, were assigned and then corrected; comprehension was assessed but not taught. Recent studies have demonstrated that explicit instruction of comprehension strategies improves students' comprehension of new texts and topics (Hiebert et al., 1998). As previously noted, Guided Comprehension strategies include the following:

- previewing—activating background knowledge, predicting, and setting a purpose
- self-questioning—generating questions to guide reading
- making connections—relating reading to self, text, and others
- visualizing—creating mental images while reading
- knowing how words work—understanding words through strategic vocabulary development, including the use of the graphophonic, syntactic, and semantic cue systems to figure out unknown words

- monitoring—asking "Does this make sense?" and clarifying by adapting strategic processes to accommodate the response

- summarizing—synthesizing important ideas

- evaluating—making judgments

Duffy (2001) notes that comprehension strategies can be taught, and Duke and Pearson (2002) concur. In fact, Duke and Pearson suggest using balanced comprehension instruction, which incorporates "both explicit instruction in specific comprehension strategies and a great deal of time and opportunity for actual reading, writing, and discussion of text" (p. 206). Pressley (2001) states that comprehension instruction should begin in the early grades with the teaching of comprehension skills, such as sequencing and questioning, and a few strategies, such as predicting and summarizing, occurring as early as kindergarten.

Linking skills and strategies can facilitate comprehension. Comprehension strategies are generally more complex than skills and often require the orchestration of several skills. Effective instruction links comprehension skills to strategies to promote strategic reading. For example, the comprehension skills of sequencing, making judgments, noting details, making generalizations, and using text structure can be linked to summarizing, which is a comprehension strategy (Lipson, 2001). These and other skills including generating questions, making inferences, distinguishing between important and less important ideas, and drawing conclusions facilitate students' use of one or more comprehension strategies. For example, students' ability to generate questions permeates all the Guided Comprehension strategies. (See Chapter 2, particularly Figure 2 on page 20, for more detailed information about questioning.)

Fielding and Pearson (1994) recommend a framework for comprehension instruction that encourages the release of responsibility from teacher to student. This four-step approach includes teacher modeling, guided practice, independent practice, and application of the strategy in authentic reading situations. This framework is supported by Vygotsky's (1934/1978) work on instruction within the zone of proximal development and by scaffolding, the gradual relinquishing of support as the students become more competent in using the strategy.

After explaining and modeling strategies, teachers scaffold instruction to provide the support necessary as students attempt new tasks. During this process teachers gradually release responsibility for learning to the students, who, after practicing the strategies in a variety of settings, apply them independently.

Guided Comprehension connection: This tenet is a core underpinning of Guided Comprehension because the Model is designed to promote comprehension as a strategy-based thinking process. It incorporates the explicit teaching of comprehension strategies and the skills that enable their use. The Model also provides multiple opportunities for practice and transfer of learning.

Dynamic Assessment Informs Comprehension Instruction

Dynamic assessment captures students' performance as they engage in the process of learning. It is continuous, provides an ongoing record of student growth, and has the ability to afford insights into students' understandings at any given point in the learning experience. Dynamic assessment reflects constructivist theory and is viewed not as an add-on but rather as a natural component of teaching and learning (Brooks & Brooks, 1993).

Dynamic assessments, which are usually informal in nature, can be used in a variety of instructional settings. This includes scaffolded learning experiences in which students have varying degrees of teacher support. Assessing in this context captures the students' emerging abilities and provides insights that may not be gleaned from independent settings (Minick, 1987).

Guided Comprehension connection: Assessment permeates the Guided Comprehension Model, occurring for multiple purposes in a variety of settings. Dynamic assessment provides insights into students' thinking as they engage in all stages of the Model. This, in turn, informs future teaching and learning.

As delineated in this chapter, the Guided Comprehension Model for the Primary Grades has a sound theoretical framework. It is dynamic in nature and accommodates students' individual needs, employs a variety of texts and settings, and uses active, ongoing assessment. Chapter 2 details the Model by describing its three stages: teacher-directed whole-group instruction, teacher-guided small-group instruction and student-facilitated independent practice, and teacher-facilitated whole-group reflection and goal setting.

The Guided Comprehension Model for the Primary Grades

Guided Comprehension is a context in which students learn comprehension skills and strategies in a variety of settings using multiple levels and types of text. It is a three-stage process focused on direct instruction, application, and reflection. In Stage One, teachers use a five-step direct instruction process: explain, demonstrate, guide, practice, and reflect. In Stage Two, students apply the strategies in three settings: teacher-guided small groups, student-facilitated comprehension centers, and student-facilitated comprehension routines. In Stage Three, teachers and students engage in reflection and goal setting. Student engagement with leveled text and placement in small groups are dynamic and evolve as students' reading abilities increase.

The Guided Comprehension Model for the Primary Grades is a framework designed to help teachers and students think through reading as a strategy-based process. The Model is based on existing research, knowledge of best practice, and personal experience. It integrates the following:

- direct instruction of comprehension strategies
- leveled independent, instructional, and challenging texts
- dynamic assessment
- scaffolded instruction (varying levels of teacher support, with eventual relinquishing of control to students)
- various genres and text types
- reading, writing, and discussion
- strategy instruction and application in a variety of settings
- independent practice and transfer of learning in multiple settings
- reflection and goal setting

THE GUIDED COMPREHENSION MODEL

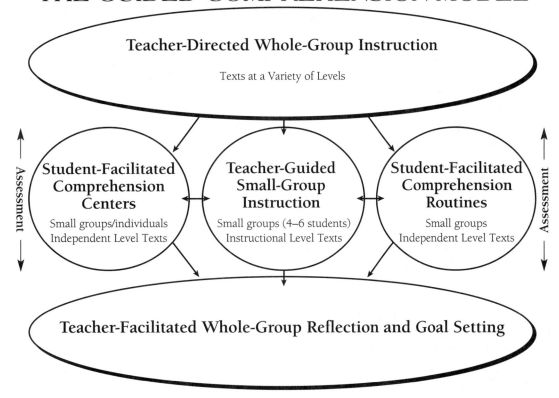

Structurally, the Model has three stages that progress in the following sequence:

Stage One: teacher-directed whole-group instruction

Stage Two: teacher-guided small-group instruction and student-facilitated independent practice

Stage Three: teacher-facilitated whole-group reflection and goal setting

Naturally situated within the context of balanced literacy, the Guided Comprehension Model is active for both teachers and students. For example, teachers engage in direct instruction and select texts and strategies based on student needs, which are assessed continually. Teachers also participate by facilitating students' engagement in reading, writing, and discussion. Students' active roles in Guided Comprehension include thinking through the reading process, using strategies, transacting with text in multiple settings, and responding in a variety of ways.

The Guided Comprehension Model includes opportunities for whole-group, small-group, paired, and individual literacy experiences. Students transact daily with texts at a variety of levels. Teachers direct whole-group instruction, explicitly teach comprehension skills and strategies, and work daily with Guided Comprehension small groups. Teachers also observe and assess students as they engage in their independent comprehension activities.

The Model progresses from explicit teaching to independent application and transfer (see Figure 1). All stages of the Model are necessary to ensure that students can independently apply comprehension strategies in multiple settings. Assessment permeates every aspect of the Model, facilitating the gathering of information about student progress, which continually informs teaching and learning.

Figure 1. Overview of Guided Comprehension Instruction in the Primary Grades

STAGE ONE

Teacher-Directed Whole-Group Instruction—Teaching a comprehension strategy using easy, just right, or challenging text.

Explain the strategy of the day and how it relates to the class goal.

Demonstrate the strategy using a Think-Aloud and read-aloud.

Guide student practice by reading additional sections of text aloud and having students apply the strategy with support. Monitor students' applications.

Practice by having students apply the strategy to another section of text you have read, providing minimal support. Applications can occur in small groups or pairs.

Reflect by having students think about how they can use this strategy on their own.

STAGE TWO

Students apply the comprehension strategies in teacher-guided small groups and student-facilitated comprehension centers and routines. In these settings, students work with varying levels of support and use appropriate instructional and independent level texts.

Teacher-Guided Small-Group Instruction—Applying comprehension strategies with teacher guidance using instructional level texts and dynamic grouping (four to six students).

Review previously taught strategies and focus on strategy of the day.

Guide the students to apply the strategy of the day as well as previously taught strategies as they read sections of the instructional level (just right) text or the text in its entirety. Prompt the students to construct and share personal meanings. Scaffold as necessary, gradually releasing support as students become more proficient. Encourage discussion and repeat with other sections of text.

Practice by having students work in pairs or individually to apply the strategy. Encourage discussion. Have students record their strategy applications in their Guided Comprehension Journals and share them during reflection in either small or large groups.

Reread, Retell, and Reflect by having students engage in a second reading of the text, retell what they read, and share ways in which the strategy helped them to understand the text. Talk about ways in which students can apply the strategy in comprehension centers and routines.

Student-Facilitated Comprehension Centers and Routines—Applying comprehension strategies individually, in pairs, or in small groups using independent level (easy) texts.

Comprehension Centers are independent activities that provide opportunities to practice strategy application and extend understandings.

Comprehension Routines are procedures that foster habits of thinking and promote the comprehension of text.

STAGE THREE

Teacher-Facilitated Whole-Group Reflection and Goal Setting—Reflecting on performance, sharing experiences, and setting new goals.

Share performances from Stage Two.

Reflect on ability to use the strategy.

Set new goals or extend existing ones.

ASSESSMENT OPTIONS

Use authentic measures in all stages.

(adapted for the primary grades from McLaughlin & Allen, 2002a)

The Guided Comprehension Model for the Primary Grades is adapted from the original Guided Comprehension Model, which was developed for grades 3–8 (McLaughlin & Allen, 2002a). The primary-grade Model differs from the original Model in a number of ways. First, shared reading and interactive read-alouds are often integrated into direct instruction in this Model. Second, teacher-guided small-group instruction has been expanded to include rereading and retelling. The comprehension centers include a variety of language-based activities. The comprehension routines have also been adapted; they now include Literature Circles, Reciprocal Teaching, and Cross-Age Reading Experiences.

STAGE ONE: TEACHER-DIRECTED WHOLE-GROUP INSTRUCTION

In Stage One of Guided Comprehension, the teacher engages in direct instruction by using a five-step process: explain, demonstrate, guide, practice, and reflect. The class is organized as a whole group during the first two steps, but flexible grouping occurs in the guide and practice steps. Stage One concludes with whole-class reflection. During this stage, the level of text may be easy, just right, or challenging because the teacher is reading aloud.

Organizing for Stage One

In Stage One of the Model, whole-group instruction provides students with a positive sense of belonging to a community of learners. The sense of community is fostered by student-teacher and student-peer interactions, print-rich environments, opportunities to engage with authentic texts from a variety of genres, students who are active learners, and teachers who are knowledgeable about their students and current best practice.

Because the instruction in Stage One of Guided Comprehension is teacher directed and allows us to fully support student learning, we can choose to teach from texts that range in level from easy to challenging. For example, if we choose a text that is interesting to the students and works well when teaching a particular strategy but is challenging in nature, we can share it with students through a read-aloud.

Engaging in Direct Instruction

In working with a wide variety of literacy professionals, I have heard many note that reading educators often describe teaching comprehension strategies as "going over" the strategies with students or "telling" the students about the strategies. Effectively teaching comprehension strategies requires more than "going over" these ideas; it requires direct instruction—explaining, demonstrating, guiding, practicing, and reflecting.

When engaging in direct instruction, we use authentic text, and assessment is a natural part of the process. As previously noted, there are a variety of comprehension strategies incorporated into the Model. They include previewing (activating prior knowledge, setting a purpose for reading, and predicting), self-questioning, making connections, visualizing, knowing how words work, monitoring, summarizing, and evaluating. Which strategies are taught at a particular grade level will depend on the students' stage of literacy development and their abilities. For example, the focus in kindergarten is often teaching comprehension skills and just a few strategies—usually previewing and summarizing. To facilitate teaching comprehension strategies at your students' levels, consider active, strategic readers in the intermediate grades, take a step back, and contemplate what you can teach your students to help them become such readers.

Steps in Direct Instruction

Regardless of the skill or strategy being taught, the direct instruction process remains the same. It includes the following steps:

Explain the skill or strategy: Describe how the skill or strategy works and how it contributes to text comprehension. Describe a related teaching idea (see Appendix C) and explain how it works.

Demonstrate the skill or strategy: When introducing a skill or strategy at the primary level, use a read-aloud, a Think-Aloud, and an overhead projector, chalkboard, whiteboard, or poster paper. Using a Think-Aloud allows us to share our reasoning process with our students and provide a model for students to think through their strategy use. As we think aloud, we orally explain precisely what is triggering our thoughts and how it is affecting our understanding. (For a detailed description of Think-Alouds, see Appendix C, page 223.) This can lead to the development of personal connections, questions for clarification, and refined predictions. Duffy (2001) notes the importance of wording the Think-Aloud. For example, he suggests using the following format when modeling predicting:

> Let me show you how I would make a prediction about this book. When I read the title, *Circus Animals*, I know from having been to a circus that it is probably going to have animals in it like elephants, lions, and tigers. I didn't see frogs or turtles at the circus, so I probably won't see them at this circus. The secret of making predictions is to think about what you already know from your own experience with the circus.

When using the Think-Aloud to demonstrate strategies, we need to explain our thinking so students have a clear idea of the cognitively active process readers experience as they transact with text.

Guide the students to apply the strategy: Read aloud the next section of the text and guide the students to apply the strategy just taught, prompting and offering assistance as necessary. When the students are comfortable with the strategy, continue scaffolding instruction by having the students work in pairs or small groups.

Practice the skill or strategy: Students begin to practice the skill or strategy independently in small groups, as we gradually relinquish control of the process.

Reflect on strategy use: Have the students reflect on how using the strategy helped them to understand the text. Discuss the ideas shared.

When engaging in direct instruction, always focus on the following:

- explaining the skill or strategy and how it works
- demonstrating using a Think-Aloud
- guiding students to practice, prompting and offering assistance as necessary
- providing settings for group, paired, and independent practice
- affording opportunities to reflect on strategy use

This stage also provides multiple opportunities for authentic assessment. These often include observation, discussion, informal writing, and sketching.

Throughout this framework, students' learning is scaffolded. When students learn how the strategy works, they have our total support. When they engage in guided practice, they have our support as necessary. When they apply the strategy independently, our support is diminished and the students are in control.

Comprehension Strategies: Focus on Teaching

During Stage One of the Model, a number of teaching ideas can be used to clarify and reinforce students' understanding and application of the comprehension skills and strategies. Although these ideas are used as frameworks for teaching individual strategies, our goal is for students to eventually develop a repertoire of strategies they can use independently. This section provides a definition of each comprehension strategy and a list of related teaching ideas. These lists are not exhaustive, but they do include those that are used most frequently at the primary level. Appendix C contains a step-by-step process for direct instruction of each teaching idea, as well as the idea's links to comprehension strategies, types of text, and reading stages.

Previewing is a way of introducing the text. It includes activating background knowledge, setting a purpose for reading, and predicting. The following teaching ideas support this strategy:

- Anticipation/Reaction Guide
- Predict-o-Gram
- Probable Passages
- Semantic Map and Semantic Question Map
- Storybook Introductions
- Story Impressions

Self-questioning involves generating questions to guide thinking while reading. Teaching ideas that support this strategy include the following:

- "I Wonder" Statements
- K-W-L and K-W-L-S
- Paired Questioning
- Question-Answer Relationship (QAR)
- Thick and Thin Questions

Making connections occurs when students think about the text in relation to connections they can make to self, to texts, and to others (Keene & Zimmermann, 1997). Teaching ideas that support this strategy include the following:

- Coding the Text
- Connection Stems
- Double-Entry Journal
- Drawing Connections

Visualizing is creating mental images while reading. Teaching ideas that support this strategy include the following:

- Draw and Label Visualizations
- Graphic Organizers/Visual Organizers
- Mind and Alternative Mind Portraits
- Open-Mind Portrait
- Sketch to Stretch

Knowing how words work is understanding words through strategic vocabulary development, including the use of the graphophonic, syntactic, and semantic cueing systems to figure out unknown words. The graphophonic cueing system involves creating grapheme (written letter)-phoneme (sound) matches. The syntactic cueing system deals with the structure of the language. The semantic cueing system focuses on meaning. Readers use all three cueing systems, along with other knowledge of words, to effectively engage with text. Ideas that support this comprehension strategy include the following:

- Concept of Definition Map
- Context Clues
- List-Group-Label
- RIVET
- Semantic Feature Analysis
- Text Transformations

Monitoring involves asking, "Does this make sense?" and clarifying by adapting strategic processes to accommodate the response. Monitoring is knowing if meaning is being constructed and what to do if it is not. The following teaching ideas support this strategy:

- Bookmark Technique
- Cueing Systems Check
- Patterned Partner Reading
- Say Something
- Think-Alouds

Summarizing involves extracting essential information, including the main idea and supporting details from text. Teaching ideas that support this strategy include the following:

- Bio-Pyramid

- Lyric Retelling and Lyric Summary
- Narrative Pyramid
- QuIP (Questions Into Paragraphs)
- Retelling
- Story Map
- Summary Cube

Evaluating means making judgments. The following teaching ideas support this strategy:

- Discussion Web
- Evaluative Questioning
- Journal Responses
- Persuasive Writing

Skills That Underpin the Comprehension Strategies

As stated earlier, comprehension strategies are more complex than skills and may require the orchestration of several comprehension skills. In the primary grades, students often begin by learning comprehension skills and then progress to learning strategies. The following list of skills is not exhaustive, but it offers a good sampling of the kinds of skills that underpin comprehension strategies:

- Decoding Skills
- Generating Questions
- Recognizing Text Structures
- Sequencing
- Distinguishing Important From Less Important Ideas

These skills are essential components of the reading process, and they need to be taught. For example, the ability to generate questions is a skill that underpins every comprehension strategy (see Figure 2). For this reason, we should assure that the students understand how to create questions by engaging in direct instruction.

When teaching students about questioning, we can explain what questions are, discuss their purposes, and delineate their multiple levels. We can explain that there are many reasons for generating questions, including information seeking, connected understanding, historical speculation, imagination, and research. Busching and Slesinger (1995) note that the best way to help students develop meaningful questions is to encourage them to engage extensively in reading, writing, speaking, listening, and viewing.

Ciardiello (1998) suggests that students generate questions at four levels: memory, convergent thinking, divergent thinking, and evaluative thinking. He also provides the following signal words and cognitive operations for each category:

Memory Questions

Signal words: *who, what, where, when?*

Cognitive operations: naming, defining, identifying, designating

Figure 2. Generating Questions: A Skill That Supports Comprehension Strategies

Comprehension Strategy	Narrative Text (*The True Story of the Three Little Pigs*)	Informational Text (*Whales*)
Previewing	What is the story about? What might happen in this story?	What do I already know about whales?
Self-Questioning	Why is the wolf telling this story?	Why are whales mammals?
Making Connections	How does this little pigs story compare/contrast to the original?	How do the text description and illustrations compare to the video we saw about whales? To the article we read in *National Geographic World*?
Visualizing	Is my mental picture of the wolf still good? Why should I change it?	What do orcas look like? How do they compare/contrast with gray whales?
Knowing How Words Work	Does the word make sense in the sentence?	What clues in the text can I use to figure out the word *baleen*?
Monitoring	Does what I'm reading make sense? If not, what can I do to clarify?	Does what I'm reading make sense? If not, what can I do to clarify?
Summarizing	What has happened so far?	What is the most important information in the book?
Evaluating	Do I believe the wolf's story? Why? How does this story rank with other little pigs stories I've read?	How would our lives be different if whales did not exist?

(adapted for the primary grades from McLaughlin & Allen, 2002a)

Convergent Thinking Questions

Signal words: *why, how, in what ways*?

Cognitive operations: explaining, stating relationships, comparing and contrasting

Divergent Thinking Questions

Signal words: *imagine, suppose, predict, if/then*

Cognitive operations: predicting, hypothesizing, inferring, reconstructing

Evaluative Thinking Questions

Signal words: *defend, judge, justify/what do you think?*

Cognitive operations: valuing, judging, defending, justifying

The teacher explains each question type and then models, first with life experiences and then with authentic text. Students engage in guided practice in a variety of settings and finally engage in independent application and transfer.

STAGE TWO: TEACHER-GUIDED SMALL-GROUP INSTRUCTION AND STUDENT-FACILITATED COMPREHENSION CENTERS AND ROUTINES

Stage Two of the Guided Comprehension Model focuses on three instructional settings: teacher-guided small groups, student-facilitated comprehension centers, and student-facilitated comprehension routines.

Organizing for Stage Two

In Stage Two of Guided Comprehension, students have opportunities to apply the comprehension skills and strategies in a variety of settings with varying levels of support. Texts in this stage vary from the instructional level texts used in the teacher-guided small groups to the independent level texts used when students work independently in comprehension centers and routines.

Because students can work in three different settings in this stage, having an organizational plan is essential. One way to manage this time is to use a chart that illustrates the settings in which students should be at given times (see Figure 3). (Other organizational plans can be found in Appendix D.)

Teacher-Guided Small-Group Instruction

Although Stage Two is characterized by three different instructional settings, only one is teacher-guided. In this small-group setting, students of similar abilities apply their knowledge of strategies to leveled texts to become active, engaged readers. Students are dynamically grouped and progress at individual rates, changing groups as they become prepared to transact with increasingly challenging levels of text.

When organizing for teacher-guided small-group instruction, we need to consider the following factors:

- All students in the group need to have similar instructional levels; this means that all the students in this Guided Comprehension setting should be able to read the same texts with some teacher support.

- What we are teaching is determined by students' needs and use of skills and strategies while constructing meaning.

Figure 3. Organizing for Stage Two

Centers	Session 1	Session 2
ABC		
Drama		
Making Words		
Theme		
Writing		

Routines	Session 1	Session 2
Literature Circles		
Reciprocal Teaching		
Cross-Age Reading Experiences		

Teacher-Guided Small Groups		

- While teaching in this setting, we also need to monitor students who are working independently in the comprehension centers and routines.

Once the small groups are formed and the appropriate text is matched to students' abilities, the teacher meets with one or more guided small groups every day. During this time with the students we should use the following Guided Comprehension small-group lesson format:

Review previously taught strategies and focus on the strategy of the day.

Guide the students to apply the strategy of the day, as well as previously taught strategies, as they read a section of the instructional level text or the text in its entirety. Prompt the students to construct personal meanings. Incorporate word study as needed. (See Appendix B and selected centers in Chapter 3 for examples of teaching ideas to use for word study.) Scaffold as necessary, gradually releasing support as students become more proficient. Encourage discussion and repeat this process with other sections of text.

Practice by having the students work in pairs or individually to apply the skills and strategies as they read the text (silently or in whisper tones).

Reread, retell, and reflect by having students do a second reading of the text, retell it, and share ways in which the skill or strategy helped them to understand the text. Extend learning by incorporating word study (see Appendix B), discussion, and related activities (see Appendix D). Discuss the text and ways in which the students can apply the skill or strategy in the comprehension centers and routines. The second reading of the text offers an opportunity to complete a running record with a student. (See Chapter 5 for information about running records.)

Review the strategies.   Begin each guided group by reminding students about skills and strategies that have been taught previously. It is helpful to have these posted on a chart in the classroom or listed on a bookmark or other quick reference for the students. Keene and Zimmermann (1997) suggest creating "Thinking Records" using the following steps:

- Use chart paper to create a separate record for each strategy.
- Record strategy definitions.
- Include examples generated by children.
- Add questions and insights about the use of the strategy.
- Display the Thinking Records in the classroom.
- Add information about the strategies as they are learned and used.

This review is designed to remind students that even though they need to learn each strategy, the ultimate goal is to use them in concert—developing a repertoire of strategies to use as needed to construct personal meaning. After this quick review, the focus shifts to revisiting the strategy and related teaching idea featured in that day's whole-group setting.

Guide students.   Begin by introducing the text and helping students preview. When the students will be reading narrative text, Marie Clay's Storybook Introduction (1991) (see Appendix C, page 210) can be used to introduce the text. Then have each student read silently or in whisper tones a designated portion of the text. Having the students read in whisper tones allows you to check on fluency and observe strategy use. After reading, integrate word study as needed and guide students to discuss understandings. To facilitate this, you may revisit predictions, verbalize connections, or share visualizations. You may ask, "What does this remind you of?" "Have you ever had an experience like this?" "How is this character like…?" You can also revisit students' original predictions and have students determine why their thinking has changed or remained the same. After this, the students read another predetermined section of the text and stop for more guided discussion.

Practice.   When students are actively engaging with the text and constructing meaning, they practice reading and using the focus strategy. For example, they may make connections as they finish reading the text independently and then discuss it with the members of the small group. If the text appears challenging for the students, you may choose to continue guiding their comprehension until they are more successful.

Reread, retell, and reflect.   The final component of teacher-guided small-group instruction includes rereading the text, retelling it, and reflecting on the text and strategy through discussion. Students may make personal responses and share new information or insights at this point. You may choose to incorporate word study and guide students to make broader connections to other texts and extend their understandings. These may be documented through writing, drawing, dramatization, or oral response. Students reread the text to enhance understanding and practice fluency. The rereading also provides an opportunity to do a running record with one of the students. This is also a good time to observe student responses and connections; this information will inform dynamic grouping, future student-text matches, and instructional planning. During discussion, it is important to ask students to reflect on their reading and review the strategies they used to make sense of the text. This will remind students to transfer what they have learned in whole-class instruction and in their Guided Comprehension small groups to their reading of other texts. The Guided Comprehension Model provides students with two settings for such independent practice: comprehension centers and comprehension routines.

Student-Facilitated Comprehension Centers and Routines

Comprehension centers provide purposeful, authentic settings for students to integrate and apply their comprehension strategies. Students may work in small groups, with partners, or on their own when they are engaged in the centers. Theme-based center activities promote the integration of reading, writing, and discussion. Ideas for organizing and managing centers as well as descriptions of a variety of centers are delineated in Chapter 3.

Students also practice and transfer what they have learned in comprehension routines. Comprehension routines are those habits of thinking and organizing that facilitate reading and response in authentic contexts. These are independent settings: This implies that students are knowledgeable about the strategies and routines, that they are provided with texts at their independent levels, and that they have ample time for practicing and transferring these processes. Routines used in Guided Comprehension at the primary level are described in detail in Chapter 4.

STAGE THREE: TEACHER-FACILITATED WHOLE-GROUP REFLECTION AND GOAL SETTING

In this stage of the Model, the students and teacher gather to reflect on what they have learned. This stage follows a three-step process: share, reflect, and set new goals.

Organizing for Stage Three

In this setting we encourage students to think about what they have accomplished in the first and second stages of the Model. We want them to actualize their learning and be accountable for it. Bringing the class together also provides opportunities for closure and celebration of new knowledge.

The cyclical process of setting goals, engaging in learning experiences, reflecting on performance, and setting new goals helps students to perceive themselves as empowered, successful learners. It encourages students to think critically, observe progress, and take ownership of their learning.

It is these active roles that students are taking, not reflection itself, that is new to the educational process. In 1933, Dewey suggested that teachers become reflective practitioners to gain better understandings of teaching and learning. In 1987, Schon noted that reflection offers teachers insights into various dimensions of teaching and learning that can lead to better understanding. In the 1990s, when reflection became a valued component of evolving assessment practices, students were encouraged to engage actively in the process (Darling-Hammond, Ancess, & Falk, 1995; Hoyt & Ames, 1997; McLaughlin, 1995).

Self-reflection focuses on what students have learned and how they feel about their learning (Cooper & Kiger, 2001). It includes both self-assessment, which addresses process and product, and self-evaluation, which makes judgments about performance. Questions raised for self-assessment purposes include "What is confusing me?" and "How did I contribute to the discussion?" Questions that foster self-evaluation include "What did I do well?" and "Did I achieve my goal?"

Self-reflection offers insights into students' thinking. It not only illustrates that they are thinking but also details how they are thinking. According to Hoyt and Ames (1997), "Self-reflection offers students an opportunity to be actively involved in internal conversations while offering teachers an insider's view of the learning and the student's perception of self as learner" (p. 19). This focus on internal conversations parallels Tierney and Pearson's (1994) idea that "literacy learning is an ongoing conversation with oneself.... If we view learning as dynamic in character, as that evolving dialogue with oneself, then even major shifts become little more than the natural, almost inevitable, consequence of human reflection" (p. 514).

Reflection and Goal Setting in Guided Comprehension

Goal setting is a natural outgrowth of reflection. As Hansen (1998) notes, "Learning proceeds from the known to the new" (p. 45). What students have learned to a given point influences what they learn next; this is the foundation of goal setting. Students reflect on what they have learned and set future personal goals for continuous improvement. When students actively engage in creating both personal and class goals, they appear to be more motivated and take more responsibility for their learning (Clemmons, Laase, Cooper, Areglado, & Dill, 1993; Hill & Ruptic, 1994).

Because direct instruction of reflection and goal setting is necessary, we apply the steps shared in Stage Two to this process. This is especially important in the primary grades, because students may not have strong background experiences in reflection; in fact, many may not even be familiar with the concept.

- *Explain* what reflection is and how it works.
- *Demonstrate* how to reflect.
- *Guide* students to apply reflection to something they have learned. Reflection forms can be used to facilitate this process (see Appendix E).
- *Practice* by providing students with multiple opportunities for application.

After engaging in reflection, students create new personal goals. The following are examples of new goals that were shared in student-teacher conferences in various grade levels:

- My goal is to read a Big Book with a buddy. (kindergarten)
- My new goal is to write more sentences in my stories. (grade 1)
- My new goal is to tell more of my ideas when I am in my Literature Circle. (grade 2)
- My new goal is to ask bigger questions, ones that have bigger answers. (grade 3)

When students become comfortable with reflection and goal setting, they engage in transfer of their learning. In Guided Comprehension, students have opportunities to reflect on their performance as members of a whole group, small group, or pair, as well as individually (see Appendix E).

Because reflection and goal setting are essential components of Guided Comprehension, it is important to maintain student interest in them. The following are additional teaching ideas to foster students' engagement in these processes.

Vary the components. When planning reflection and goal setting, we make selections from the following four categories:

1. Type of goal: individual or whole group, short term or long term
2. Reflection setting: whole group, small group, paired, or individual
3. Reflection mode: speaking, writing, illustrating, or dramatizing
4. Sharing setting: whole group, small group, paired, or individual

Choices can vary according to lesson content, student learning styles, or student interest. For example, students can create new personal goals by working in pairs to reflect on their learning, create sketches to illustrate their thinking, and then share them with a small group.

There are several formats for engaging students in written reflection, two of which are Guided Comprehension Journals and Tickets Out:

Guided Comprehension Journals: Students can use Guided Comprehension Journals during all stages of the Model. For example, they can use the journals to record notes for Literature Circles, jot down questions that arise during the stages of Guided Comprehension, and engage in reflection. In Stage Three, students can use the journals to record their reflections and set new goals.

Tickets Out: This is a favorite teaching idea because it fosters reflection, helps monitor students' learning, and takes very little time. It is called Tickets Out because students hand their tickets to the teacher as they exit the classroom at the end of the period or the end of the day. To participate in this activity, students use a half sheet of paper. On the first side, they write the most important thing they learned that day. On the other side, they write one question they have about something they learned that day. Whether students put their names on their tickets is the teacher's choice.

To complete this activity, students need only about five minutes. As the students leave the room, collect the tickets with side one facing up. After students have left the room, read side one of their tickets first. During this part of Tickets Out, put aside any tickets that need clarification.

Next, turn over the entire pile of tickets and read the questions students have about their learning. Some days, more than one student will raise the same question, and other days, not every student will have a question. During this part of Tickets Out, put aside questions that you deem valuable. Respond to these questions, which usually number between four and six, at the start of the next day's class. This helps students understand that we value their thinking and also enhances the continuity from class to class.

Tickets Out is not a time-consuming process, but it does provide valuable information. For example, it offers insight into what students value about their learning and also gives us an opportunity to monitor and clarify any misconceptions they may have. (A graphic organizer for Tickets Out can be found in Appendix E, page 329.)

Provide prompts. Providing prompts can assist students when reflecting and creating new goals in a variety of settings. Prompts help to focus students' thinking on various dimensions of learning.

Questions to guide reflection:
- What was your goal today? Did you reach it?
- What did you learn today?
- What did you do today that you have never done before?
- What strategies did you find most helpful?
- What confused you today? How did you figure it out?
- How did your group do? What contributions did you make to your group? What contributions did others make?
- What questions do you have about what you learned today?
- How do you think you will use what you learned today?

Reflection stems:
- I was really good at…
- The best thing I learned today was…
- I found out that…
- I contributed…to our literature discussion.
- I read…and found out that…
- When I was confused today, I…

Questions to guide goal setting:

- What do you need to work on?

- Where will you start next time?

- What do you hope to accomplish?

- What is your new goal?

Goal-setting stems:

- I need more work on…

- Tomorrow, I hope to…

- My goal for tomorrow is to…

Students can think about one or more of these prompts and then share their responses. Sharing can take place with a partner, a small group, or the whole class. I often use Think-Pair-Share (McTighe & Lyman, 1988) as a framework for this. Students *think* about their learning, *pair* with a partner to discuss ideas, and then *share* their thoughts with the class. Students also can write their reflections in their Guided Comprehension Journals and then use Think-Pair-Share. This technique also can be adapted for goal setting. First, students *think* about their performance and new goal(s), then they write it. Next, they *pair* with a partner to discuss their new goal(s). Finally, they *share* their goal(s) with the whole class. Sharing with the whole class is beneficial because it shows that everyone values reflection and goal setting and provides good models for the other students.

The Guided Comprehension Model for the Primary Grades provides a variety of settings for student learning. These include student-facilitated comprehension centers and routines, settings in which the students engage in independent practice. These components of Stage Two are examined in detail in Chapters 3 and 4.

CHAPTER 3

Creating, Organizing, and Managing Comprehension Centers

Comprehension centers provide purposeful, authentic settings for students to independently integrate and apply their comprehension strategies. Students may work in small groups, in partners, or on their own in this setting. Comprehension centers promote the integration of reading, writing, and discussion and provide a variety of ways for students to integrate and practice their comprehension strategies.

Student-facilitated comprehension centers are described in detail in this chapter. It begins by explaining the nature of the primary-level centers and delineating their purposes. Next, issues related to organization and management, including scheduling and student accountability, are explored. Finally, descriptions of a variety of comprehension-based centers and sample activities are presented.

CREATING GUIDED COMPREHENSION CENTERS

The time students spend in the centers should be meaningful. This means that we need to be aware of students' abilities to work independently. Once students have acquired such skills, it is important to take time to teach them the purpose of each center and how it functions. The five steps of direct instruction—explain, demonstrate, guide, practice, and reflect—facilitate this process.

Center activities should accommodate a variety of learning levels, be open-ended, and be able to be completed independently—in small groups, pairs, or individually. The activities should be purposeful, address a variety of interests and intelligences, and help students to think critically and creatively. The activities also should be engaging, foster discussion, extend learning, and promote decision making and student ownership of learning.

The centers are usually located around the perimeter of the classroom and away from teacher-guided small-group instruction. The centers vary in appearance from tabletop displays to file folders, pizza boxes, and gift bags. It is important to remember that the content of the center is more important than its physical appearance.

A variety of centers can be used when implementing the Guided Comprehension Model. Some centers may be specific to reading skills such as the ABC center; others, such as the mystery center, represent a theme-related genre; still others, such as the listening center and the writing center are process based. Centers may be permanent throughout the year, but the topics addressed may change with themes. For example, in the poetry center, the resources could change from poems about animals to poems about transportation or weather, depending on the current theme.

During center time, students can work independently or in small groups to make words, apply strategies while reading theme-related texts, write stories or poems, complete projects, or engage in other theme-related activities. The teacher should provide a structure for these projects but make sure that the activity is open-ended to allow for students to apply thinking and personal interpretations.

Although there are many activities that can be completed in literacy centers, it is important to remember that in Guided Comprehension, center activities are designed to promote the students' development and application of comprehension skills and strategies. (A graphic organizer to facilitate planning literacy centers can be found in Appendix D, page 275. Suggested centers, accompanying open-ended projects, and other extensions for learning are described in this chapter; additional center activities are embedded in the theme lessons in Part Two of this book.)

ABC Center

Students participate in a wide variety of language activities ranging from word sorts to creating alphabet books of varying levels of complexity.

A-B-C Watch Me Read! (Page, 2001): Students fold a piece of paper into eight sections. At the top of each section, they write one of their favorite lowercase letters. Next, they look around the room and in familiar literature to find words they can read that begin with each of the chosen letters. Then they copy the words onto their charts.

Alphabet Books—Individual: When students know 10 letters, they begin making their own alphabet books. They continue adding to the books as they learn the remaining letters.

Students continue making alphabet books through the elementary grades. These books are often theme based. Titles of student books might include *Poetry Alphabet Book*, *Mystery Alphabet Book*, *Eric Carle Alphabet Book*, or *Community Alphabet Book*. (See Appendix D, page 272, for a list of published alphabet books that serve as great models for this activity.)

Class Alphabet Book: Students can create individual pages to contribute to a class alphabet book.

Sentence Strips: Sentence strips from a variety of stories are kept at this center. Students can use these for numerous activities including practicing sequencing; reviewing the beginning, middle, and end structure of stories; and reading and retelling the story.

Sorts: A variety of sorts can be kept at this center. Students may use these cards or manipulatives to create sound, word, or concept sorts. (For more information about sorts, see Appendix B.)

Art Center

Students use materials at the art center to visually represent their understandings of texts or to create illustrations for the texts they are writing. A variety of materials and examples of specific art techniques should be available at the center. The following materials are suggested:

- all kinds of paper—colored, lined, construction, large, textured, adhesive notes
- all kinds of writing and illustrating utensils—markers, crayons, paints, colored pencils, pencils, water colors, texture paints
- scraps of fabric, scraps of wallpaper, contact paper, cotton balls, and macaroni (and other items to provide texture for illustrations)
- glue sticks, white glue, tape
- scissors—straight and patterned—and hole punches
- stamps—alphabet, textures, symbols, designs
- printmaking supplies
- wire, yarn, sticks, ribbon, rubber bands
- magazines, catalogs

The center should include samples and directions for a variety of art techniques, such as drawing, collage, painting, printmaking, and puppetry.

Drama Center

In this center, students use acting to demonstrate their understandings. They can plan and rehearse their acting performances. The following are some ideas for implementing drama in the classroom:

Puppet Theater: Students use puppets provided at this center to engage in storytelling and retelling. Puppets may be created from paper bags, wooden spoons, or other materials.

Readers Theatre: Students use minimal theatre to dramatize stories. They first transcribe a story or other text into a play format, and then they rehearse the dramatization using voice, facial expressions, and movement to portray characterizations. They use scripts during the performance.

Genre Center

The focus of the genre center changes as the year progresses. Possible topics include biography, brochures, traditional and transformational fairy tales, fantasy, folk tales, mystery, and poetry. (For examples of genre centers, see the descriptions of mystery and poetry centers in this section.)

Making Words Center

Students use a variety of activities to construct words. (For related blackline masters, see Appendix D, pages 291–292.)

Making Words (Cunningham, 2000): Students manipulate the letters of a mystery word to create other words. They begin with short words and progress to longer ones. They may create the words based on clues or just list as many words as possible. Then they guess the mystery word. When creating the words, students may manipulate plastic letters, arrange magnetic letters on a cookie sheet, or use letter tiles.

Making and Writing Words (Rasinski, 1999a): In this adaptation of Making Words, students write the words they create from the letters in a mystery word.

Making and Writing Words Using Letter Patterns (Rasinski, 1999b): In this adaptation of Making Words, students use rimes (word families) and other patterns as well as individual letters to create words. Then students transfer their knowledge to create new words. Finally, they cut up the organizer to create word cards, which they use to practice the words in games and sorts.

For example, in a unit on Eric Carle, the word *caterpillar* might be the mystery word. Then we would ask the students to make and write as many words as they can using the letters in that word. Following are some of the words they might create.

- two-letter words: *at, it*
- three-letter words: *cat, rat, pat, pit, lit, car, par, tar, all, ill, lip, tip, rip, air, act, ape, are, arc, art*
- four-letter words: *rate, late, care, rare, pare, pear, pair, tall, call, clip, trip, pill, pact, cape, ripe, cart, race*
- five-letter words: *trail, liter, alert, peril, price, alter, plate, trial, pleat, pearl, petal, relic, taper, crate, crept, crier, lilac, alert, later*
- six-letter words: *pillar, carpet, pirate, taller, triple, parcel, caller, cellar, crater*

Mystery Center

Students read mysteries and use the elements of the genre to create mysteries in a variety of formats.

Create-a-Mystery: Label bags or boxes with the major components of a mystery (i.e., suspects, clues, victims, detectives, criminals, motives, crimes, and crime scenes). The students will record on index cards examples of each from mystery novels they have read, and then they will place the index cards in the appropriate bag or box. Other students will select one index card from each box and use that information to create a mystery. After writing the mystery, students can illustrate it and share it with the class. The students can then extend this activity by participating in a Mystery Theater.

Suspicious Suspects: The students organize their thoughts about the suspects in a mystery by completing the Mystery Suspect Organizer (see Appendix D, page 295). Based on the clues, the students can easily come to a conclusion about who committed the crime. The organizer also can be completed as a planner for writing a mystery.

Write Your Own Mystery: The students will use the Write Your Own Mystery graphic organizer to record information to help them plan mysteries they will write (see Appendix D, page 311). The organizer also can be used to help students summarize a mystery they are reading. On the organizer they draw, describe, or explain the crime scene. They write four clues and describe a main character, and they also write a brief description of how the mystery is solved. As an alternative writing activity, students can create mysteries based on photos or story starters placed at the center. Following is a mystery written by a second-grade student:

The Mistery of the Wieyuld Amagenaeshans in the Adik
by Francesca

CREEK! CREEK! The foot steps of the adik CREEK. Each time it gets lawder and lawder and lawder! This one little gurl named Emma and some of her friens found an owld box. Emma owpind it, nothing happend. Well, nouw I know wy my perints did not wont me to opin it because there is nothing in it. "Come on" said Emma "lets go."

They whent down staz. Emma hrad a SKREECH! "What was that?" said Emma. Cluck! CLUK! Ok now I'm getting a little skard. Emma hrd lawd strange foot steps. She saw the shadoe of a man throo the door "Ahhh!" "What's that?" Jeska skreemd.

Deeng dong! Emma and her friens shiverd. The door nob turnd. The door owpined "AHHH!" "Whoos there?" Lizzie shatid!

"Gurl's kom down" said her mom. "mom, dad I owpind the box the one in the adik you no the one that you toed me not to opin." I said. "Oh that wan that's the one that maekes kids amagenaeshans wieyuld." her mom said. "But what about evrytheeng" "But what about the shatoe" Emma said with a shiver. "Oh that is the new naebers" laft mom. Then what was that SKREECH?" Kate said. "That is the SKREECH from the braench SKREECHING agenst the window." The dad said surpisd. "Then what was evrytheeng els," Lise said. "Your amagnaeshan!" mom and dad both said.

The gurls were so surpisd when they found out it was just there amagenaeshans. They giguld all night. Neckst time they heer a stchrange nouse they woent be fritind.

Mystery Poetry: Students write poems about various aspects of mysteries using formats such as acrostics, bio-poems, cinquain, definition, or diamantes (see Appendix D for poetry forms beginning on page 298). For example, students may write an acrostic about one of the suspects in a mystery by writing the name and using the letters in the suspect's name as starters for the clues related to this suspect. Students can contribute their poems to a class book of mystery poems or use their poems for a Poetry Theater presentation.

Mystery Pyramid: Students can manipulate language by trying to fit all the elements of a mystery into a Mystery Pyramid (see Appendix D, page 294).

Mystery Theater: The students practice a scene from a mystery they have read and perform it for the class. The audience tries to guess what mystery the scene is from and the characters involved.

Word Detective: Using the Word Detective Sequential Roundtable Organizer, the students can create a master list or word wall of mystery words from mysteries read (see Appendix D, page 310). This can then support students' writing or be used for word sorts.

Listening Center

Students can independently apply their comprehension strategies as they listen to a variety of theme-related audio books at this center.

Making Books Center

Students can retell key events from stories, gather data and create reports on content area topics, or write creative pieces that can be published. These may be self-created or follow a familiar structure, such as alphabet books. The following is a list of book types and suggestions for using them:

- accordion—retelling, content area facts, creative stories with illustrations
- origami—word books, retelling, facts, short stories, story elements
- flip/flap—word work (parts of speech, antonyms, synonyms, rhymes, prefixes/suffixes); story elements, riddles
- slotted—journals, reading response, word books, alphabet books
- dos à dos—dialogue or buddy journal, research and report, compare/contrast
- stair-step—riddle books, sequence story events, time lines

(See Appendix D, pages 282–284, for directions for making books.)

Pattern Book Center

Students use a pattern from a familiar book and retell the story or share information using the pattern. Some effective patterns are those used in *Fortunately* by Remy Charlip (1993) and *The Important Book* by Margaret Wise Brown (1990). I have found it helpful to provide specific organizers to help students plan these books (see Appendix D, pages 296–297).

Poetry Center

Keep a large supply of poetry books and poetry cards at this center. (See Chapter 10, pages 174–177, for a list of poetry resources.) Have lots of copies of poems that students can read, act out, or illustrate. The following is a list of activities students will enjoy completing at the Poetry Center:

Poetry Acting: In small groups, students plan and practice acting out a poem. These dramatizations include minimal theatrics and props and maximum expression through voice and actions.

Poetry Forms: Students create their own poems using structured formats such as bio-poems, cinquains, and diamantes. Blacklines of poem formats (see Appendix D, pages 298–302) for students to use and examples of completed poems are available at this center.

Poetry Frames: Students create their own versions of published poems. The teacher can create frames in which students can write their own words, keeping the structure but changing the content of the original poem. (A poetry frame for "If I Were in Charge of the World" is included in Appendix D, page 287.)

Poem Impressions: Students write poems based on a series of clues provided from an existing poem, and then they share their poems. Finally, the original poem is read and discussion focuses on comparing and contrasting the impressions with the original poem.

Project Center

Students work on specific extensions or projects related to the theme or current events. These may include multiple modes of response including reading, writing, illustrating, and dramatizing. Various reference materials, from encyclopedias to books to the Internet, should be readily available.

Book Cubes: Students use the Summary Cube (see Appendix C, page 268) to present essential information about a book. For example, students can record the title, author, main character(s), setting, summary statement, and illustration.

Bookmarks: Students create bookmarks about the book they read. Students may choose what to include on the bookmark or the teacher can provide guidelines. For example, information for narrative texts may include title, author, main character(s), critique, and illustrations of characters or events. For informational texts, students can include the title, author, key ideas learned, their reactions and illustrations.

Book Mobile: Students create mobiles about books they have read. Students may create the mobile on their own or use the Book Mobile Organizer (see Appendix D, page 273) to format the information. Information may include the title, author, setting, characters, problem, resolution, and illustration. Students may also use the mobile format to share information about the author, focus on a single narrative element (e.g., character mobiles), or to review a book. Because the mobiles will be suspended from the ceiling, students can record information on both sides of the paper.

Newspaper/Newsletter: Students write newspaper articles related to a topic of study and publish them in a newspaper format. Examples include articles about pollution during an oceans theme, reviews of a new Harry Potter book or movie during a fantasy theme, and collections of comic strip summaries presented as the comics section of the newspaper.

Press Conference (McLaughlin, 2000b): This inquiry-based activity promotes oral communication. Students choose a topic to investigate. Then they peruse newspapers, magazines, or the Internet to find at least two sources of information about the topic. After reading the articles, focusing on essential points, raising questions, and reflecting on personal insights, the student presents an informal summary of his or her research to a group of classmates or the entire class. Members of the audience then raise questions that can lead to "I Wonder" Statements that students can record in their investigative journals (see the Press Conference Summary blackline in Appendix D, page 303).

Open-Mind Portraits (Tompkins, 2001): Students draw two or more portraits of one of the characters in a story. One drawing is a regular face of the character; the others include one or more that represent the mind of the character at important points in the story. The mind pages include words and drawings representing the character's thoughts and feelings.

Questions Into Paragraphs (QuIP) (McLaughlin, 1987): Students ask questions related to the topic and use two or more sources to find answers to each question. The information is recorded on a QuIP Research Grid (see Appendix C, page 265) and then used to write a summary paragraph or to organize research for a press conference.

ReWrite (Bean, 2000): In this activity, students write songs before and after content area study. For example, students write a song based on what they think they know about bats. Then they read to learn about bats and rewrite their lyrics based on the new information. The rewrite represents how students' knowledge, perceptions, and feelings have changed after studying the topic. Tunes may include familiar songs or instrumental tapes.

Choose Your Own Project: Students make selections from a list of ideas to extend their thinking about what they have read (see Appendix D, page 279).

Storytelling Center

Students can engage in storytelling, in which they focus on the narrative elements (characters, setting, problem, attempts to resolve, and resolution) with a partner or small group.

Wordless Picture Books: Students tell the story of wordless picture books, such as Alexandra Day's *Carl Goes to Daycare* (1995) or David Wiesner's *Tuesday* (1991), *Sector 7* (1999), and *The Three Pigs* (2001). Students may work in pairs or tape record their storytelling.

Storytelling Gloves: Students use Storytelling Gloves with Velcro-backed characters and other representations of the narrative elements to tell familiar songs, rhymes, and tales. Commercially available Storytelling Gloves include "Old MacDonald Had a Farm," "The Three Little Pigs," "Five Green and Speckled Frogs," "Five Little Ducks," "The Three Bears," "The Itsy Bitsy Spider," "Baa Baa Black Sheep," and "The Gingerbread Man." (Storytelling Gloves are available from Lakeshore, 800-421-5354.)

Teaching Center

In this center, students work in partners and take turns being the teacher. A variety of activities can be used in this center.

Transparency Talk (Page, 2001): In this center, a student assumes the role of the teacher. He or she places transparencies containing sentences, messages, or stories the classroom teacher has prepared on the overhead projector. The "teacher" then uses these for a variety of activities including finding and lifting words he or she can read, finding all the words that begin or end with a particular sound or pattern, or reading along with a partner. (Place the projector on the floor and use a white piece of paper for a screen.)

Read the Room: The "teacher" uses a pointer and the "student" and "teacher" take turns reading room labels, the word wall, bulletin board, or morning message as the "teacher" points to it. Then the partners switch roles.

Shared Reading: The "teacher" uses a pointer as he or she and the "student" read a Big Book together.

Theme Center

Books at a variety of levels related to the theme of study are housed in this center. Students may self-select a book to read and use it to practice and transfer comprehension strategies. Students may also select the mode of reading they will use. This often includes using the following partner-reading patterns:

Predict-Read-Discuss: Partners make predictions about material, read to confirm or disconfirm their predictions, discuss the outcome, and then renew the cycle.

Read-Pause-Retell: Partners read, stop to think, and retell what they have read to that point.

You Choose: Partners select which mode to use.

Vocabulary Center

This center may have a word wall or other display of words that can be the focus of study. These words may be structurally similar (rhymes, prefix, suffix, roots) or may be theme-related. Sentences also may be displayed, so students can use context clues to "Guess the Covered Word" (Cunningham, 2000).

This center also may include interesting word books (such as *The Weighty Word Book* by Paul Levitt [1990], *Anamalia* by Graeme Base [1996], or books by Fred Gwynne, Ruth Heller, or Marvin Terban) that can provide the impetus for word study. Students work on learning, using, and making connections to these new vocabulary words. The following is a list of activities students can complete at the vocabulary center:

Acrostics: Students write the name of a topic or character vertically, and then write words or phrases to describe the topic, each description starting with one of the letters in the name. The focus can include characters, places, people, or any other topic related to areas of study. Students can also use the acrostic form to retell key events of a story in sequential order.

Invent a Word: Students use their knowledge of prefixes, suffixes, and roots to create new words and their meanings.

Word Bingo: Students put 16 vocabulary words on a Bingo sheet. Clues such as definitions, synonyms, antonyms, or rhymes are listed on cards and placed in a bag or box. One at a time, a student pulls out a card and reads the clue, and students cover the word with a marker. The first student to get four in a row wins.

Word Sorts: Students sort vocabulary words into categories provided by the teacher (closed sort) or by self-selected categories (open sort). These might include rhyming words, parts of speech, vowel sound, syllables, and specific theme subtopics. This may be completed in a hands-on fashion, using word cards; then students can record their ideas on a word-sort sheet. This activity also may be completed in writing on a web or other organized structure.

Word Storm: A visual display—such as a picture from a book, a piece of art, or a poster—provides the impetus for word brainstorming. Students look at the visual and brainstorm and record words that come to mind. Then they use some or all of the words to create a detailed sentence or paragraph about the visual.

Writing Center

This center is a place for free and structured writing. Students may write informally or use the writing process. You may also structure the writing using one or more of the following ideas:

Informational Writing: Students write restaurant menus and checks; create brochures about theme-related topics; write newspaper articles; write letters; and develop book, movie, and music reviews.

Journals: Students write about self-selected topics or respond to teacher-provided prompts.

Patterned Writing: Students use patterned books, poetry forms, fractured fairy tales, and nursery rhymes as formats for writing.

Sticker or Stamp Stories: Students use stickers or stamps to create an illustration with action and then write a story to accompany the picture.

Story Bag: Students pull out one item at a time from a bag of story-related props the teacher has prepared. They create a story based on the props as they remove them from the bag.

Story Collages: Instead of writing a story and then illustrating it, students create textured illustrations first and then develop stories based on them. Because the illustrations are textured (pine cones, aluminum foil, felt, sand), students can use their tactile modalities (Brown, 1993).

Story Impressions: Students write a story based on approximately 10 clues from a story. Each clue is from three to five words, and the clues are placed sequentially and connected with downward arrows. The title of the original story may or may not be shared. When the story is completed and the students read it, the original author's story is read for comparison and contrast.

Story Trifold: Students write a story using a graphic that folds into three labeled parts: beginning, middle, and end (see Appendix D, page 309).

ORGANIZING AND MANAGING COMPREHENSION CENTERS

Students can move from center to center in a variety of ways, depending on the structure of the literacy schedule and the students' level of independence. The following methods are used frequently:

Menu Board: One way to organize center time is to use a menu board that provides a visual organizational overview of Stage Two (see Figure 3 on page 22). The students who will meet for teacher-guided small-group instruction are listed on the menu board. Center choices are also provided and students put their names under the center name where they will work. The number of students who may work at a given center or at a given activity within a center is designated at that center and on the menu board. For example, three is the designated number of students for the making words center as posted at the activity site and on the menu board. Students continue working at their assigned center until they complete the work they have scheduled for that day. For example, students may choose to work on word study at the ABC center or use a partner-reading pattern to read a book at the theme center. This assures that choice is being accommodated on multiple levels: Students can choose what goals they are trying to achieve that day, which centers to visit, how long to stay, and how to manage their time.

Required and Optional Centers: We can also provide students with a framework for required and optional centers (see Appendix D, page 308). Sometimes we may choose to assign students to the centers where they will begin, but they may choose to move later, as openings at other centers occur.

Rotating Schedule: Some teachers prefer to move the students using a rotating schedule. With this, students move among three or four activities, changing every 15 to 20 minutes. This rotational format provides maximum control by the teacher, but limits students' opportunities for choice and opportunities for learning to manage their own time.

Student Accountability

It is important to have accountability for the time students spend at the centers. Using a record-keeping system helps to keep track of which centers each student visits during the week. We can use a whole-group chart to monitor who visits which centers each week, or we can place charts at individual centers for students to record their visits. Students may also keep track of their work in their Guided Comprehension Journals (see cover sheet in Appendix D, page 286).

Student self-assessment can also contribute to our understanding of how students used their center time. Providing self-assessment forms that indicate which centers students visited, what they did, and how they think they progressed toward their goal on a particular day facilitates this process (see Appendix D, page 278).

Students can keep their center work and reflections in a two-pocket folder, where the teacher can review them weekly or biweekly. Students also can share their work with the teacher in individual conferences. Including a checklist, rubric, or other evaluative tool at each center facilitates this process (see Appendix D). At the end of Stage Three, selected works will be transferred to the students' Guided Comprehension Profiles.

Regardless of what the centers include or how they are managed, it is important to remember that the centers are places for independent exploration by students. The centers should accommodate a variety of abilities, have clear directions, and provide activities that are familiar to students so they can use them independently.

Ford and Opitz (2002) suggest the following guidelines for using centers to facilitate this process:

- Operate with minimal transition time and management concerns.
- Encourage equitable use of centers and activities among learners.
- Include a simple built-in accountability system.
- Allow for efficient use of teacher preparation time.
- Build the centers around classroom routines.

In the next chapter, another setting in which students independently apply reading skills and strategies, student-facilitated comprehension routines, is described in detail. The comprehension routines discussed include adapted versions of Literature Circles, Reciprocal Teaching, and Cross-Age Reading Experiences.

CHAPTER 4

Organizing and Managing Comprehension Routines

In addition to comprehension centers, primary-grade students practice and transfer what they have learned in comprehension routines, another Stage Two setting for independent application. Comprehension routines are those habits of thinking and organizing that facilitate reading and response in authentic contexts. These are independent settings, which implies that students are able to work on their own, are knowledgeable about comprehension skills and strategies, know how to use the routines, have access to texts at their independent levels, and have ample time for practicing and transferring these processes.

Routines are courses of action that are so ingrained that they can be used successfully on a regular basis. Routines that are most effective for promoting comprehension in both whole-group and small-group settings at the primary level are Literature Circles, Reciprocal Teaching, and Cross-Age Reading Experiences.

Before students can use these comprehension routines independently, they need to understand the purpose of the routines, why they are engaging with them, and how they function. These needs can be accommodated by using the five-step direct instruction process—explain, demonstrate, guide, practice, and reflect—to teach the routines. This assures that students' learning is scaffolded. The teacher can begin by offering total support, and, as learning progresses, he or she gradually releases control of the routines to the students.

It is important to note that students engage in the various routines as appropriate for their developmental stage. For example, students can begin engaging in Cross-Age Reading Experiences in kindergarten, but they may only begin to learn some skills associated with the other routines at that level. For this reason, teaching models for Literature Circles and Reciprocal Teaching for each grade level are included.

This chapter is organized into three sections, one for each routine. Within each section, the information is divided into two parts: what we know about the routine and how we can use the routine in the primary grades.

LITERATURE CIRCLES: WHAT WE KNOW

Groups of students can share their insights, questions, and interpretations of the same or theme-related texts in Literature Circles. The basic goal of Literature Circles is to provide students with a setting in which to converse about texts in meaningful, personal, and thoughtful ways (Brabham & Villaume, 2000). In Guided Comprehension, this means that students are integrating their comprehension skills and strategies as they construct personal meaning.

Implementing Literature Circles

To facilitate students' use of Literature Circles, we need to directly teach the concept and engage in active demonstration. Brabham and Villaume (2000) caution against a cookie-cutter version of how to implement Literature Circles and instead recommend designing and using them in ways that emerge from our students' needs and challenges. These circles may not all have the same format, but they all encourage the implementation of grand conversations about texts (Peterson & Eeds, 1990). It is particularly important to remember this when using Literature Circles in the primary grades. Although the procedural decisions about the implementation of Literature Circles need to emerge from specific classrooms, there are some structures that do facilitate their use. (Literature Circle models designed by primary-grade teachers are presented later in this chapter.)

It is important to remember that Literature Circles are a time of exploration and construction of personal meaning for the students. Their personal interpretations drive the discussion. This routine is not a list of literal questions to be answered after reading. The focus is on students' inquiries, connections, and interpretations. During direct instruction, we should make a point of modeling how to converse in critical ways during the demonstration step. Using Think-Alouds will facilitate this process.

Daniels (1994) and Tompkins (2001) suggest 10 guiding principles for using Literature Circles:

1. Students self-select the books they will read.

2. Temporary groups are formed based on book choice.

3. Each group reads something different.

4. Groups meet on a regular basis, according to predetermined schedules.

5. Students use drawings or writings to guide their conversations.

6. Students determine the topics for discussions and lead the conversations.

7. The teacher acts as a facilitator, not an instructor or leader.

8. Assessment can be completed through teacher observation or student self-reflection.

9. Students are actively involved in reading and discussing books.

10. After reading the books, the students share their ideas with their classmates, choose new books to read, and begin the cycle anew.

Noe and Johnson (1999) suggest that we expand students' opportunities to respond to text by encouraging them to participate in extension activities. These activities provide students with another mode for exploring meaning, expressing their ideas about the text, making connections, and using a variety of response formats. Examples of extension projects adapted for use at the primary level include the following:

Accordian Book: Make an illustrated accordion format book that includes a title page and unfolds to reveal the beginning, middle, and end of the story. An alternative is to design the book to reveal the narrative elements: characters, setting, problem, attempts to resolve, and resolution.

Quilt Square: Design a quilt square to represent the book and add it to the class book quilt. Include the book's title and author and create an illustration to represent the book. Use the yarn provided to connect your square to the existing quilt. Class book quilts may feature theme-related texts, be genre-specific (our favorite poetry books, biographies, mysteries, etc.), or focus on the work of a favorite author.

(For more ideas about extending students' thinking after reading, see Appendix D and the Theme Resources sections of Chapters 6–10.)

Choice, literature, and response are Tompkins's (2001) suggestions for the key features of Literature Circles.

Choice. Students make many choices within the framework of Literature Circles: They choose the books they will read, the group they will join, the schedule they will follow, and the direction of the conversation. We can set the parameters for students to make these choices by providing a variety of texts at multiple levels for student selection, setting minimum daily or weekly reading requirements, and prompting ideas for conversations. However, the ultimate responsibility for each group rests with the students.

Literature. The books from which the students choose should be high-quality authentic literature or informational text that relates to their experiences. It should also help students make personal connections and prompt critical reflection (Brabham & Villaume, 2000). The books should include interesting stories with well-developed characters, rich language, and relevant themes that are engaging and meaningful and that generate interest from students (Noe & Johnson, 1999; Samway & Wang, 1996).

While reading, students can jot ideas in their Guided Comprehension Journals to share during discussion. Providing prompts to help students focus their thoughts is beneficial. Examples of prompts include the following:

- I wonder…
- I want to ask my group about…
- I think it is funny (sad, surprising, scary) that…
- I think it is interesting that…
- I think it is confusing that…
- The illustrations in this text…
- A vocabulary word I think our group should talk about is…
- This book reminds me of…

Using the Bookmark Technique (McLaughlin & Allen, 2002a) is a viable alternative for documenting students' ideas (see Appendix C, page 221). In this activity, students record their thoughts on four different bookmarks. The first contains their ideas about what they found most interesting; the second features a vocabulary word they think the group needs to discuss; the third provides information about something that was confusing; and the fourth contains ideas about illustrations, maps, or other graphics featured in the text (see Appendix C, pages 259–260, for Bookmark blacklines). The students record the page number and their thoughts on the bookmarks and place them at appropriate points in the text. Then the students use the completed bookmarks to support their contributions to the discussion.

Response. Response is the final feature to keep in mind when implementing Literature Circles. After reading, students gather in their small group to share understandings from the text and make personal connections. This public sharing, in the form of a conversation, helps the students to broaden their interpretations and gain new perspectives from the other members of the group.

Organizing and Managing Literature Circles

There are several ways to structure and manage Literature Circles. There is no right way, but rather choices must be made to accommodate the needs and challenges of not only each grade level but also of each student in the class. Any of the existing plans for Literature Circles may be used to create successful formats (see Figure 4). Specific models for using Literature Circles in the primary grades appear in the next section. Once a meaningful plan has been selected, we make decisions about text choice, forming groups, and structuring the conversations.

Text selection. Texts for Literature Circles can be novels, picture books, poetry books, magazine articles, informational books, or selections from anthologies. The material that is selected will need to accommodate a wide range of student interests and abilities.

There are multiple options for selecting texts for Literature Circles. One way is to choose books that relate to a theme, topic, genre, or author (Noe & Johnson, 1999). When using this method, the teacher should choose several texts on varying levels, and the students should make reading choices based on interest and ability. Another way to select text is to create collections of text sets related to a theme or topic (Short, Harste, & Burke, 1996). Texts within each set are related but can vary in level of difficulty. Students select the theme or topic and then choose the reading material from within that set. A third way to choose reading material is to allow students to self-select and then form groups based on text similarities.

Introducing text. After selecting the texts to be used in Literature Circles, we match the books with readers. Although there are various methods for doing this, these two are especially effective:

Book passes: Several books are passed among students. Each student peruses a book for a few minutes, noting the title, reading the book cover, and leafing through the opening chapter. If the students find a book appealing, they jot the title in their Guided Comprehension Journal and pass the book to the next person. After previewing several titles, students make choices. Groups are then formed on the basis of the book selections.

Book talks: This is a short oral overview of the book, focusing on the genre, the main characters, and the plot. After the book talks, students make choices and groups are formed.

Figure 4. Literature Circle Formats

OPTION 1 (Daniels, 1994)
Roles:

Required	*Optional*
Discussion director	Researcher
Literary luminary/passage master	Summarizer/essence extractor
Connector	Character captain
Illustrator/artful artist	Vocabulary enricher/word master
	Travel tracer/scene setter

Books: All participants use the same text.
Process:
• Meet to set reading goals.
• Read independently, complete role sheets.
• Meet to discuss role sheets and other text connections.
• Set new reading goals, rotate roles.
• Read independently, complete role sheets.
• Meet to discuss role sheets and other text connections.

Continue this process until finished.
Celebrate by class sharing of project related to the book.

OPTION 2 (Klein, 1995)
Books: Teacher selects and introduces several according to theme; students make choices.
Group: Teacher composes groups based on student text choices.
Process:
• Groups meet, choose format for reading: whole group—read aloud; independent—silently.
• Weekly—each group reads four days, responds two days, meets to talk about the book one day.
• Groups prepare response projects to share books with the class.

We may need to guide some students in making appropriate text choices. If text sets are used, we can introduce the theme of the set and the kinds of texts that are in it. If selections are used from an anthology, we can introduce them through book talks.

Grand conversations: Schedules, talk, and roles. Once the Literature Circles are formed, students meet and develop a schedule to determine how much they will read and to create meeting deadlines. At first, the teacher can provide the schedule as a way to model how to set these goals. Once reading goals are set, students read the text on their own or with a partner. At the designated group meeting time, the students gather to discuss the texts. Notes or sketches from their reading that have been recorded in their Guided Comprehension Journals or their Literature Circle Bookmarks inform this discussion. Prior to this point, we model how to respond to text and how to use these responses to get the group conversations started.

The time spent in Literature Circles varies by length of text, but usually 10 to 20 minutes is sufficient. We can use a minilesson to demonstrate a particular literary element—such as plot, theme, or characterization—on which the students may focus their discussion. It is important, though, that we allow each group's conversation to evolve on its own.

Gilles (1998) has identified four types of talk that often occur during Literature Circles: talk about the book, talk about the reading process, talk about connections, and talk about group process and social issues. Teachers can encourage all types of talk with demonstrations and gentle prompts during the Literature Circle conversations.

Some teachers prefer to use assigned roles and responsibilities as a way to guide the conversations. Daniels (1994) has found that the following roles, which students rotate, provide a wide level of conversation within the Literature Circle:

- The *discussion director* takes on the leadership of the group and guides the discussion. Responsibilities include choosing topics for discussion, generating questions, convening the meeting, and facilitating contributions from all members.

- The *literary luminary/passage master* helps students revisit the text. Responsibilities include selecting memorable or important sections of the text and reading them aloud expressively.

- The *connector* guides the students to make connections with the text. Responsibilities include sharing text-self, text-text, and text-world connections and encouraging others to do the same.

- The *illustrator/artful artist* creates a drawing or other symbolic response to text. Responsibilities include making the visual response and using it to encourage others to contribute to the conversation.

The advantage of using these roles is that they represent response in a variety of learning modes, including linguistic, dramatic, and visual. The disadvantage is that this structure may stifle responses. I have found that starting with clearly defined roles and then relaxing or relinquishing them as the students gain competence in Literature Circles is effective. Daniels (1994) concurs, noting that role-free discussions are the ultimate goal.

Assessment in Literature Circles

There are several ways to assess students' comprehension, contributions, and cooperation within Literature Circles. Options include self-reflection, observation, and response sheets or journal entries.

- Students may self-reflect on their contributions to the circle and the group's ability to function. Providing forms for students to record their self-reflections facilitates this process (see Appendix D, pages 289–290).

- Although the students meet independently, we can observe their conversations and make anecdotal notes or keep a checklist of the content and depth of discussions (see Appendix E, page 325). We can note who is contributing to the discussion and if full participation is lacking. We can use this data to teach the students additional ways to include all group members. We also can observe the scope of the discussion. If the students are focused on basic recall of story events, we can choose to do a minilesson on making meaningful connections with texts.

- Students' response sheets, Guided Comprehension Journals, or Literature Circle Bookmarks provide another opportunity for assessment. In this format, students take notes about the text, document understandings, and make personal connections to bring to the discussion. These written or drawn artifacts provide a window into the students' thinking about the text.

The most important thing to remember about assessment in Literature Circles is to use the assessment results. These should contribute to decisions about future instruction.

USING LITERATURE CIRCLES IN THE PRIMARY GRADES

When working with primary-grade students, adaptations can be made to Literature Circles. I always suggest observing intermediate-grade Literature Circles, taking a step back, and contemplating what we could teach in third grade, second grade, first grade, and kindergarten to help students function successfully in those settings.

For example, in kindergarten, the focus may be teaching students the importance of personal response when discussing read-alouds. Teachers may even choose to have students arrange their chairs in a circle and describe such discussion times as Literature Circles. In first grade, teachers may build on what students learned in kindergarten by having the whole class meet in small groups to discuss texts read aloud by the teacher, texts read in teacher-guided small groups, or texts from shared reading. During this process, teachers may monitor the groups' discussion, prompting as necessary. As time progresses, students may discuss texts they have read independently. Second-grade teachers may choose to build on and refine this process. Third-grade teachers may then find themselves working with students who are very familiar with the Literature Circle process. Self-assessment can also be integrated in first grade and become more refined and detailed as the students progress through the grades. (Forms to facilitate student self-assessment can be found in Appendix D.)

The next section features teacher-designed models for using Literature Circles in the primary grades. These models are working successfully in the grades designated, but it is important to note that your students' needs and abilities will inform your decision to use one of these models or adapt one or more of them for use in your classroom. To access an additional resource for using Literature Circles at the primary level, see "Literature Circles With Primary Students Using Selected Reading" at http://www.readwritethink.org, a website maintained by the International Reading Association and the National Council of Teachers of English.

Model One: Tanya Kubrakovich's Kindergarten Class

Format for discussion: I do not do formal Literature Circles, but I do teach my students the value of discussion and how it contributes to understanding.

Preparation: Most of what I do to prepare my students to eventually participate in Literature Circles comes in the form of discussions before, during, and after a read-aloud and shared reading with Big Books. The following are often components of our discussions:

- predicting what may happen and confirming what actually happens (we use a chart to record our results—drawings and writing)

- looking at the pictures and discussing how they help us understand the story and how the pictures were made (we try and re-create several illustrators' work)

- comparing a book to another author's book or to the author's other work

- making "quick clouds" (children draw a picture in a cloud quickly)—this represents the thought they are having in their heads about the story; we share these ideas in small groups (see Appendix D, page 304, for a Quick Cloud blackline)

- talking about questionable or tricky words (words students have questions about; the word's meaning is usually the focus)

- playing detective with the Big Books (students are given a word and asked to locate the word by placing Wikki Stix [yarn coated with wax] around the word)

Comments: We recently read *My Apron: A Story from My Childhood* by Eric Carle (1995) and had quite the discussion about the apron and how the apron was used for something different than the children thought an apron would be used for. Our discussion of the apron led to everyone making personal connections, which truly enriched our grand conversation.

My students enjoy discussing what they read. I can see their abilities to respond through discussion increase as the year progresses.

Model Two: Leslie Fisher's First-Grade Class

Format for discussion: The whole class organizes into groups of four or five for Literature Circles. Students take turns being the discussion director, word finder, feeler, illustrator, and summarizer. The discussion director develops his own questions, although I do teach students how to develop effective questions before we begin using Literature Circles. The word finder locates and discusses tricky words. The feeler finds the part of the text he liked best and shares it with the group, explaining why he selected it. The group then uses it as a point of discussion. The illustrator creates a drawing in response to the text and encourages the group to discuss it. The summarizer shares the most important ideas from the text and the discussion. Students often write or sketch in their Guided Comprehension Journals while reading. They use this information to support their contributions to the discussion. I use direct instruction to teach students about Literature Circles.

Each group has a Literature Circle folder that contains the group's schedule, role rotation, student work, and group assessments. I review this at the end of each day that we do Literature Circles. If the group accomplished all of its tasks and worked well together, I place a sticker in the folder.

Students choose each time whether they will read the text chorally, individually, or with a buddy. When they have finished reading, each assumes one of the roles.

When the discussions are complete, students engage in an extending activity. They choose a way to share what they have read with the class. They have shared poster-size story maps, alternative endings, murals, lyric summaries, and talk-show segments about the texts they have read.

Preparation: I find that my first-grade students are accustomed to talking about what they read, but I do spend time reviewing or teaching skills they need to effectively participate in Literature

Circles. For example, we practice guidelines for cooperative learning, including speaking one at a time, respecting everyone's ideas, and assuring that everyone has opportunities to contribute to the discussion. We also discuss each group member's responsibility to the group as a whole and practice using group reflections for assessment purposes.

Text: Students read and discuss theme-based trade books and a variety of leveled texts.

Comments: My first graders are very enthusiastic about Literature Circles. They enjoy reading and sharing their ideas. I use direct instruction to teach the students about Literature Circles, and I continue to scaffold their learning by providing support as needed when they are in their groups. I should note that once students become totally comfortable with this routine, they seem to take pride in helping their circle be successful and enjoy working independently.

One of the most interesting things I have observed is students negotiating meaning through discussion. This has also been evident when they have worked on their extension activities. For example, when one group completed a poster-size draw-and-label retelling to share their reading with the class, group members discussed the characters, setting, problem, and solution in great depth, assuring that all the important details were present in the sketches and sentences.

Model Three: Victoria Principe's Second-Grade Class

Format for discussion: Students are working independently in groups of four. No roles other than book club leader are used. The leaders open the conversations with a question or statement either by using a prompt card or creating one of their own. This role is modeled for students prior to their engaging in Literature Circles independently.

Preparation: Students need to know how to have a conversation, choose texts, and work cooperatively in order to have successful experiences in Literature Circles. I directly teach these processes prior to beginning Literature Circles.

Text: We have a book club board in our classroom. The students sign up in the morning for the text set of their choice. The text sets may be collections of books written by the same author, different versions of the same story, or books about a particular genre, theme, or concept. For example, we have poetry books, Jan Brett books, books about the ocean, and books about the moon. Six text sets are being used at one time, and the sets are rotated until the children have had a chance to read at least one book from each set. The children understand that if they are not able to use a particular text set on a certain day, they will have an opportunity to use it soon.

Comments: Because I teach second grade, I engage in direct instruction of Literature Circles to scaffold students' learning and assure that students understand the process. I also make some modifications and adaptations to accommodate my students. These include the following:

- Audio books for nonreaders are provided for students who have difficulty reading so they may be included in the discussions.

- Partners for reading, including peers, upper-grade students, parent helpers, and tutors are available if needed.

- General prompts to promote discussion are provided for each group. Questions include "How are the characters the same?" "How are they different?" "How were the stories alike and different?" "If you were in the story, which character would you want to be? Explain your choice." The question prompts help the students stay on task and promote discussions, while leaving it open-ended at the same time.

Model Four: Samantha Shyka's Grade 2/3 Combined Class

Format for discussion: I organize my students in discussion groups based on interest, not on reading levels. I do use roles, and I am careful to teach the roles to the students before the Literature Circles begin.

Preparation: To explain the concept of Literature Circles to parents, I often tell them that Literature Circles are the equivalent of book clubs for adults. This statement seems to make parents comfortable and more interested in the concept of Literature Circles. It also helps parents to realize that children need to talk about what they are reading.

I introduce the students to Literature Circles by asking them if they have ever talked to anyone about their favorite book, movie, or television show. This always meets with a positive response. When I ask them what they have talked about, their responses usually include the people, the places, what happened, and why they liked it. Then I draw parallels between their responses and the characters, the setting, the story summary, and making connections.

Before starting Literature Circles, I teach the students the roles that they will be using— discussion director, word wizard, clever connector, interesting illustrator, passage picker, and summarizer. Once the students are comfortable with book discussions, the next step begins: learning the Literature Circle roles. In order to successfully participate in a Literature Circle, all students should be comfortable and confident with all the roles. I usually begin by teaching the role of the interesting illustrator and then move through the remaining roles to the discussion director. During this time, I read aloud and all the students practice the same role. This allows for discussion on that specific role and assists me in locating any students who may require extra help. After all the roles have been learned and reviewed, Literature Circles begin.

Once the students are organized into groups, they meet, decide their roles, and read the text. Reading the text may take several forms. Once the students have read the text, they work on their roles independently. When the students have developed their roles and recorded information on the corresponding forms, the group meets to discuss the book. During the book discussion, each group member assumes his or her role (in no particular order).

Text: Students are offered a choice from four or five texts. I present the texts to the class, and the students list their preferences. I use this information to organize the discussion groups.

Comments: The students usually complete very high-quality work in Literature Circles. I attribute this to their reading, their knowledge of their roles, and knowing that the rest of the group is counting on them for a specific purpose.

Model Five: Joseph Walsh's Third-Grade Class

Format for discussion: Students work independently in small groups of four. They take turns assuming the roles of discussion director, literary luminary, connector, and illustrator.

Preparation: Even though my students used Literature Circles in second grade, I engage in a very detailed review of the skills, strategies, and processes necessary for Literature Circles to function successfully. This helps students to reconnect with the process and refine their understanding before they engage in Literature Circles independently. I also introduce the text sets and remind students that writing ideas and drawing sketches in their Guided Comprehension Journals while reading will help them to engage in more meaningful discussions.

I find that it is beneficial to review self-assessment techniques before students engage in Literature Circles independently. I explain and model how to use a self-reflection form to record ideas about personal and group performance (see Appendix D, pages 289–290). After discussing this process, I guide students through their initial use of the form and focus on how to use their reflections to set new goals. I find that self-assessment helps students to understand that they are accountable for the time they spend in Literature Circles.

Text: My students use text sets as the basis of their Literature Circles. The sets are theme-based and support whatever theme we are currently studying.

Comments: When I first started using Literature Circles, I was truly surprised by the depth and quality of student discussion in this independent setting. They assume their roles, contribute meaningful ideas to discussion, and engage in negotiation of meaning.

I do provide adaptations to accommodate students' needs. They include the following:

- I have recorded many of the books in the text sets on tape as a resource for struggling readers. I am grateful to parent volunteers and upper-grade students for their help in facilitating this.

- Students choose which text set they want to read after we engage in book passes. I make certain that every text set contains titles that accommodate students' reading levels.

Regardless of whether you use one of the models presented or create your own adaptation, it is important to remember that we share common goals when using Literature Circles. We are promoting student exploration, fostering reader response, and encouraging students to be independent thinkers.

RECIPROCAL TEACHING: WHAT WE KNOW

Reciprocal Teaching involves scaffolded instruction and discussion of text based on four comprehension strategies: predicting, questioning, clarifying, and summarizing. The students as well as the teacher take on the role of "teacher" in leading the discussion about the text (Palincsar & Brown, 1984).

Reciprocal Teaching has three purposes:

1. to help students participate in a group effort to bring meaning to a text

2. to teach students that the reading process requires continual use of the four strategies (predicting, questioning, clarifying, summarizing) for effective comprehension

3. to provide students with the opportunity to monitor their own learning and thinking

Duke and Pearson (2002) describe a Reciprocal Teaching session in the following way:

> A typical Reciprocal Teaching session begins with a review of the main points from the previous session's reading, or if the reading is new, predictions about the text based on the title and perhaps other information. Following this, all students read the first paragraph of the text silently. A student assigned to act as teacher then (a) asks a question about the paragraph, (b) summarizes the paragraph, (c) asks for clarification if needed, and (d) predicts what might be in the next paragraph. During the process, the teacher prompts the student/teacher as needed, and at the end provides feedback about the student/teacher's work. (p. 225)

Implementing Reciprocal Teaching

In Guided Comprehension, students learn Reciprocal Teaching through direct instruction before using it as an independent comprehension routine. The following steps will facilitate this process:

- Explain the procedure and the four strategies, noting their definitions, why they are important, and how they help us comprehend.
- Model thinking related to use of the four strategies by using an authentic text and Think-Alouds.
- Guide the students, in a whole-class setting, to think about their reading by providing responses for each of the strategies using verbal prompts, such as those suggested by Mowery (1995):

    Predicting:

    > I think…
    >
    > I bet…
    >
    > I wonder…
    >
    > I imagine…
    >
    > I suppose…

    Questioning:

    > Who? Where? When? What? How? Why?

    Clarifying:

    > I did not understand the part where…
    >
    > I need to know more about…
    >
    > This changes what I thought about…

    Summarizing:

    > This paragraph is about…
    >
    > The important ideas in what I read are…

- Practice by organizing the students in groups of four and provide each group with a text to read and use as the basis of their Reciprocal Teaching.
- Assign one of the four strategies and suggested prompts to each group member.
- Have students engage in Reciprocal Teaching using the process modeled.

- Reflect by providing time for discussion and self-assessment forms (see Appendix D) to facilitate students' thinking about how strategy use affected their comprehension and what their future goals will be.

This process provides students with opportunities to share their thinking in a reciprocal fashion. While students are participating in their groups, we can monitor their activity and scaffold the dialogue when appropriate. Once the students are skilled at using Reciprocal Teaching, they can use it as an independent comprehension routine.

Studies by Palincsar and Brown (1984) demonstrate that students with a wide variety of abilities can use Reciprocal Teaching successfully. Although originally designed to help students who could decode well but had weak comprehension skills, all students benefit from this type of instruction because it allows them to read and understand more challenging texts (Palincsar & Brown, 1984).

Text Selection

In Reciprocal Teaching, the level of text is determined by students' abilities and the instructional setting in which this routine is being used. For example, when students have learned how to use Reciprocal Teaching and teacher support is available, narrative texts should have complex story lines and require critical thinking. Expository texts should have complex organizations and enough information for students to distinguish essential from nonessential information. When students are learning how to use Reciprocal Teaching in a whole-class setting or if students are using Reciprocal Teaching independently to practice using multiple comprehension strategies, texts should be at students' easy or independent reading levels.

Assessing Reciprocal Teaching

Teachers can assess students in Reciprocal Teaching groups by observing their ability to successfully use the strategies (see Appendix E, page 325). Students may self-reflect on contributions (see Appendix D, page 307) or may keep notes of the ideas they contributed. These data will help teachers create whole-class or small-group minilessons on using the strategies.

USING RECIPROCAL TEACHING IN THE PRIMARY GRADES

Although Reciprocal Teaching is used more often in the intermediate and middle grades, it also can be used successfully in the primary grades (Palincsar & Brown, 1986). Observing an intermediate class successfully using Reciprocal Teaching as an independent routine may inform how you will use Reciprocal Teaching in your primary classroom. While observing, consider your students' needs and abilities and what you can do to help prepare them for using Reciprocal Teaching.

For example, kindergarten teachers may support the process by teaching related comprehension skills—such as generating questions and sequencing—as well as how to predict and retell. Students may also practice assuming the role of the teacher in center activities such as Transparency Talk and A-B-C Watch Me Read! In first grade, students may learn additional skills and strategies and use the Reciprocal Teaching process as a heavily scaffolded whole-group activity. Second graders may begin using Reciprocal Teaching as an independent routine, a process that may be refined and extended in third grade. Teachers at all levels may wish to create Thinking Records (Keene & Zimmermann, 1997) for each strategy. This involves defining the strategy on a long piece of paper that is adhered to the wall. Students complete the Thinking Records by providing examples of how they used the strategies while reading. When engaging in Reciprocal Teaching, students may also benefit from using Reciprocal Teaching Bookmarks (Allen, 2002) (see Appendix D, pages 305–306), which contain the four strategies and prompts that facilitate their use.

Examples of teachers' ideas for using Reciprocal Teaching in the primary grades follow. Each teacher provides some information about the class he or she taught and what was done to promote students' engagement in Reciprocal Teaching.

Model One: Madeline Apfel's Kindergarten Class

I would describe what I did with my students as "Getting Started With Reciprocal Teaching." I observed third-grade classes first to get a sense of what Reciprocal Teaching looked and sounded like. After those experiences, I observed second- and first-grade classes. After numerous discussions with the teachers of the classes I observed and colleagues who teach kindergarten, I thought about the abilities and needs of my students and began "Getting Started With Reciprocal Teaching."

First, I knew I would need to use a whole-class setting. Next, I revisited predicting and summarizing, two strategies that I had modeled early in the year and that we—as a class—had become proficient in using. Then I introduced the role of the teacher and the students delighted in it. We used "I Wonder" Statements—one of their very favorite methods of predicting—and Summary Sentences to engage in our adapted version of this routine. I prompted the students to engage in questioning and clarifying as necessary, but the students took turns being the teacher for the predicting and summarizing phases of the routine during the rest of our Reciprocal Teaching experiences.

Model Two: Karen Bell's First-Grade Class

My first-grade students had a true mix of reading abilities, but I found that Reciprocal Teaching benefited all of them. I think the fact that I always tried to use engaging text and that students thoroughly enjoyed being the teacher contributed to its success.

As my teaching of Guided Comprehension progressed and students became increasingly aware of the reading strategies and the need to use them in concert, I began teaching Reciprocal Teaching in a whole-class setting. In the beginning, I provided copies of an easy text for the students in the class as well as the members of my demonstration group. I reviewed the comprehension strategies involved in the process and reminded the students about the variety of ideas we had learned to apply the strategies. Then I modeled Reciprocal Teaching through Think-Alouds, as I played the role of the teacher in a small demonstration group. I did this on multiple occasions to provide modeling with a variety of texts and to assure that every student had an opportunity to participate in a demonstration group. Seeing Reciprocal Teaching in action helped the students to understand the process. It also clarified the role of the teacher for me. I gained a better understanding of how to word meaningful prompts to encourage quality responses. Next, I guided students to assume the role of the teacher in similar demonstration sessions. In the spring, I began organizing Reciprocal Teaching groups of four students within the whole-class setting. We used a read-think-write pattern throughout the process. We would read a paragraph, pause to think and write an idea in our Guided Comprehension Journals, and then engage in the four-step strategy process. Whole-class sharing and reflection always followed this.

Model Three: Kevin Gress's Second-Grade Class

By the time the students arrived in my second-grade classroom, they had a good background in using Reciprocal Teaching. They had used it as a whole-group process in first grade.

I began by reviewing the necessary comprehension skills and strategies and focusing on the importance of knowing a repertoire of strategies to use as needed. I explained that we would begin by organizing Reciprocal Teaching groups in a whole-class setting and then add Reciprocal Teaching to Literature Circles and Cross-Age Reading Experiences we used as independent small-group routines in Stage Two of Guided Comprehension.

The whole-class experience worked well, and we were able to integrate Reciprocal Teaching as a routine sooner than I expected. The students had a good command of the strategies and thoroughly enjoyed being the teacher. I was somewhat surprised that the struggling students were so secure with the process, but they successfully engaged in every aspect of Reciprocal Teaching. In discussions with teaching peers, we reasoned that their proficiency was the result of scaffolded instruction and use of the routine.

My students completed self-assessments of personal and group performance in Reciprocal Teaching (see Appendix D, page 307) and shared the highlights of their Reciprocal Teaching experiences, as well as their work from the other routines and comprehension centers, in Stage Three of Guided Comprehension. This provided an additional forum for discussion of student performance.

Model Four: Judy Burke's Third-Grade Class

At the beginning of the year I talked with my students about Reciprocal Teaching. Most of them were familiar with this routine, so my goals included reviewing this routine and the strategies it involved, organizing and managing the routine, and teaching the students how to be accountable when using Reciprocal Teaching.

I began by describing the multiple-strategy nature of Reciprocal Teaching, reviewing the strategies, and demonstrating the process. After I explained and demonstrated, we practiced by engaging in Reciprocal Teaching in groups of four within a whole-class setting. Students used Reciprocal Teaching Bookmarks (Allen, 2002) (see Appendix D, pages 305–306), which featured strategy prompts during this process. We did this on several occasions before integrating Reciprocal Teaching into our comprehension routines. During this process, students also practiced reflecting on individual and group performance during Reciprocal Teaching. Once we began using Reciprocal Teaching as one of our routines, it became a natural part of our Guided Comprehension lessons.

How you support students' use of Reciprocal Teaching will depend on their needs and abilities. To decide what you will do to contribute to students' understanding and use of this routine, you may wish to meet with your fellow primary-grade teachers. This will provide an opportunity to develop a general plan for integrating Reciprocal Teaching across the primary grades. The plan may be revised during the year, as students have opportunities to demonstrate their abilities.

CROSS-AGE READING EXPERIENCES: WHAT WE KNOW

Cross-Age Reading Experiences generally involve a novice working on a specific task with a more knowledgeable person for a particular period of time. This type of learning is especially applicable in education, in which practitioners frequently model and scaffold learning for less-experienced learners. Forman and Cazden (1994) note that such educational practices reflect Vygotsky's thinking about adult-child relationships and offer an alternative to traditional adult-child interactions. In educational contexts, there are a variety of people who may play the role of the more knowledgeable other in cross-age relationships with our students. These people include community volunteers, upper-grade students, and classroom aides.

In Guided Comprehension, Cross-Age Reading Experiences are routines that involve exploration, strategy application, and the construction of personal meaning. The resulting learning experiences are meaningful and memorable for all involved.

Implementing Cross-Age Reading Experiences

When planning Cross-Age Reading Experiences, there are options to consider. To begin, the cross-age partners must be identified. Students from upper grades, community volunteers, and classroom aides are among those who may volunteer for this position. Once the partners are selected, a few informal training sessions should be held. These meetings may focus on modeling read-alouds, reviewing comprehension strategies, demonstrating upcoming teaching ideas, and discussing the role of the partner in the cross-age experience. It is important that the partners understand that this routine is part of the Guided Comprehension Model and that it is a time for students to practice and transfer comprehension strategies. It is also helpful to introduce a range of texts to the partners.

Scheduling is another important consideration. The partners will need to be available during the reading/language arts block. Community volunteers and classroom aides should be able to work with students on a consistent basis. Upper-grade students may be available only once a week for a limited amount of time, but they still provide important models for students. Examples of Cross-Age Reading Experiences situated within theme-based Guided Comprehension lessons can be found in Chapters 6–9.

Text Selection

The texts used in Cross-Age Reading Experiences will vary by type and genre according to the theme of study. However, they should be easy-level texts so the students can use them without teacher assistance.

Assessment in Cross-Age Reading Experiences

Self-assessments similar to those that emerge from Literature Circles and Reciprocal Teaching also can be used for Cross-Age Reading Experiences (see Appendix D, page 281, and Appendix E, page 323).

USING CROSS-AGE READING EXPERIENCES IN THE PRIMARY GRADES

Cross-Age Reading Experiences are easily situated in the primary grades. They provide a setting for a wide variety of meaningful comprehension-related activities, including student read-alouds and skill and strategy applications, including multiple modes of response. When first beginning Cross-Age Reading Experiences, primary teachers often organize them as a whole-class activity.

Model: Leslie Fisher's First- and Third-Grade Reading Buddies

My first-grade students have Cross-Age Reading Experiences with third graders. Every Friday my students meet with their third-grade reading buddies, either in our room or theirs. Before we start with our Reading Buddy Program, I go to the third-grade class for a period, while the third-grade teacher takes my class. I talk to the third graders about when they learned how to read and what they remember. We talk about the different strategies they use when they read and I teach them the strategies I want them to use when helping my first graders with their reading. I give them each a strategy bookmark with pictures that will help guide their first-grade readers when they get stuck on a word. I also talk to them about helping to motivate their readers by using positive talk and by making the reading experience fun for them. We talk about questioning and ways to get the first graders thinking about the story. I usually meet with the third graders two or three times before they actually start working with their first-grade buddies.

Each week my students bring a book on their independent level, their instructional level, and a book that they would like their buddy to read with them to these meetings. The third graders bring a book of their choice that they think their buddy would enjoy. They often check out books from the library, the class library, or from home. They read a story to their buddy and use prompts to promote discussions. The third-grade teacher gives them an assignment on Thursday to find a book to read, practice it, and come up with some questions for their buddy. They read their story and then help my students read their books using the strategies to help their buddies.

In addition to Guided Comprehension, we do lots of other fun activities with the students like have a pajama party where we all dress in our pajamas and read with our flashlights and stuffed animals. We also do interviews, pen pal with each other, dress as our favorite character, give book talks, and celebrate with holiday parties and Lunch Bunch (we eat lunch with our buddies in our room). We also celebrate All About Our Buddy Day.

My students look forward each week to reading with their buddies. The third graders have already told me they have seen great progress in their first-grade readers. When I initially went to the third graders about working with my students, one boy said I should pay him for helping. I told him he would receive an award, but it wouldn't be something he could touch. He didn't understand what I meant. I explained to him that the reward would be how good he felt inside from helping and seeing his buddy learn to read. A few weeks ago he came up to me and told me he already got his reward that day. It made me realize how important this program is not only to my students but also to the third graders.

Stage Two of Guided Comprehension provides students with a variety of meaningful settings in which to practice comprehension skills and strategies. In teacher-guided small-group instruction, students' reading has teacher support as needed. In student-facilitated comprehension centers and routines, students engage in independent applications. Student assessment and leveled texts are integral to all three of these settings.

In the next chapter, the roles of assessment and leveled text are examined in detail. A variety of practical assessments are described, information about leveled texts is presented, and student-text matches are discussed.

CHAPTER 5

Assessment and Leveled Texts

Dynamic assessment and leveled texts are integral components of Guided Comprehension. Assessment provides information about our primary-level students. Leveling provides information about our materials. The results of assessment and leveling inform our teaching and help us to make meaningful student-text matches.

This chapter provides information about both topics. The first part of the chapter focuses on assessment in Guided Comprehension. It describes the dynamic nature of assessment and makes connections to state standards. The assessment section also features descriptions of a number of practical, informative primary-level assessments and introduces the Guided Comprehension Profile, an organizational framework for documenting student progress. The second part of the chapter makes connections between assessment and leveled texts by delineating the role of each in creating student-text matches. The final section focuses on leveled texts and factors that influence accessibility. Topics discussed include student accessibility, choosing appropriate texts, methods of leveling, and classroom text organization. (Appendixes E and F, which contain a variety of reproducible assessments and sources of leveled texts, support this chapter.)

ASSESSMENT IN GUIDED COMPREHENSION

Assessment in Guided Comprehension is dynamic in nature. It occurs in an ongoing manner, offers insights into the learning process, chronicles student development, and is a natural component of teaching and learning (McLaughlin, 2002). This aligns with constructivist thinking that purposeful assessments should be an inherent part of teaching and learning (Brooks & Brooks, 1993; Tierney, 1998). Dynamic assessment also supports Vygotsky's belief that assessment should extend to scaffolded experiences to capture students' emerging abilities (Minick, 1987).

Assessment in Guided Comprehension has several purposes, including the following:

- to provide an approximate range of reading levels for students
- to offer insights into student attitudes and interests
- to facilitate student-text matches

- to inform grouping for teacher-guided instruction
- to provide windows to students' thinking
- to document students' performance
- to provide information for evaluation

Assessment permeates every stage of the Model and occurs in a variety of forms and settings. For example, diagnostic assessments are used to group students for teacher-guided instruction in Stage Two. The teacher employs formative measures to monitor student learning in a continuous, ongoing manner in all stages of the Model and uses summative assessments to examine what students have learned over time. The measures used for diagnostic and formative purposes tend to be informal and flexible, focused on process. Summative assessments are often more formal and fixed, focused on product (McMillan, 1997).

Connections to State Assessments

As educators, we are all well aware that students are required to take state assessments at multiple points during their K–12 careers. In fact, students' engagement with high-stakes testing often extends beyond their school years to university entrance and professional certification requirements. Although our personal thinking about these measures may be more closely aligned with the position statements issued by the American Education Research Association, International Reading Association, and National Council of Teachers of English, we know that student performance on state assessments affects schools, districts, curricula, teachers, students, and materials. For these reasons, demonstrating how Guided Comprehension supports student performance on these measures is vital.

Some state departments of education are taking active roles in making connections between the state assessments and classroom instruction. For example, the Pennsylvania Department of Education has created a website (http://www.pde.state.pa.us) that contains instructional strategies that focus on connecting the Pennsylvania Academic Standards and the Pennsylvania System of School Assessment. The site includes sample classroom assessment items and rubrics for four levels: primary, intermediate, middle school, and high school. Also in Pennsylvania, the Partnership for Educational Excellence Network has published *Early Childhood Learning Continuum Indicators*, which addresses students' learning in literacy and math in grades K–3 (see http://www.pde.state.pa.us/nclb/lib/nclb/earlychildhoodcontinuum.pdf).

The Guided Comprehension Model for the Primary Grades supports the aspects of comprehension addressed in U.S. national standards, state standards, and related documents. The Model has a comprehension focus, promotes knowledge of text structure, encourages question generation at multiple levels, and supports making connections—text-self, text-text, and text-others. The Model and the state documents also strongly support the focuses of *Put Reading First: The Research Building Blocks for Teaching Children to Read* (Partnership for Reading, 2001): phonemic awareness, phonics, fluency, vocabulary, and comprehension. (See Appendix B for practical teaching ideas for each of the emphasized areas.)

Assessment is an integral facet of Guided Comprehension and a focus of state departments of education. Assessments used in Guided Comprehension are described in the next section.

Practical Assessment Measures

When preparing to teach Guided Comprehension, we assess to gather information about students' reading backgrounds, to determine approximate range of reading levels, and to gain insights into students' knowledge and use of comprehension strategies. Results of these assessments inform several aspects of our planning, including lesson content, student-text matches, and grouping students for guided instructional settings.

This section presents a number of practical, effective assessments divided into two categories: assessments that provide information about students' backgrounds and assessments that provide information about students' current reading abilities and strategy use. Descriptions of the assessments and their connections to the Guided Comprehension Model for the Primary Grades are included.

Assessments to learn about students' backgrounds. Some assessments provide insights into students' pasts that enable us to better understand their present attitudes toward and performance in reading. Examples of these measures include attitude surveys, interest inventories, literacy histories, and motivation profiles. (Reproducible copies of these measures are included in Appendix E.)

Attitude surveys are designed to illuminate students' feelings about their literacy experiences. The most common formats are question and response, sentence completion, and selected response. How students feel about various aspects of reading and writing, how they would define reading and writing, and how they would describe successful readers and writers are among the topics often addressed. Information gleaned from these surveys also provides insights into factors that may have contributed to students' current attitudes toward literacy. (Reproducible primary-level reading and writing attitude surveys can be found in Appendix E, pages 313–314.)

Guided Comprehension connection: Completed surveys contribute to our understanding of students' perceptions of literacy and resulting motivational needs.

Interest inventories are informal surveys designed to provide information about students' literacy habits and general backgrounds. Topics typically addressed include students' reading preferences, hobbies, and special interests. The most common formats for interest inventories are question and response or sentence completion. These surveys are relatively easy to complete and provide information about numerous topics including genre and author preferences, what students are currently reading, and whether students choose to read beyond required assignments. (Interest inventories appropriate for the primary grades can be found in Appendix E, pages 317–318.)

Guided Comprehension connection: Completed inventories inform our decisions about text selection and student-text matches.

Literacy histories chronicle students' literacy development from earliest memory to present day (McLaughlin & Vogt, 1996). They facilitate students' ability to make connections between their past literacy experiences and their current beliefs.

To create their personal literacy histories, students engage in questioning and reflection. Sources they use to construct their histories range from family memories to early-grade writing samples to copies of favorite books. Students can choose the mode of presentation, and I have received everything from time lines to scrapbooks replete with family photos. To model this assessment, share your literacy histories and provide students with prompts to guide the process. (Reproducible literacy history prompts for the primary grades are included in Appendix E, page 319.)

Guided Comprehension connection: Literacy histories offer insights into students' development that contribute to our understanding of the students and their current attitudes toward literacy.

The **Motivation to Read Profile** (Gambrell et al., 1996) consists of two instruments: the Reading Survey and the Conversational Interview. The cued response survey, which requires 15 to 20 minutes for group administration, assesses the self-concept of a reader and value of reading. The interview, which features open-ended free-response questions and requires 15 to 20 minutes for individual administration, assesses the nature of motivation, such as favorite authors and interesting books. The Conversational Interview (see Appendix E, pages 320–322) has three emphases: narrative text, informational text, and general reading.

Guided Comprehension connection: Knowledge of what motivates students to read both narrative and informational text enhances our understanding of our students and informs meaningful text selection.

Attitude surveys, interest inventories, literacy histories, and motivation profiles provide background information that informs our understanding of individual students and their literacy needs. These measures contribute vital information as we seek to provide optimum literacy experiences for our students. These assessments are easy to administer, require little time, and provide insights that may not be discerned from other literacy assessments.

Assessments to learn about students' reading levels and strategy use.

Some assessments provide insights into students' ability to use comprehension strategies to comprehend text. Examples of these measures include metacognitive strategy inventories, miscue analysis, student writing samples, and observation. (Reproducible copies of many of these measures are included in Appendix E.)

Miscue analysis (Goodman, 1997) assesses students' use of the graphophonic, syntactic, and semantic cueing systems. Miscues indicate how a student's oral reading varies from the written text. Miscue analysis is used for three purposes: to determine oral reading accuracy, to code and analyze miscues to determine needs for strategy instruction, and to evaluate the retelling for insights into student comprehension.

To analyze miscues, Goodman, Watson, and Burke (1987) suggest that teachers use the following four questions:

1. Does the miscue change the meaning?
2. Does the miscue sound like language?
3. Do the miscue and the text word look and sound alike?
4. Was an attempt made to self-correct the miscue?

To facilitate the use of the miscue analysis in Guided Comprehension, the teacher selects some "anchor books"—both fiction and nonfiction—and has students do an informal oral reading, which is tape recorded. At this point the teacher codes and analyzes the students' miscues. The students also do a brief retelling based on this text. These two pieces of information provide approximate student reading levels and insights into their strategy use and comprehension. There are some defined accuracy percentages that may influence the determination of a reader's range of levels: below 90%, frustration; 90–95%, instructional; 96–100%, independent. However, when assessing students' levels we also need to consider factors such as background experience with the content, interest in the text, and supports within the text.

There are a number of published resources that facilitate the administration of miscue analysis. The Qualitative Reading Inventory (QRI), which ranges from preprimer to high school, is detailed in the next section. Other published resources include the following:

Leveled Reading Passages Assessment Kit (Houghton Mifflin, 2001): This assessment offers word lists, leveled reading passages, benchmarks, and scoring forms for levels ranging from kindergarten/ beginning grade 1 to grade 6.

PM Benchmark Introduction Kit (Rigby, 2001): This assessment includes leveled reading passages, benchmarks, and scoring forms for grades K–5.

Classroom Reading Miscue Assessment (Rhodes, Shanklin, & Valencia, 1990): This alternative view of miscue analysis includes specific points of observation and retelling criteria (see Appendix E, page 315).

Guided Comprehension connection: Miscue analysis provides approximate reading levels, helps the teacher make matches between readers and texts, and informs instruction.

The **Qualitative Reading Inventory–3** (QRI) (Leslie & Caldwell, 2000) is a comprehensive assessment that ranges from preprimer to high school. It includes fluency and comprehension measures that enable us to estimate students' reading levels, match students with appropriate texts, and verify suspected reading difficulties. Because there are so many components to this measure, we need to make choices when using it. For example, we may choose to do the miscue analysis and then use either the retelling checklist or the comprehension questions that accompany each leveled passage to determine students' instructional levels.

Guided Comprehension connection: The QRI provides information necessary to place students in teacher-guided small groups and create student-text matches.

Running records were developed by Marie Clay (1993a) as a way to observe, record, and analyze what a child does in the process of reading. The teacher assumes the role of a neutral observer for the purpose of taking a record of the child's independent reading behavior. Running records provide qualitative and quantitative information about what a reader knows and what needs to be learned next. In addition, running records help the teacher to make informed decisions concerning instructional needs, approximate reading levels, grouping for guided reading, and making student-text matches. (To learn how to use running records, see *Running Records: A Self-Tutoring Guide* [2000] by Johnston and *Assessment and Instruction of Reading Difficulty* [2003] by Lipson and Wixson.)

Guided Comprehension connection: Running records are used to assess students for placement and advancement purposes in teacher-guided small groups and to inform the teacher's understanding of students' reading.

Student writing is a flexible assessment. It can be used for numerous purposes including applying strategies, using text structures, and recording personal responses. It can also be used as a mode of reflection and goal setting. We observe and analyze student writing for multiple purposes including language structure, use of vocabulary, knowledge of sight words and spelling patterns, and organization.

Guided Comprehension connection: Writing is a mode of expression for students' thinking that informs all stages of the Model.

Observation is one of the most flexible assessments because it can offer information about virtually any aspect of literacy in which students engage. For example, we can observe if we want to assess students' fluency, record ideas about their engagement, or comment on their roles in cooperative learning activities.

Before we begin observing, we need to establish a purpose and determine how we will record the information gleaned from this measure. For example, if we are observing a student who is doing an oral retelling, we can use a checklist that includes information such as the characters, setting, problem, attempts to resolve, and resolution and that has a section for us to record additional comments. In contrast, if we are observing a student's contribution to a cooperative activity, the checklist might include items such as the student's preparation for the group's work, engagement with peers, and contributions. (Reproducible observation guides can be found in Appendix E, pages 323–325.)

Guided Comprehension connection: This informal technique can be used in all stages of the Model to gain insights into students' performance.

What we want to know about our students determines which assessments we use. Therefore, our goal is not to use all these measures to assess each reader but rather to make choices and use the measures that provide the information we need. The assessments described in this section are practical, can be used for multiple purposes, and offer valuable insights into students' backgrounds and abilities.

In addition to the measures described, informal assessment opportunities are embedded in all stages of the Guided Comprehension Model. These formative measures are situated in a variety of instructional settings and provide occasions for students to demonstrate what they know through multiple modes of response including reading, writing, discussion, illustration, drama, and music. For example, one of the most authentic measures of students' abilities to use the comprehension strategies is simply evidence of their application. We can observe students using the strategies while reading, and we can also review their applications in formats such as Concept of Definition Maps, Story Impressions, Retellings, and Lyric Summaries.

Guided Comprehension Profiles

Guided Comprehension Profiles were designed to facilitate organizing and managing student assessments over time. The profiles house examples of student strategy applications, assessments, and other indicators of student progress. Teachers select assessment information to include in the Profile (interest inventories, literacy histories, running records, retellings, etc.). Some measures such as student writing, observations, and comprehension strategy applications are included systematically. Teachers use these assessments to document student progress, refine guided instruction groups, and inform future instruction.

The Guided Comprehension Profile Summary provides an overview of the assessment information contained in the Profile. It features space for the teacher to summarize students' background information at four points during the school year and space to record students' reading levels and observations of strategy use. The Guided Comprehension Profile Summary provides an at-a-glance view of student progress and facilitates evaluation and reporting. (A reproducible copy of this organizer is included in Appendix E, page 316.)

LINKING ASSESSMENT AND LEVELED TEXT

Once assessments are used to determine students' approximate reading levels, we can group students for teacher-guided small-group instruction, placing students of similar abilities together. It is important to remember that grouping in this stage of the Model is dynamic in nature; students will move to groups using more challenging levels of text as they become more proficient.

Assessment results also inform student-text matches. When students' approximate reading levels and interests are known, we can make meaningful matches to encourage student engagement in all stages of the Model. Student access to a variety of genres and levels of text is an essential component of this process.

For example, a second-grade student may have a third-grade instructional level and a second-grade independent level. This student's book basket would contain both levels of text—third-grade books for guided small-group instruction and second-grade books for independent practice. Similarly, if a third-grade student has a second-grade instructional level and a first-grade independent level, he or she would need access to second-grade texts for guided small-group instruction and first-grade texts for independent practice. As the students become more proficient and move to groups using more challenging text, their access to texts would change accordingly.

The process of choosing appropriate text for each student is challenging because there are so many variables to consider. Assuring that text is accessible involves not only leveling the texts themselves but also making good matches between the readers and the texts. Two factors that influence these decisions are student information and text information.

Student Information

Before planning meaningful Guided Comprehension instruction, the teacher needs to determine each student's independent and instructional level. We use this information for two purposes: to form teacher-guided small groups and to inform teacher-directed whole-group instruction and students' independent applications in the comprehension centers and routines. Miscue analysis

(Goodman, 1997), which assesses students' oral reading and comprehension, is a viable source of this information.

Hunt (1996/1997) suggests that students also contribute to determining text accessibility. He recommends that students engage in self-evaluation during independent reading by responding to questions such as the following:

- Did you have a good reading period today?

- Were you able to concentrate as you read independently?

- Did the ideas in the book hold your attention?

- Were you bothered by others or outside noises?

- Could you keep the ideas in the book straight in your mind?

- Did you get mixed up in any place? Were you able to fix it?

- Were there words you did not know? How did you figure them out?

- Were you hoping the book would end, or were you hoping it would go on and on?

Although these queries require only yes or no responses, they do provide insights into students' perceptions of their performance. This information can be useful when determining the appropriateness of a text for the reader.

We also need to gather data on student experiences and interests. This can be accomplished through interviews, observations, or interest inventories.

Text Information

Once information about each student is gathered, we need to consider what texts we will use. The following three steps can be used to facilitate this process:

1. Identify the texts already available in the classroom. These may include basals, anthologies, trade books, textbooks, magazines, poetry books, and picture books.

2. Organize the texts to facilitate Guided Comprehension. The following questions can be used to accomplish this:

   - Does this text add to existing content area study or knowledge?

   - Can this text be used in a genre study?

   - Does this text exemplify a particular style, structure, language pattern, or literary device? Can this text be used to teach a comprehension strategy?

   - Are there multiple copies of the text available?

   - Does this text match a particular student's interests?

   - Is this a good example of a text structure?

   - Is this text part of a series?

   - Is it written by a favorite author?

These questions can be used with both narrative and expository texts, including individual stories in literature anthologies as well as individual articles within magazines.

3. Acquire additional materials to assure ample accessible texts for all readers. It is important to have some small sets of books to use during teacher-guided comprehension groups, but it is also necessary to have a wide array of texts, varying in type, genre, length, and content. All students must have a multitude of accessible books within the classroom. These books must represent a wide range of readability and genre. It is important to include novels of varying lengths, nonfiction trade books, picture books, poetry books, and magazines.

Keep in mind the following ideas when adding to your classroom collections:

- content areas—nonfiction and narrative text to supplement studies in math, science, and social studies
- student interests—a variety of texts (fiction, nonfiction, poetry) to match students' interests
- read-alouds—texts that offer examples of a variety of text structures and engaging story lines to be used to demonstrate comprehension processes and fluency
- anchor books—texts used in whole-group and small-group instruction to demonstrate a specific strategy or routine
- sets of books—small sets (four to six copies) of books to be used in Guided Comprehension small groups; these should be based on students' levels as well as the strategies that can be taught and used
- text sets—series books, favorite author, genre, topic; several books that have a common characteristic

Once we have accumulated the texts, we need to organize them to accommodate all stages of the Model.

LEVELED TEXT IN GUIDED COMPREHENSION

Authentic text is a mainstay of Guided Comprehension. The Model is motivational, dynamic, and real, but none of these characteristics matter if the text is not accessible to students. Readers need opportunities to engage with multiple levels of texts in a variety of instructional settings. The Guided Comprehension Model for the Primary Grades accommodates that need.

This section of the chapter focuses on making text accessible to students. It begins by describing the various levels at which text can be accessible and the factors that influence accessibility. This is followed by the rationale for using leveled texts, ideas for text organization, and suggestions to facilitate leveling. Finally, commercially published leveled texts are discussed and connections are made to Appendix F, which features leveled book resources.

Students' Reading Levels and Accessible Texts

Students can usually engage with multiple levels of text if they have appropriate teacher support. Students can engage with independent level or easy text when working on their own; they can

Figure 5. Accessible Texts

Text Level	Teacher Support	Guided Comprehension
Independent	No teacher support needed.	Stage Two: independent centers and routines
	Just right when students are reading on their own and practicing strategy application.	
Instructional	Some teacher support needed.	Stage Two: teacher-guided small groups
	Just right when guiding small groups.	
Challenging	Full teacher support needed.	Stage One: teacher-directed whole groups
	Just right when doing read-alouds in whole group.	
	(*Note*: Because full teacher support characterizes this setting, independent and instructional level texts also can be used.)	

engage with instructional level or "just right" text when they have some teacher support; and they can engage with independent, instructional, and challenging texts when they have full teacher support, such as during teacher-directed whole-group instruction. This means that even though students should work with independent level texts when reading on their own, they can engage with text at a challenging level if we share it through a read-aloud. Figure 5 illustrates how these texts are generally situated in the Guided Comprehension Model. It is important to remember that descriptions of texts at these levels are approximations and that factors beyond the text influence student accessibility.

Accessible text is a core component of comprehension instruction. For students to learn to use reading strategies to enhance comprehension, it is important that they learn within their zone of proximal development (Vygotsky, 1934/1978), the context in which learners can be successful if their learning is scaffolded by a more knowledgeable other. In Guided Comprehension, teachers are the more knowledgeable others, and we can scaffold students' learning in a variety of ways including the use of modeling, thinking aloud, prompting/reminding, or coaching (Brown, 1999/2000; Roehler & Duffy, 1991).

Factors That Influence Accessibility

There are several factors that influence the accessibility of a text; some reside in the reader, others are determined by the text. Reader factors include background knowledge and prior experience with language and types of texts, motivation, and critical thinking. Text factors include type and structure, page layout, content, and language structure (Fountas & Pinnell, 1999; Weaver, 2000).

Reader factors.   Readers' **background knowledge** of text content, language, and text type influence accessibility. If students have background knowledge, they will be more familiar with vocabulary and concepts. This would also provide a greater brain framework to make relevant connections to the new information. This is true for both narrative and expository texts and is influenced by the amount of time spent reading each type.

Motivation to read also is influenced by students' prior experience with texts. Students who have spent years reading textbook chapters and answering the questions at the end of chapters can have negative feelings when asked to read for information. This is also true for students who have had stories so chopped up for vocabulary study or detail recall that the major themes and meaning have been lost. Students who have had positive, successful experiences with texts have greater motivation to try more challenging or longer texts.

Once students begin to read more challenging or longer texts, **thinking critically** and reading between the lines become essential for comprehension. Texts that have supports, such as pictures and examples, may be a better match for students who lack higher levels of critical thinking. On the other hand, students who have the ability to make connections and inferences will be able to read more challenging texts.

Text factors.   Students' knowledge of and experience with **text type and structure** can affect accessibility. This means that if students have a greater background in reading narrative text—which is generally based on characters, setting, problem, attempts to resolve, and resolution—they may find reading expository text more difficult. One reason for this may be that expository text has a greater variety of structures including problem-solution, comparison-contrast, sequence, description, and cause and effect (Vacca & Vacca, 2002). Students' familiarity with these structures facilitates their transaction with texts.

Goldman and Rakestraw (2000) have drawn the following three conclusions from existing research on students' knowledge of text structure:

1. Readers use their knowledge of structure in processing text.
2. Knowledge of structural forms of text develops with experience with different genres, and is correlated with age/time in school.
3. Making readers more aware of genre and text structure improves learning. (p. 321)

The **page layout**—such as the size of print, the number or availability of pictures or other visual cues, the range of punctuation, the layout and organization of print, and the number of words per page—are the influential factors in this category.

Often the **text content** requires background knowledge by the reader in order to be fully interpreted. Students who have a vast amount of knowledge of a specific topic will find the text more accessible simply because the vocabulary and concepts are familiar. This will allow them to make interpretations and connections with the information provided. Similarly, with narrative texts, a student who has good experience reading mysteries will be able to read many levels of mysteries because the process of looking for clues and an unlikely suspect is familiar.

Texts with unfamiliar **language structure**—such as difficult or technical vocabulary—tend to be more difficult for students to read and comprehend. When the vocabulary is challenging, readers often spend more energy decoding, thereby decreasing fluency and comprehension. Similarly, texts with complex and unusual sentence structures pose challenges for readers who lack the background knowledge or language familiarity to make connections and interpretations. The use of literary language and devices—such as metaphor, simile, or onomatopoeia—also may be challenging for readers unfamiliar with them (Fountas & Pinnell, 1999).

Considering all these text features is essential when we choose texts and create student-text matches. Because some of these features may pose challenges to the reader, we need to be familiar with the texts and what, if any, supports each has to offer students. Supports include illustrations, support information (such as table of contents or book jacket summary), text set up (including font size and sentence layout), dialogue, book and chapter leads, and chapter formats (such as continuation from chapter to chapter and length) (Szymusiak & Sibberson, 2001). Harvey (1998) suggests supports specific to nonfiction texts: fonts and special effects, textual cues ("similarly," "for instance"), illustrations and photographs, graphics, and text organization.

We need to help students understand these supports and how to use them to facilitate comprehension. The more blatant the supports, the easier it is for the reader to understand and make connections.

Classroom Text Organization

Our goal is to organize the texts efficiently to promote their optimum use. This includes texts for us to use in whole-class and small-group teaching as well as texts for students to use during independent routines and comprehension centers.

To facilitate accessing text for teaching, Harvey and Goudvis (2000) suggest accumulating a master list of titles and organizing them according to what they have to offer as teaching models. For example, Nancy Shaw's (1995) *Sheep Out to Eat* and Eric Carle's (2002) *Does a Kangeroo Have a Mother, Too?* might be organized with books that promote phonemic awareness and phonics. Patterned books, such as *Brown Bear, Brown Bear, What Do You See?* (Martin, 1967) and *We're Going on a Bear Hunt* (Rosen, 1997), might be placed with books that promote fluency. *The Little Red Hen Makes a Pizza* (Sturges, 1999) and *Cook-a-Doodle-Doo!* (Stevens & Crummel, 1999) might be organized with books that foster predicting or making connections. Books also can be organized by genre, author study, or title. (For lists of books to use when teaching phonemic awareness, phonics, and fluency, see Appendix B; for a list of alphabet books, see Appendix D, page 272; for extensive lists of themed texts, see Chapters 6–10 and Appendix G.)

To provide accessible texts for student-facilitated comprehension centers and routines, you might use the following methods of organization:

Class book baskets: Creating book baskets by author, series, content, or approximate reading level is one method. With the teacher's help, students can then make selections from a whole collection of books in the basket.

Individual book baskets: We can also help students to create individual book baskets in which they keep an ongoing collection of books they want to read. This eliminates any "down time" when students need to select text for independent reading.

Individual student booklists: Students keep these lists in the back of their Guided Comprehension Journals. Titles can be added to the list in an ongoing manner to accommodate student progress. These books would be stored in the classroom book baskets.

To further facilitate text organization, Szymusiak and Sibberson (2001) recommend that books in classroom collections be placed face out so readers can easily see the covers and preview the texts and that sections for fiction, nonfiction, and poetry be marked clearly.

Methods for Leveling Texts

All text levels are approximations, and there is no specific rule for determining them. Text ease or difficulty is determined by both text and reader factors. Each text will need to be evaluated with specific readers in mind. Leveling systems, teacher judgment, paralleling books, and using leveled lists developed by others facilitate this process.

Leveling systems. Several systems exist that will help determine the approximate level of a text. These take into consideration factors such as format, language structure, and content (Weaver, 2000). The following are examples of these formulas: the Primary Readability Index (Gunning, 1998), Reading Recovery (Clay, 1985), and the Fountas and Pinnell Leveling System (1996, 1999).

Teacher judgment. Although these leveling systems provide a starting point for leveling texts and have been used in the primary grades, teacher judgment may be the most often used method in leveling texts for the upper grades. The following processes can be used for leveling texts:

- Separate books into fiction, nonfiction, and poetry.
- For each type of book, divide the books into harder and easier.
- Take each pile of books and sort by hardest to easiest (repeat this process as necessary).
- Label or color code levels for student access.

The process of leveling texts works best when several teachers work together and discuss the decision-making process.

Paralleling books. Another way to level texts is to parallel classroom books with titles from published lists. Factors such as length, font size, number of illustrations, and type of text can be matched with lists of published leveled books to determine approximate levels. The lists provide model books to represent approximate levels (see Appendix F, pages 331–333).

Published lists and websites for leveled books. Using published resources is another method of leveling books. These collections provide titles at various levels that can be used in creating student-text matches and in all stages of Guided Comprehension. We can use these lists as resources for identifying anchor books and for assessment purposes. Many sets of leveled books, which include narrative and expository texts, are available for purchase. (Information about these sources, including websites, is detailed in Appendix F.)

GUIDED COMPREHENSION: FAVORITE AUTHOR ERIC CARLE
SUMMARIZING: DRAW AND LABEL RETELLING

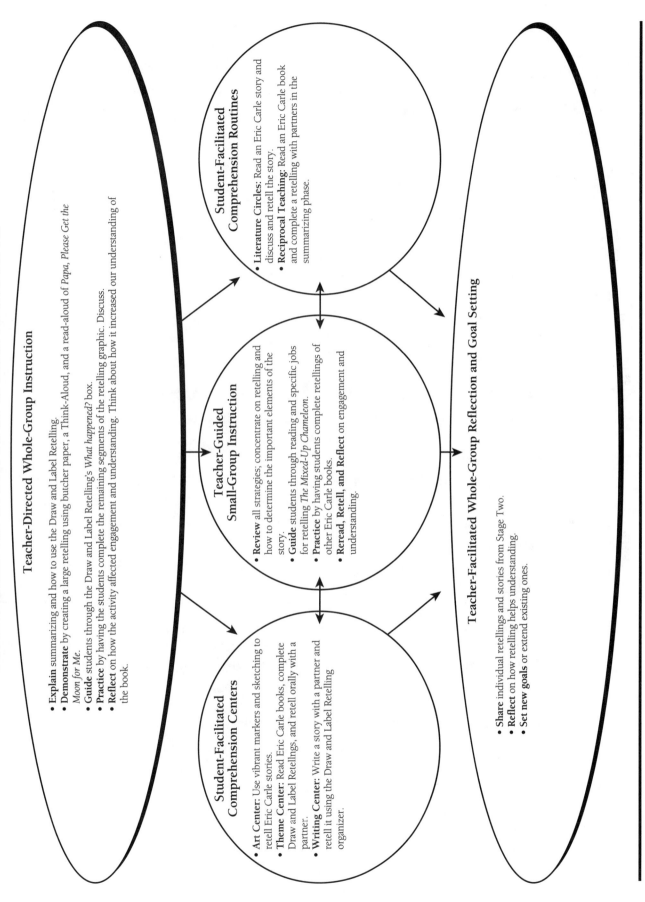

Teacher-Directed Whole-Group Instruction

- **Explain** summarizing and how to use the Draw and Label Retelling.
- **Demonstrate** by creating a large retelling using butcher paper, a Think-Aloud, and a read-aloud of *Papa, Please Get the Moon for Me*.
- **Guide** students through the Draw and Label Retelling's *What happened?* box.
- **Practice** by having the students complete the remaining segments of the retelling graphic. Discuss.
- **Reflect** on how the activity affected engagement and understanding. Think about how it increased our understanding of the book.

Student-Facilitated Comprehension Centers

- **Art Center:** Use vibrant markers and sketching to retell Eric Carle stories.
- **Theme Center:** Read Eric Carle books, complete Draw and Label Retellings, and retell orally with a partner.
- **Writing Center:** Write a story with a partner and retell it using the Draw and Label Retelling organizer.

Teacher-Guided Small-Group Instruction

- **Review** all strategies; concentrate on retelling and how to determine the important elements of the story.
- **Guide** students through reading and specific jobs for retelling *The Mixed-Up Chameleon*.
- **Practice** by having students complete retellings of other Eric Carle books.
- **Reread, Retell, and Reflect** on engagement and understanding.

Student-Facilitated Comprehension Routines

- **Literature Circles:** Read an Eric Carle story and discuss and retell the story.
- **Reciprocal Teaching:** Read an Eric Carle book and complete a retelling with partners in the summarizing phase.

Teacher-Facilitated Whole-Group Reflection and Goal Setting

- **Share** individual retellings and stories from Stage Two.
- **Reflect** on how retelling helps understanding.
- **Set new goals** or extend existing ones.

Guided Comprehension in the Primary Grades by Maureen McLaughlin ©2003. Newark, DE: International Reading Association. May be copied for classroom use.

Please Get the Moon for Me.) I continued to model by thinking aloud as I looked back through the book to find out about the setting. When I found the necessary information, I drew a picture of the setting in the designated box. Then I wrote a sentence to label my drawing.

Guide: I continued to the *What happened?* box and guided the students in completing the box. The students worked in small groups and drew what happened in the designated box on forms I had provided for them. Then each group wrote a sentence to label their drawing and shared their responses with the class. After discussing their efforts, I quickly sketched what happened on the large graphic and wrote a sentence to label my drawing.

Practice: Students practiced by completing the *How did it end?* box in their small groups. They shared their drawings and sentences with the class and, based on their responses, I completed the Draw and Label Retelling I had posted on the board. Then we used the information on the organizer to create a whole-class oral retelling of *Papa, Please Get the Moon for Me.*

Reflect: After retelling the story, we talked about how summarizing helps us to remember the important information about what we have read. One of the students observed that drawing what was important made summarizing fun. Another commented that the form was like a map telling us what to do next. We concluded our discussion by sharing ideas about how we could use the Draw and Label Retelling in Stage Two.

STAGE TWO: Teacher-Guided Small-Group Instruction

Text: *The Mixed-Up Chameleon* (1998) (Texts varied according to students' abilities.)

Review: I reviewed summarizing, the story elements, and things good readers do to determine the most important events.

Guide: I guided the students through the reading of *The Mixed-Up Chameleon*. Then we discussed the Draw and Label Retelling organizer, and students completed the *Who?* and *Where?* boxes. They shared their responses with the group, and we discussed their ideas. Then students shared and discussed their sketches.

Practice: Students continued by completing the *What happened?* and *How did it end?* boxes on the Draw and Label Retelling. Then they used the completed organizer to retell the story orally. I observed the students' progress during this activity. (Figure 14 shows examples of Tanika's and Jesse's Draw and Label Retellings.)

Reread, Retell, and Reflect: When students finished rereading the story, we engaged in an oral group retelling. Then we talked about Eric Carle, his stories, and how the Draw and Label Retelling extended our understanding and enjoyment of his books.

Student-Facilitated Comprehension Centers

Art Center: Students used vibrant markers and the Draw and Label Retelling organizer to retell an Eric Carle story.

Theme Center: Students worked with partners and read one of the Eric Carle books I had placed in the center. After reading, they completed the Draw and Label Retelling, retold the story, and displayed their completed organizer in a space provided in the center.

Writing Center: Students worked with partners and wrote flipbook stories about an Eric Carle book of their choice. Then they completed Draw and Label Retellings of their stories. Keena

Figure 14. Draw and Label Retellings for *The Mixed-Up Chameleon*

Who?
Draw:
Label: KmeLin

Where?
Draw:
Label: Dazrt

What happened?
Draw:
Label: he trn in to a FLmigo

How did it end?
Draw:
Label: he is bacto nomL

Who?
Draw:
Label: Chameleon

Where?
Draw:
Label: Zoo

What happened?
Draw:
Label: Mixed up

How did it end?
Draw:
Label: Wish hm self bak

and Jim's flipbook was titled *The Very Hungry Puppy*. Kyle and Stephanie's flipbook was titled *The Very Grouchy Cat*.

Student-Facilitated Comprehension Routines

Literature Circles: I adapted the Literature Circle by limiting the roles to literary luminary and discussion director. One group of students read *Walter the Baker* (1998) and used it as the basis of their discussion. Then they created a group Draw and Label Retelling.

Reciprocal Teaching: Students focused only on the predicting and summarizing phases of this routine. I provided prompts to facilitate these. In the summarizing phase, students worked with a partner to create a Draw and Label Retelling. The sets of partners then took turns retelling the story orally.

STAGE THREE: Teacher-Facilitated Whole-Group Reflection and Goal Setting

Share: Students shared in small groups the retellings they created in Stage Two of Guided Comprehension. I monitored this and then we engaged in a whole-group sharing of the stories they wrote in the writing center. Students then displayed their books in our Eric Carle gallery and put their retellings into their Guided Comprehension Profiles. (See Chapter 5 for more information on these profiles.)

Reflect: We reflected on how well we could summarize and retell stories using the Draw and Label Retelling. We also reflected on how summarizing improved our understanding of the story and the benefits of using this format.

Set New Goals: We decided we were good at using the Draw and Label Retelling and that we would extend our goal of learning how to summarize by learning about Comic Strip Summaries (McLaughlin & Allen, 2002a).

Assessment Options

I used observation, students' completed retellings, students' stories, and student self-reflections as assessments.

FINAL THOUGHTS ABOUT THE ERIC CARLE THEME

It was great fun to observe the Eric Carle theme being taught by a number of primary-grade teachers. It was clear during the theme and long after it ended that Eric Carle's writing and art were engaging topics for students and teachers alike.

As noted earlier in this book, a number of skills underpin the comprehension strategies that serve as the focus of this theme. Although space restraints prohibited sharing lessons at the skill level, I think it is important to note that lessons on a variety of aspects of language development and skills such as sequencing, generating questions, and distinguishing important from less important ideas were embedded in the theme. For example, Eric Carle titles such as *Does a Kangaroo Have a Mother, Too?* were used in kindergarten lessons to promote phonemic awareness. (For ideas about using literature to teach phonemic awareness, phonics, and fluency, see Appendix B.) *The Grouchy Ladybug*, *The Very Hungry Caterpillar*, and *The Secret Birthday Message* (1997) served as the bases of lessons about sequencing, and students engaged in repeated readings of patterned books such as *Polar Bear, Polar Bear, What Do You Hear?* (Martin 1997; illustrated by Carle) to improve fluency. Other Eric Carle titles such as *Dream Snow* and *"Slowly, Slowly, Slowly," Said the Sloth* peaked students' interest in questioning, and the illustrations in all of Eric Carle's books sparked students' interest and creativity. In addition, teachers adapted lessons for prereaders and prewriters by engaging in read-alouds and encouraging response through a variety of modes—including discussion, drawing, painting, singing, dancing, and dramatizing.

THEME RESOURCES

Texts

Carle, E. (1973). *Do bears have mothers too?* New York: HarperCollins.

Carle, E. (1988). *Do you want to be my friend?* New York: Putnam.

Carle, E. (1989). *The very busy spider.* New York: Putnam.

Carle, E. (Contrib.) (1990). *All in a day.* New York: Philomel.

Carle, E. (1990). *The foolish tortoise.* New York: Simon & Schuster.

Carle, E. (1991). *Pancakes, pancakes!* New York: Simon & Schuster.

Carle, E. (1991). *Papa, please get the moon for me.* New York: Simon & Schuster.

Carle, E. (1993). *The greedy python.* New York: Simon & Schuster.

Carle, E. (1994). *The very hungry caterpillar.* New York: Philomel.

Carle, E. (1995). *Eric Carle's treasury of classic stories for children.* New York: Cartwheel Books.

Carle, E. (1995). *My apron: A story from my childhood.* New York: Putnam.

Carle, E. (1996). *The art of Eric Carle.* New York: Philomel.

Carle, E. (1996). *Eric Carle's dragons dragons: And other creatures that never were.* New York: Putnam.

Carle, E. (1996). *I see a song.* New York: Econo-Clad Books.

Carle, E. (1997). *Draw me a star.* New York: Putnam and Grosset.

Carle, E. (1997). *Flora and Tiger: 19 very short stories from my life.* New York: Philomel.

Carle, E. (1997). *Have you seen my cat?* New York: Simon & Schuster.

Carle, E. (1997). *The secret birthday message*. New York: HarperCollins.

Carle, E. (1997). *The very quiet cricket*. New York: Penguin.

Carle, E. (1998). *Hello, red fox*. New York: Simon & Schuster.

Carle, E. (1998). *Little cloud*. New York: Philomel.

Carle, E. (1998). *The mixed-up chameleon*. New York: HarperCollins.

Carle, E. (1998). *1, 2, 3 to the zoo*. New York: Econo-Clad Books.

Carle, E. (1998). *Walter the baker*. New York: Simon & Schuster.

Carle, E. (1998). *You can make a collage: A very simple how-to book*. New York: Klutz.

Carle, E. (1999). *From head to toe*. New York: HarperCollins.

Carle, E. (1999). *The grouchy ladybug*. New York: HarperCollins.

Carle, E. (1999). *The very clumsy click beetle*. New York: Putnam.

Carle, E. (1999). *The very lonely firefly*. New York: Philomel.

Carle, E. (2000). *Dream snow*. New York: Philomel.

Carle, E. (2001). *The honeybee and the robber: A moving/picture book*. New York: Putnam Penguin.

Carle, E. (2001). *Rooster's off to see the world*. New York: Simon & Schuster.

Carle, E. (2001). *The tiny seed*. New York: Scholastic.

Carle, E. (2001). *Today is Monday*. New York: Scholastic.

Carle, E. (2002). *Does a kangaroo have a mother, too?* New York: HarperCollins.

Carle, E. (2002). *A house for hermit crab*. New York: Aladdin Paperbacks.

Carle, E. (2002). *"Slowly, slowly, slowly," said the sloth*. New York: Penguin Putnam.

Carle, E. (2002). *Watch out! A giant!* New York: Simon & Schuster.

Books Illustrated by Eric Carle

Carle, E. (1989). *Eric Carle's animals, animals*. New York: Philomel.

Green, N. (1987). *The hole in the dike*. New York: HarperCollins.

Martin, B. Jr. (1967). *Brown bear, brown bear, what do you see?* New York: Henry Holt.

Martin, B. Jr. (1997). *Polar bear, polar bear, what do you hear?* New York: Henry Holt.

McLerran, A. (2000). *The mountain that loved a bird*. New York: Aladdin.

Singer, I.B. (1987). *Why Noah chose the dove*. New York: Farrar, Straus & Giroux.

Sundgaard, A. (1991). *The lamb and the butterfly*. New York: Orchard Books.

Websites

Autobiographical Sketch of Eric Carle
www.edupaperback.org/authorbios/Carle_Eric.html

Carol Hurst's Children's Literature Site: Featured Author Eric Carle
www.carolhurst.com/newsletters/24dnewsletters.html

The Children's Literature Web Guide
www.ucalgary.ca/~dkbrown

The Eric Carle Museum of Picture Book Art
www.picturebookart.org

Eric Carle Resource Page
falcon.jmu.edu/~ramseyil/carle.htm

Grouchy Ladybug Resources
    www.eho.org/ladybug.htm

The Official Eric Carle Website
    www.eric-carle.com

Picture Book of Eric Carle's Illustrations
    www.picturebookart.org/home/index.asp

Scholastic Author Study: Eric Carle
    www.teacher.scholastic.com/lessonrepro/lessonplans/ecarle.htm

SCORE: The Very Hungry Caterpillar—Teacher Guide
    www.sdcoe.k12.ca.us/score/carle/carletg.html

Student Art Inspired by Eric Carle
    www.pausd.palo-alto.ca.us/hays/artstudio/carle_art.html

Related Websites

Brown Bears

Animal Diversity
    animaldiversity.ummz.umich.edu/accounts/ursus/u._arctos$narrative.html

California Academy of Sciences Library
    www.calacademy.org/research/library/biodiv/biblio/bears.htm

National Geographic
    www.nationalgeographic.com/bearcam

Insects: Caterpillars, Ladybugs, Fireflies

ABC Teach
    www.abcteach.com/Themeunits/Ladybugs/LadybugTOC.htm

Biodiversity Resource Center
    www.calacademy.org/research/library/biodiv/biblio/kids.htm

Butterfly Websites
    www.olemiss.edu/projects/nmgk12/curriculum/elementary/first/butterfly%20trunk/butterfly
    websites.doc

The Firefly Files
    iris.biosci.ohio-state.edu/projects/FFiles

Hairy the Caterpillar's Page for Kids
    m1.aol.com/abook4u/kidspage.htm

Learning the Secrets of Fireflies
    aso.jhs.choyo.kumamoto.jp/choyo-es/choyo-es96/choyo-es1001e.html

Insect Lore
    www.insectlore.com

Iowa State University's Tasty Insect Recipes
    www.ent.iastate.edu/misc/insectsasfood.html

National Wildlife Federation
www.nwf.org/wildlifework

The Spencer Entomological Museum
www.insecta.com/insecta/index.shtml

University of Kentucky Department of Entomology—Youth Facts
www.uky.edu/Agriculture/Entomology/ythfacts/entyouth.htm

Pretzels

Ask Yahoo
ask.yahoo.com/ask/20010627.html

Tom Sturgis Pretzels
www.tomsturgispretzels.com/Pretzel_History.htm

Videos

Eric Carle: Picture Writer. (1993). Berkeley, CA: Searchlight Films.

The Very Hungry Caterpillar *and Other Stories*. (1995). New York: Scholastic.

Performance Extensions Across the Curriculum

Art/Music/Drama

- Investigate Eric Carle's art techniques and explore how to use the techniques through resources such as the books *The Art of Eric Carle* and *You Can Make a Collage: A Very Simple How-To Book*, the videotape *Eric Carle: Picture Writer*, and the websites Picture Book of Eric Carle's Illustrations and Student Art Inspired by Eric Carle. Invite the students to become "picture writers" and create drawings to contribute to a class-authored wordless picture book.

- Watch a segment of Eric Carle's video on how he makes his "beautiful papers." Then use multiple colors of paint, large brushes, sponges, and toothbrushes to create designs on two pieces of paper with no particular picture in mind. After the papers dry, choose one to keep and use the other one to make an Eric Carle animal collage. Draw the animal's body parts on the back of the paper, cut them out, and paste them together on a contrasting sheet of construction paper. (Kimberly Burke, Mosser Elementary School)

- After reading *The Very Busy Spider*, use oil pastels to draw a spider and a fly. Then use cool colors, such as blue, green, and purple, to watercolor paint over the drawings. What the students don't know is that spider webs are predrawn on the papers with white crayon. The spider web appears before the students' eyes and the drawings become "magic pictures" because of the crayon resist. Allow the paintings to dry and write the book title on the paper. This works especially well with kindergarten students. (Kimberly Burke, Mosser Elementary School)

- Sing Eric Carle's song "Today Is Monday" from the book *Today Is Monday*. Extend students' thinking by writing a class song titled "Today Is Saturday" or other day of students' choice.

- Encourage and promote musical creativity by reading the story *I See a Song*. Have students illustrate a song they know using Eric Carle art techniques.

- Dramatize an Eric Carle story (e.g., *The Very Lonely Firefly* or *Papa, Please Get the Moon for Me*) in whole-class or small-group settings.

- Create puppets to represent the characters in an Eric Carle book or a class-authored Eric Carle-style book and use them to dramatize the story.
- Read *"Slowly, Slowly, Slowly," Said the Sloth* and create and dramatize class books such as *"Slowly, Slowly, Slowly," Said Mrs. Fisher's Class* and *"Quickly, Quickly, Quickly," Said Mrs. Baxter's Class*.
- Use *Dream Snow* as a model to develop a class book titled *Dream Fog, Dream Rain,* or *Dream Cloud*.

Mathematics
- Read the story *The Grouchy Ladybug* to introduce the concept of time to the hour, quarter hour, and half hour. Engage in class storytelling to create a parallel story that incorporates time (e.g., *The Grouchy Gorilla, The Hungry Grasshopper*).
- Discuss the story *Today Is Monday* to understand basic concepts of the modern calendar.
- Review counting skills with the book *1, 2, 3 to the Zoo*. Create a class book about the current focus of math study (e.g., *2 + 2 on the Farm, 2 x 2 at the Park*).
- Reinforce students' number sense by reading the story *Rooster's Off to See the World*.

Science
- Incorporate Eric Carle books such as *A House for Hermit Crab, Does a Kangaroo Have a Mother, Too?,* and *Eric Carle's Animals, Animals* into a unit on animals and animal habitats. Create Eric Carle stories or poems about animals being studied in class.
- Use the story *From Head to Toe* to describe and discuss the parts of the human body. Have students draw themselves and label the picture "head to toe."
- Explore the life cycle of a plant by reading the story *The Tiny Seed*.
- Discover how a spider makes a web in the book *The Very Busy Spider*.
- Introduce the process of the water cycle by reading the book *Little Cloud*.
- Read "My Father, My Teacher," a story about the nature walks Eric Carle took with his father, from *Flora and Tiger: 19 Very Short Stories From My Life* to help students understand how Carle became interested in nature. Then take the students on a nature walk and record what the class encounters in a class nature journal and have students sketch and label what they see.

Social Studies
- Use Eric Carle books to compare and contrast the feelings of characters (e.g., *The Grouchy Ladybug, The Very Lonely Firefly*).
- Use *The Mixed-Up Chameleon* to teach about self-esteem.
- Read the story *Walter the Baker* and research the invention of the pretzel and other such foods (e.g., the bagel, the doughnut).
- Explore cultures around the world through the story *All in a Day*.

Culminating Activity

We Are Authors and Illustrators Celebration: Invite parents and friends to a celebration of authors and illustrators featuring the work of Eric Carle and the students. Have students design and deliver the invitations. Display students' performances from the Eric Carle theme in the multipurpose room. These will include items such as students' books, artwork, songs, poems, plays, and completed strategy applications.

As the guests arrive, the students, who will be wearing their famous author nametags, will greet them. They will tell the guests about Eric Carle's writing and illustrations and then serve as tour guides to various displays of their performances from the theme. The students will share a few of

Eric Carle's books through read-alouds and dramatization. The class will also sing their Eric Carle songs and Lyric Summaries for their guests. Parents and other guests will be invited to write and draw on a wall-size Eric Carle-style mural titled *We Are All Writers and Illustrators*. At the conclusion of the program, students will autograph books they authored during the theme and present them to their families.

Refreshments, including grouchy ladybug cookies and very hungry caterpillar brownies, will be served to assure everyone enjoys the author celebration.

CHAPTER 7

The Neverending Adventures of Arthur the Aardvark

rthur the Aardvark is a favorite character of primary-grade students and teachers. Arthur seems to have a keen ability for getting into and out of trouble on an almost daily basis. The character's adventures in *Arthur's Computer Disaster* (1997), *Arthur's Family Vacation* (1993), and *Arthur Writes a Story* (1996) support this theory.

Arthur the Aardvark was created by Marc Brown. Brown's grandmother was a storyteller, and Brown started telling stories when his first son was born. One night he told a story about an aardvark named Arthur that hated its nose. That was the basis of the first Arthur book, *Arthur's Nose* (1986). Many of the characters featured in the Arthur series are based on people Marc Brown grew up with. For example, Buster is based on Terry Johnson, Brown's best friend in elementary school. Brown has also used ideas from his life experiences in his books. His many jobs as a truck driver, short-order cook, television art director, actor, costume designer, college professor, and farmer have provided material for his books. Brown has written a wide variety of Arthur books, including flapbooks, picture books, and chapter books.

The sample Theme-Based Plan for Guided Comprehension: The Neverending Adventures of Arthur the Aardvark (see Figure 15) offers an overview of the thinking and resources that support this theme. It presents a sampling of goals, state standards, assessments, texts, technology resources, comprehension strategies, teaching ideas, comprehension centers, and comprehension routines. The plan begins by delineating examples of student goals and related state standards. The student goals for this theme include the following:

- use appropriate comprehension skills and strategies
- interpret and respond to literature
- write a variety of types of text
- communicate effectively

Figure 15. Theme-Based Plan for Guided Comprehension: Arthur the Aardvark

Goals and Connections to State Standards

Students will

- use appropriate comprehension skills and strategies. Standard: learning to read independently
- interpret and respond to literature. Standard: reading, analyzing, and interpreting literature
- write a variety of types of text. Standard: types and quality of writing
- communicate effectively. Standards: types and quality of writing; speaking and listening

Teaching Ideas

1. Connection Stems
2. Mind and Alternative Mind Portraits
3. Draw and Label Retelling

Comprehension Strategies

1. Making Connections
2. Visualizing
3. Summarizing

Comprehension Centers

Students will apply the comprehension strategies and related teaching ideas in the following comprehension centers:

Art Center
Drama Center
Making Words Center
Poetry Center
Storytelling Center
Theme Center
Writing Center

Comprehension Routines

Students will apply the comprehension strategies and related teaching ideas in the following comprehension routines:

Literature Circles
Reciprocal Teaching
Cross-Age Reading Experiences

Assessment

The following measures can be used for a variety of purposes, including diagnostic, formative, and summative assessment:

Connection Stems
Double-Sided Mobiles
Draw and Label Retelling
Mind and Alternative Mind Portraits
Observation
Retelling
Running Records
Student Self-Assessments
Student Writing

Text	Title	Theme	Level
1.	*Arthur Writes a Story*	Arthur	2
2.	*Arthur's Family Vacation*	Arthur	2
3.	*Arthur's Computer Disaster*	Arthur	2

Technology Resources

Arthur Worldwide
www.arthurworldwide.com
PBS Kids: Arthur
www.pbskids.org/arthur
PBS Teacher Source
www.pbs.org/teachersource

These goals support the following state standards:

- learning to read independently
- reading, analyzing, and interpreting literature
- types and quality of writing
- speaking and listening

Examples of assessments used in theme-based Guided Comprehension lessons include observation, running records and retellings, skill and strategy applications, and student self-assessments. The Guided Comprehension lessons, which were designed and taught by primary-grade teachers, are based on the following strategies and corresponding teaching ideas:

- Making Connections: Connection Stems
- Visualizing: Mind and Alternative Mind Portraits
- Summarizing: Draw and Label Retelling

The texts used in teacher-directed whole-group instruction include *Arthur Writes a Story*, *Arthur's Family Vacation*, and *Arthur's Computer Disaster*. Numerous additional theme-related resources—including texts, websites, performance extensions across the curriculum, and a culminating activity—are presented in the Theme Resources at the end of the chapter.

In this theme, students' independent strategy applications occur in the comprehension centers and comprehension routines. The centers include art, drama, making words, poetry, storytelling, theme, and writing. The routines include Literature Circles, Reciprocal Teaching, and Cross-Age Reading Experiences. Sample websites complete the overview.

The three Guided Comprehension lessons that follow are presented through first-person teacher commentaries. Examples of student work are featured throughout the lessons.

GUIDED COMPREHENSION LESSONS

The Neverending Adventures of Arthur the Aardvark
Guided Comprehension Strategy: Making Connections
Teaching Idea: Connection Stems

STAGE ONE: Teacher-Directed Whole-Group Instruction

Text: *Arthur Writes a Story* (1996)

Explain: I began by explaining making connections, noting that the connections we make are usually text-self, text-text, and text-world. Next, I explained that a Connection Stem is part of a sentence that connects something that happened in the story with an experience we might have had. I noted it could also be an experience someone else might have had or remind us of something that happened in another book. I pointed to sentence strips containing the following stems and read them aloud.

That reminds me of…

I remember when…

I have a connection…

An experience I have had like that…

If I were that character, I would…

Demonstrate: I introduced *Arthur Writes a Story* by sharing the cover and reading aloud the opening pages. Next, I used a Think-Aloud to share my connections to the story. I began by thinking aloud about the cover, the title, and the first two pages of the story. As I spoke, I noted my text-self, text-text, and text-world connections. I noted that I could make a text-self connection because Arthur was writing a story, and that reminded me of how much I like to write stories. I said that I could make a text-text connection because *Arthur Writes a Story* reminded me of *Author: A True Story* (Lester, 1996), a book about writing that I read aloud a few weeks ago. I shared my text-world connection that Arthur's being a school student reminded me that school students often write stories. Next, I read page three of *Arthur Writes a Story* aloud. I held up a sentence strip on which I had written the Connection Stem, "I remember when…" and I made a text-self connection by recalling a time when I was in second grade and wrote a story about my dog, Smokey. Then I reminded students that I could make connections to Arthur's writing experience because I had been a student, I had written stories, I had read other stories about writing, and I knew what writers were expected to do. (See Connection Stems in Appendix C, pages 242–243.)

Guide: After reading aloud another section of *Arthur Writes a Story*, I held up a sentence strip on which I had written "I have a connection.…" I completed the Connection Stem by saying, "I have a connection to the way Arthur asked his friends what they were going to write. I remember starting to write a story and then talking to my friends. I thought the ideas they had for their stories were better and more interesting than what I was writing in my story." I reminded the students that I was able to make a text-self connection to Arthur's experience because I had experienced something

GUIDED COMPREHENSION: THE NEVERENDING ADVENTURES OF ARTHUR THE AARDVARK
MAKING CONNECTIONS: CONNECTION STEMS

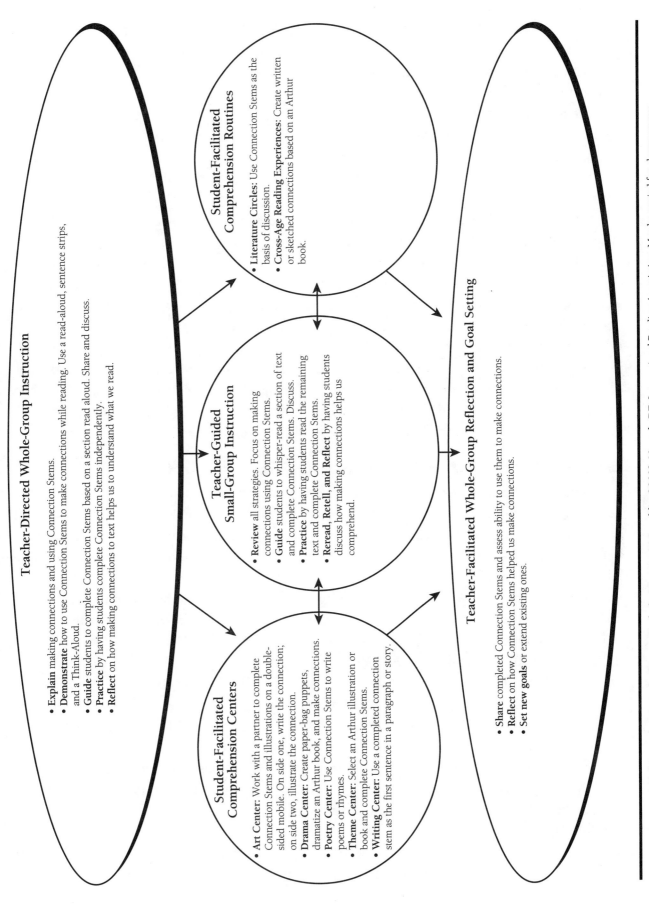

Teacher-Directed Whole-Group Instruction

- **Explain** making connections and using Connection Stems.
- **Demonstrate** how to use Connection Stems to make connections while reading. Use a read-aloud, sentence strips, and a Think-Aloud.
- **Guide** students to complete Connection Stems based on a section read aloud. Share and discuss.
- **Practice** by having students complete Connection Stems independently.
- **Reflect** on how making connections to text helps us to understand what we read.

Student-Facilitated Comprehension Routines

- **Literature Circles:** Use Connection Stems as the basis of discussion.
- **Cross-Age Reading Experiences:** Create written or sketched connections based on an Arthur book.

Teacher-Guided Small-Group Instruction

- **Review** all strategies. Focus on making connections using Connection Stems.
- **Guide** students to whisper-read a section of text and complete Connection Stems. Discuss.
- **Practice** by having students read the remaining text and complete Connection Stems.
- **Reread, Retell, and Reflect** by having students discuss how making connections helps us comprehend.

Student-Facilitated Comprehension Centers

- **Art Center:** Work with a partner to complete Connection Stems and illustrations on a double-sided mobile. On side one, write the connection; on side two, illustrate the connection.
- **Drama Center:** Create paper-bag puppets, dramatize an Arthur book, and make connections.
- **Poetry Center:** Use Connection Stems to write poems or rhymes.
- **Theme Center:** Select an Arthur illustration or book and complete Connection Stems.
- **Writing Center:** Use a completed connection stem as the first sentence in a paragraph or story.

Teacher-Facilitated Whole-Group Reflection and Goal Setting

- **Share** completed Connection Stems and assess ability to use them to make connections.
- **Reflect** on how Connection Stems helped us make connections.
- **Set new goals** or extend existing ones.

Guided Comprehension in the Primary Grades by Maureen McLaughlin ©2003. Newark, DE: International Reading Association. May be copied for classroom use.

similar. Next, I shared a variety of Connection Stems I had written on sentence strips and attached them to the board. Then I encouraged the students to use the Connection Stems to create their connections to that section of text. Students shared their connections with partners and then some of the students shared with the class. We discussed the students' connections and determined if they were text-self, text-text, or text-world. For example, Kaleena said, "I have a connection to when Arthur shared his story with D.W. because whenever I read my stories to my sister, she doesn't like them either." When I asked Kaleena which type of connection she had made, she said that she thought it was text-self because her connection was about something that had happened to her. The class agreed.

Practice: I continued reading aloud, and the students practiced by creating connections and sharing them with the class. We used this process throughout the book. As the story progressed, students became more comfortable sharing the type of connection as well as the connection itself. When the students were sharing their final connections to the story, Matt said that he had a text-self connection to Arthur doing what his teacher suggested and writing his story about his dog, Pal, because he liked writing stories about his yellow lab puppy, Cody.

Reflect: We reflected on how making connections helped us to understand what we read. Students observed that the more they knew about the topic of the story and the more experiences they had with it, the more connections they could make. They especially liked the text-self connections because they could share their life experiences. Finally, we talked about how we could use Connection Stems in other settings and with other types of text to help us comprehend.

STAGE TWO: Teacher-Guided Small-Group Instruction

Text: *Arthur's Baby* (1990) (Texts varied according to students' abilities.)

Review: I reminded the students about the comprehension strategies good readers use and focused on using Connection Stems. We discussed making connections between the text and themselves, the text and another text, and the text and the world. We noted student-created examples of Connection Stems from Stage One that were on display.

Guide: I introduced *Arthur's Baby* by sharing the cover and reading the opening pages. Students immediately noted connections about their younger brothers and sisters. I asked the students if this book reminded them of any other book we had read recently. They recalled that we had read *Julius, the Baby of the World* (Henkes, 1995), a book about a child's feelings toward a new family member. We discussed these connections and recalled that the students had made text-self and text-text connections. I reminded students to think about making connections as they whisper-read a section of *Arthur's Baby*. Students stopped at a predetermined point (I had placed stop-sign stickers in the text) and shared their connections. We discussed their ideas.

Practice: Students practiced by continuing to make connections by using the Connection Stems as they finished reading the text. They wrote at least three connections as they read, and we discussed their written connections at the conclusion of the story.

Reread, Retell, and Reflect: Students reread the story with a partner and we completed a group oral retelling. We reflected on how Connection Stems helped us to understand what we read and talked about how we could use this technique with informational texts.

Student-Facilitated Comprehension Centers

Art Center: Students worked with partners to create Connection Stem mobiles. They read Arthur books of their choice and completed at least three Connection Stems. Then they recorded the book title and author's name on their mobile. On each piece of the mobile, students wrote a connection on side one and drew an illustration on side two. Next, the students used yarn to fasten the parts of the mobile. When the mobiles were complete, students hung them in our theme gallery.

Drama Center: Students created paper-bag puppets and used them to dramatize an Arthur book of their choice. Students then completed the Connection Stems "This reminds me of…" and "If I were a character in this book…."

Poetry Center: Students chose one of their Connection Stems ("That reminds me of…," "I have a connection to…") and wrote a poem or rhyme. Some students used poem forms such as acrostics to write their poems. For example, Rick used a Connection Stem he had written about D.W. ("D.W. reminds me of my sister.") and wrote this acrostic using the word *sister*:

Susan is six

Is my little sister

She's ok for a sister

Teddy is her bears name

Every day she goes to sckool

Reading is one of her favrit things to do

Theme Center: Some students chose from a variety of illustrations picturing Arthur and his friends in various situations and completed Connection Stems about the illustrations. Other students selected an Arthur book and completed Connection Stems about the story.

Writing Center: Students used one of the Connection Stems to begin a theme-related paragraph or story that they wrote and illustrated.

Student-Facilitated Comprehension Routines

Literature Circles: The discussion director used completed Connection Stems as a basis for discussing the book the students read.

Cross-Age Reading Experiences: Students worked with a cross-age partner to read an Arthur book and create connections through either writing or sketching.

STAGE THREE: Teacher-Facilitated Whole-Group Reflection and Goal Setting

Share: We began by sharing Connection Stems from Stage Two. The students seemed to enjoy sharing the connections they had made. All the students seemed confident in their abilities to use Connection Stems, and their applications from Stage Two supported their thinking.

Reflect: We reflected on how Connection Stems helped us to make the three different kinds of connections and how that helped us understand what we read. Students also talked about how we could use Connection Stems with many different kinds of text including poetry, plays, song lyrics, newspaper articles, and hypertext.

Set New Goals: We decided to extend our goal about making connections by learning about drawing connections.

Assessment Options

Observation and review of students' Connection Stems, mobiles, and student-authored stories and poems informed my understanding of students' abilities to use this strategy. I also used running records and retellings to assess students' progress during this lesson.

The Neverending Adventures of Arthur the Aardvark
Guided Comprehension Strategy: Visualizing
Teaching Idea: Mind and Alternative Mind Portraits

STAGE ONE: Teacher-Directed Whole-Group Instruction

Text: *Arthur's Family Vacation* (1993)

Explain: I explained visualizing as creating pictures in our heads based on what we were reading. Then I explained Mind and Alternative Mind Portraits (McLaughlin, 2001), noting that we would sketch heads as we had done with Open-Mind Portraits (Tompkins, 2001), but this time we would be looking at the text from the perspective of two different characters and recording their thoughts by sketching and writing words inside the portraits. We discussed how we can look at any situation from more than one point of view and focused on examples such as a student being late for school (student, teacher, parent) and bedtimes (child, parent).

Demonstrate: I chose to use *Arthur's Family Vacation* to model this strategy because the book started off with the end of school and summer vacation just ahead. Also, in this story, Arthur himself is visualizing what his best friend Buster might be doing at camp. I began by introducing the story and explaining that, as I was reading, I would be thinking about the different perspectives or points of view from which the story could be told. Then I would choose two different characters and record the ideas they were thinking—either in words or sketches—inside the portraits I had drawn. I read the opening pages and began creating Mind and Alternative Mind Portraits (see Appendix C, page 255) for Arthur and D.W. because they viewed Arthur's vacation in different ways.

Guide: I continued reading the next section of the book, in which discussion of the vacation took place. I prompted the students to contribute ideas and recorded them inside the appropriate Mind Portrait as students added to their blackline masters.

Practice: While I read the rest of the book to the students, I stopped periodically to ask students' ideas about what we should add to each portrait. They recorded their ideas and sketches on the portraits on the overhead projector, and then we discussed how Arthur and D.W. visualized their vacation differently. Figure 16 shows Anna's and Marian's completed Mind and Alternative Mind Portraits for *Arthur's Family Vacation*.

Reflect: We focused on how visualizing contributes to our understanding of the text and how using Mind and Alternative Mind Portraits helped us to understand what we read. One of the students said that using the Mind Portraits helped her to think about the characters in different ways. Another student observed that looking at the story through different characters reminded him of *The True Story of the 3 Little Pigs!* (Scieszka, 1996) and other books that told fairy tales from different views.

STAGE TWO: Teacher-Guided Small-Group Instruction

Text: *Arthur's First Sleepover* (1994) (Texts varied according to students' abilities.)

Review: I reviewed the strategies good readers use and focused on visualizing and using Mind and Alternative Mind Portraits.

Guide: I introduced the story and explained that while we were reading we should be thinking about which characters we would use for our Mind and Alternative Mind Portraits. I guided

GUIDED COMPREHENSION: THE NEVERENDING ADVENTURES OF ARTHUR THE AARDVARK
VISUALIZING: MIND AND ALTERNATIVE MIND PORTRAITS

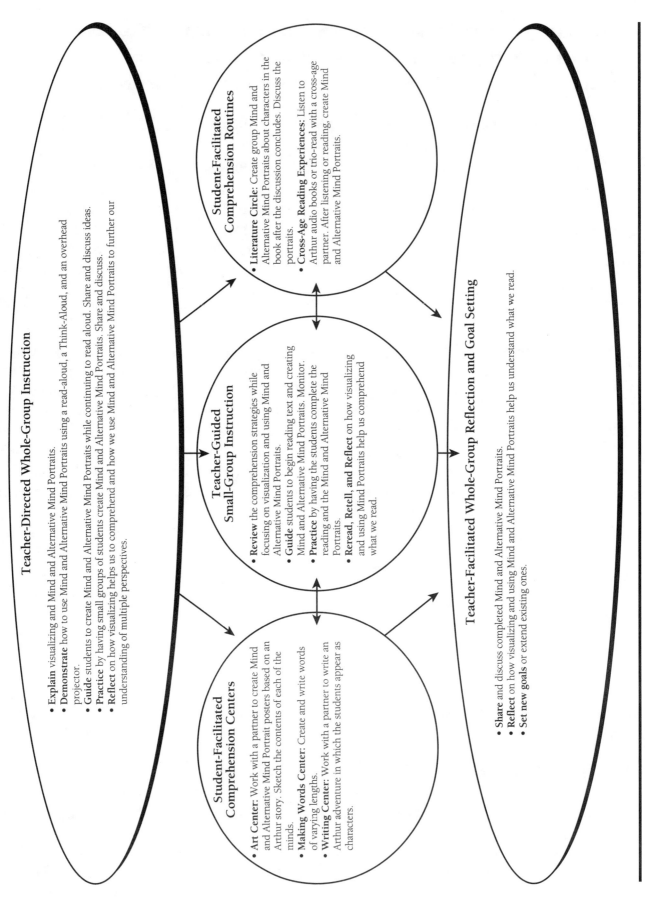

Teacher-Directed Whole-Group Instruction

- **Explain** visualizing and Mind and Alternative Mind Portraits.
- **Demonstrate** how to use Mind and Alternative Mind Portraits using a read-aloud, a Think-Aloud, and an overhead projector.
- **Guide** students to create Mind and Alternative Mind Portraits while continuing to read aloud. Share and discuss ideas.
- **Practice** by having small groups of students create Mind and Alternative Mind Portraits. Share and discuss.
- **Reflect** on how visualizing helps us to comprehend and how we use Mind and Alternative Mind Portraits to further our understanding of multiple perspectives.

Student-Facilitated Comprehension Routines

- **Literature Circle:** Create group Mind and Alternative Mind Portraits about characters in the book after the discussion concludes. Discuss the portraits.
- **Cross-Age Reading Experiences:** Listen to Arthur audio books or trio-read with a cross-age partner. After listening or reading, create Mind and Alternative Mind Portraits.

Teacher-Guided Small-Group Instruction

- **Review** the comprehension strategies while focusing on visualization and using Mind and Alternative Mind Portraits.
- **Guide** students to begin reading text and creating Mind and Alternative Mind Portraits. Monitor.
- **Practice** by having the students complete the reading and the Mind and Alternative Mind Portraits.
- **Reread, Retell, and Reflect** on how visualizing and using Mind Portraits help us comprehend what we read.

Student-Facilitated Comprehension Centers

- **Art Center:** Work with a partner to create Mind and Alternative Mind Portrait posters based on an Arthur story. Sketch the contents of each of the minds.
- **Making Words Center:** Create and write words of varying lengths.
- **Writing Center:** Work with a partner to write an Arthur adventure in which the students appear as characters.

Teacher-Facilitated Whole-Group Reflection and Goal Setting

- **Share** and discuss completed Mind and Alternative Mind Portraits.
- **Reflect** on how visualizing and using Mind and Alternative Mind Portraits help us understand what we read.
- **Set new goals** or extend existing ones.

Guided Comprehension in the Primary Grades by Maureen McLaughlin ©2003. Newark, DE: International Reading Association. May be copied for classroom use.

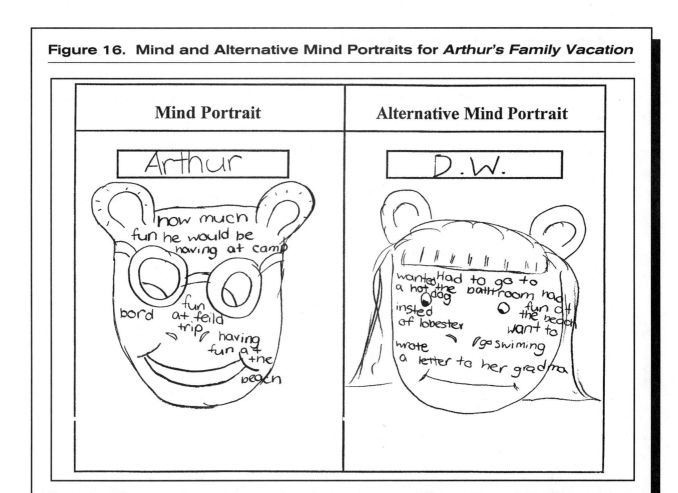

Figure 16. Mind and Alternative Mind Portraits for *Arthur's Family Vacation*

Mind Portrait	Alternative Mind Portrait
Arthur	D.W.

students' reading of the text. Next, we discussed the story and decided that we would make Arthur and D.W. the subjects of our Mind and Alternative Mind Portraits.

Practice: Students practiced by revisiting the text as they completed their Mind and Alternative Mind Portraits. Then they shared their portraits with the group and we discussed them.

Reread, Retell, and Reflect: Students reread the story silently. I completed a running record with one of the students during that time. Then we engaged in an oral group retelling. Finally, we reflected on how viewing the story from different points of view helped us comprehend.

Student-Facilitated Comprehension Centers

Art Center: Students worked with a partner to create Mind and Alternative Mind Portrait posters for Arthur books they had read. They used sketching to record the ideas. After the posters were completed, they hung them in our theme gallery. They shared their work with the class during Stage Three.

Making Words Center: Students engaged in making and writing words using letter patterns, which they recorded on organizers I had provided (see Appendix D, pages 291–292). Students concluded their work by sorting their word cards by word family, number of syllables, or parts of speech.

Writing Center: While working with a partner, students wrote their own Arthur stories in which they appeared as characters. These turned out to be quite interesting. Titles included "Arthur's First Football Game," "Arthur's Spider Disaster," and "Arthur's Motorcycle Adventure." When they had finished writing their stories, students individually created Mind and Alternative Mind Portraits that featured an Arthur character and themselves.

Student-Facilitated Comprehension Routines

Literature Circles: After reading and discussing their Arthur books, students created Mind and Alternative Mind Portraits as an extending activity. They used the completed portraits to spark further discussion.

Cross-Age Reading Experiences: Students listened to Arthur audio books or trio-read with a cross-age partner. Then they created Mind and Alternative Mind Portraits and discussed them.

STAGE THREE: Teacher-Facilitated Whole-Group Reflection and Goal Setting

Share: The students shared their portraits in small groups and then with the class. We discussed the examples and how viewing the story from different points of view helped us to understand it better.

Reflect: We reflected on how visualization helps us to understand and remember what we read. We also discussed learning about different points of view. Students thought that Mind and Alternative Mind Portraits were a "neat new way" to view characters and to help us understand what we read.

Set New Goals: We discussed how successful we were in using visualization—and particularly Mind and Alternative Mind Portraits—to help us understand what we read. We decided that we were comfortable using this technique, but we wanted more opportunities to apply it. So, we extended our existing goal and planned to apply Mind and Alternative Mind Portraits to other types of text.

Assessment Options

I observed the students in all stages of Guided Comprehension and commented on their completed Mind and Alternative Mind Portraits. I used student self-assessments from the centers and routines to learn more about their ability to visualize using Mind and Alternative Mind Portraits. I also completed running records with a number of students.

The Neverending Adventures of Arthur the Aardvark
Guided Comprehension Strategy: Summarizing
Teaching Idea: Draw and Label Retelling

STAGE ONE: Teacher-Directed Whole-Group Instruction

Text: *Arthur's Computer Disaster* (1997)

Explain: I explained summarizing to the students and focused on retelling. I offered several examples from our lives of when we might retell something, including if a friend missed a birthday party or an episode of a favorite television program, and we would share what had happened by recounting it from beginning to end. I pointed out that whenever we engaged in retelling it was important to remember to tell what had happened in the same order or sequence in which the events had occurred. Then I demonstrated how we use retellings in our everyday lives by retelling what happened in school yesterday to a student who had been absent. Next, I explained that when we retell stories we need to make sure that we include who was in the story, where it took place, what happened, and how it ended.

Demonstrate: I demonstrated by using a Think-Aloud, a read-aloud, and a sheet of poster board that I had attached to the chalkboard. I had previously sketched the Draw and Label Retelling form (see Appendix C, page 266) on the poster board, and I began by introducing the organizer and its components: who was in the story, where it took place, what happened, and how it ended. Next I introduced *Arthur's Computer Disaster* by sharing the book cover and reading the first three pages. I reminded students that as I was reading we should be thinking about what information from the story we would need to include in our retellings. I again referred them to the Draw and Label Retelling form on the poster board. Then I revisited the book title and asked the students what they thought *disaster* meant. They offered a variety of ideas including "something really bad" and "something that couldn't be fixed." We discussed a few examples of disasters we had experienced. Next, I asked the students what they thought the title of the story meant, and their replies included, "Arthur must have broken the computer," "Arthur needed to know something, but he didn't know how to use the computer to find it out," and "Arthur did something he wasn't supposed to do." I continued reading the book, stopping periodically to verify students' predictions and make new ones. When I finished reading, we discussed the story and made connections to times we had used computers, times we thought we had broken them, and times we had done things we had been told not to do. Several students commented that every time someone in their families thought they had a computer disaster, they turned the computer off and then on again and it was fine. I added that I often use that same method.

Next, I used the Draw and Label Retelling format I had created on poster board to review all the elements we would need to include. Then I started to sketch in the first frame of the Draw and Label Retelling organizer. I drew a picture of Arthur and his family. When I finished, I wrote *Arthur and his family are characters in the story*. In the frame marked "Where?" I drew a picture of Arthur's house and wrote *The story takes place in Arthur's house*. I was careful to write in complete sentences to provide a good writing model for the students.

Guide: I guided the students to work with a partner to complete the third frame on organizers I had provided. They sketched and wrote a variety of ideas, but most of them focused on Arthur

GUIDED COMPREHENSION: THE NEVERENDING ADVENTURES OF ARTHUR THE AARDVARK

SUMMARIZING: DRAW AND LABEL RETELLING

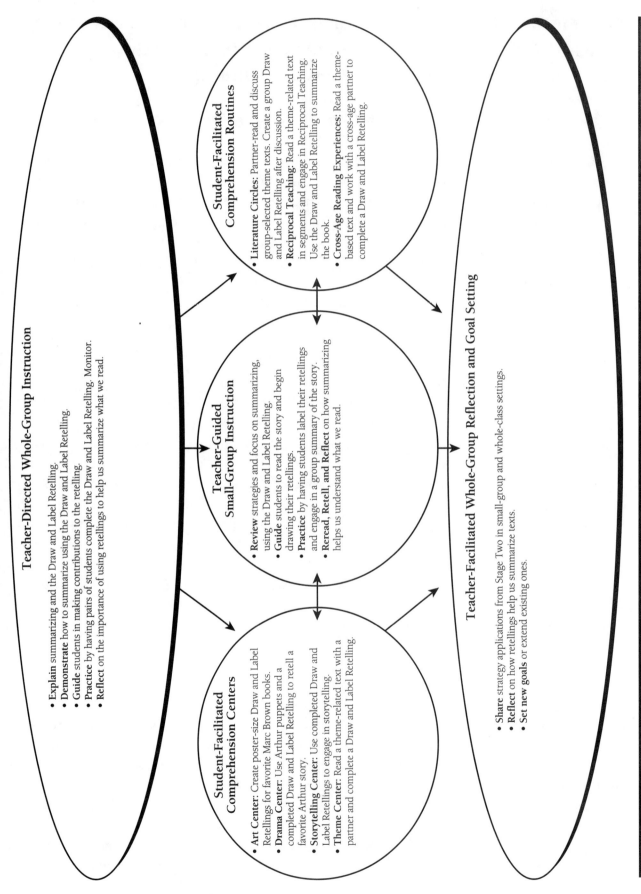

Teacher-Directed Whole-Group Instruction

- **Explain** summarizing and the Draw and Label Retelling.
- **Demonstrate** how to summarize using the Draw and Label Retelling.
- **Guide** students in making contributions to the retelling.
- **Practice** by having pairs of students complete the Draw and Label Retelling. Monitor.
- **Reflect** on the importance of using retellings to help us summarize what we read.

Student-Facilitated Comprehension Centers

- **Art Center:** Create poster-size Draw and Label Retellings for favorite Marc Brown books.
- **Drama Center:** Use Arthur puppets and a completed Draw and Label Retelling to retell a favorite Arthur story.
- **Storytelling Center:** Use completed Draw and Label Retellings to engage in storytelling.
- **Theme Center:** Read a theme-related text with a partner and complete a Draw and Label Retelling.

Teacher-Guided Small-Group Instruction

- **Review** strategies and focus on summarizing, using the Draw and Label Retelling.
- **Guide** students to read the story and begin drawing their retellings.
- **Practice** by having students label their retellings and engage in a group summary of the story.
- **Reread, Retell, and Reflect** on how summarizing helps us understand what we read.

Student-Facilitated Comprehension Routines

- **Literature Circles:** Partner-read and discuss group-selected theme texts. Create a group Draw and Label Retelling after discussion.
- **Reciprocal Teaching:** Read a theme-related text in segments and engage in Reciprocal Teaching. Use the Draw and Label Retelling to summarize the book.
- **Cross-Age Reading Experiences:** Read a theme-based text and work with a cross-age partner to complete a Draw and Label Retelling.

Teacher-Facilitated Whole-Group Reflection and Goal Setting

- **Share** strategy applications from Stage Two in small-group and whole-class settings.
- **Reflect** on how retellings help us summarize texts.
- **Set new goals** or extend existing ones.

Guided Comprehension in the Primary Grades by Maureen McLaughlin ©2003. Newark, DE: International Reading Association. May be copied for classroom use.

breaking the computer and trying to get help to fix it. Their labels included *Arthur thought he broke the computer and tried to get it fixed* and *Arthur thought he broke the computer and asked a lot of people for help*. After the students shared their ideas, I sketched Arthur looking very worried as he was reading the computer manual and asking others for help. I wrote *Arthur thought he broke the computer and read the computer book to try to fix it*. I was careful to encourage students to share their ideas before I shared my thoughts.

Practice: The students worked with their partners to complete the fourth frame—how the story ended. Their drawings showed Arthur listening to his mom and Arthur's mom playing the game on the computer. As the students worked, I monitored by walking around the room and assisting when asked. After students had shared their final frame, I sketched Arthur's mom telling him he couldn't play computer games and her sitting at the computer playing the game. To label my drawing, I wrote *Arthur's mom said he couldn't play computer games, but then she did*. Then I reviewed my Draw and Label Retelling for the class and orally summarized the story. Following this, students reviewed their retellings with another set of partners and orally summarized the story. Figure 17 shows our completed Draw and Label Retelling.

Reflect: To conclude Stage One of Guided Comprehension, we discussed how summarizing using retellings helped us to understand what we read. The students liked that they could use drawing to retell. I explained that we could also retell orally and by writing, dramatizing, and singing. Then we discussed how we could use retellings with other texts in other settings.

Figure 17. Draw and Label Retelling for *Arthur's Computer Disaster*

Who?	Where?
Draw:	Draw:
Label: Arthur and his family are characters in the story.	Label: The story takes place in Arthur's house.

What happened?	How did it end?
Draw:	Draw:
Label: Arthur thought he broke the computer and read the computer book to try to fix it.	Label: Arthur's mom said he couldn't play computer games, but then she did.

STAGE TWO: *Teacher Guided Small-Group Instruction*

Text: *Arthur's Lost Puppy* (2000) (Texts varied according to students' abilities.)

Review: First, I reviewed the comprehension strategies that good readers use and focused on summarizing using retellings. I reminded the students that we needed to be careful to include information about the story when we were retelling, just as we did in Stage One.

Guide: I introduced *Arthur's Lost Puppy* and had a brief discussion about pets with the students. Next, I shared the Draw and Label Retelling organizers with the students and guided them to whisper-read the story. I reminded them to think about the information needed for the retelling while reading. When they had finished reading, we briefly discussed the story and reviewed the elements needed for the Draw and Label Retelling.

Practice: The students practiced by completing the Draw and Label Retellings and sharing them with the group. Then we created a group oral summary based on their retellings.

Reread, Retell, and Reflect: Students read the story a second time and we used our Draw and Label Retellings as the basis of a group oral retelling. We ended our session by reflecting on how we can use retellings to help us understand what we read. We also talked about how well we could retell what we had read. Shanika commented that retelling helped us to know the story better. Tommy noted that we could retell any story we read and stories we wrote, too.

Student-Facilitated Comprehension Centers

Art Center: At this center, students worked with partners to create poster-size Draw and Label Retellings of their favorite Marc Brown books. When completed, students displayed these retellings in our theme gallery.

Drama Center: Students worked in partners or trios and used Draw and Label Retellings they had already completed to perform puppet retellings of favorite Arthur stories.

Storytelling Center: Students worked with partners and used Draw and Label Retellings they had already completed to retell one of their favorite Marc Brown stories. Some students used story gloves, others used story-bag manipulatives.

Theme Center: I placed a variety of Arthur books at this center. (For sample titles, see the Theme Resources at the end of this chapter.) Working in pairs the students read a theme-related text and completed a Draw and Label Retelling. Then they used their retellings as the basis of orally summarizing the story. Kevin and Karen's Draw and Label Retelling appears in Figure 18.

Student-Facilitated Comprehension Routines

Literature Circles: The students selected a theme-related text and read it in the partner-reading read-pause-retell pattern. Then they discussed the book in their circle and created a group Draw and Label Retelling.

Reciprocal Teaching: Students read a theme-related text in segments and engaged in the four strategies of Reciprocal Teaching. Afterward, they completed a group Draw and Label Retelling to summarize the book.

Cross-Age Reading Experiences: Pairs of students worked with cross-age partners to listen to or read a new theme-related text or reread a familiar text to practice fluency. After reading, they completed Draw and Label Retellings and used them to orally summarize the story.

Figure 18. Draw and Label Retelling for *Arthur's First Sleepover*

STAGE THREE: *Teacher-Facilitated Whole-Group Reflection and Goal Setting*

Share: Students shared their Draw and Label Retellings and summaries from Stage Two in small groups. Then we discussed the retellings as a whole class.

Reflect: We reflected on the strategy applications from Stage Two and how using retellings and summarizing helped us understand what we were reading. Stephanie said that retelling was easy because we already knew how to use the story elements in our Story Maps and in our story writing. Jake said that we needed to read the story really carefully to do a good retelling.

Set New Goals: The students decided—and their retellings and summaries supported—that they felt comfortable using the Draw and Label Retellings. Based on this information, we decided to expand our understanding of retelling and summarizing by learning how to use other techniques such as Lyric Retellings and Summaries (McLaughlin & Allen, 2002a).

Assessment Options

I observed students during the stages of Guided Comprehension, focusing on their ability to retell and summarize. I reviewed and commented on students' completed retellings and the summaries they recorded in their Guided Comprehension Journals. I also used students' self-assessments to inform my understanding of their ability to retell and summarize. In addition, I completed running records with several students during this lesson.

FINAL THOUGHTS ABOUT THE ARTHUR THE AARDVARK THEME

Arthur the Aardvark was a welcomed member of all the primary classes I observed using this theme. Students readily accepted him as a friend and teachers and students alike delighted in his amazing ability to get into trouble and problem-solve his way out of it.

As noted in the previous chapter, it is important to acknowledge that lessons on a variety of skills that underpin comprehension strategies were taught during this theme. For example, aspects of language development, such as phonemic awareness and phonics, and skills such as sequencing, generating questions, and distinguishing important from less important ideas were embedded in the theme. (For ideas about how to use literature to teach phonemic awareness, phonics, and fluency, see Appendix B.) For example, Marc Brown titles such as *Arthur Goes to School* (1995) and "How I Got My Puppy Pal" from *Arthur Writes a Story* were used to teach sequencing. *Arthur's First Sleepover* and *Arthur's Pet Business* (1990) served as the bases of lessons about cause and effect and problem and solution. Students also used a variety of Marc Brown titles in Readers Theatre to improve fluency. Because many of the Arthur stories have clearly defined dilemmas, they sparked question generation and reflection. Students' abilities to relate in personal ways to Arthur, his family, his friends, and his adventures motivated students to read and promoted their engagement in learning. In addition, teachers adapted lessons for prereaders and prewriters by engaging in read-alouds and encouraging response through a variety of modes—including discussion, drawing, painting, singing, dancing, and dramatizing.

THEME RESOURCES

Texts

Picture Books

Brown, M. (1982). *Arthur goes to camp*. Boston: Little, Brown.

Brown, M. (1983). *Arthur's Halloween*. Boston: Little, Brown.

Brown, M. (1983). *Perfect pigs*. Boston: Little, Brown.

Brown, M. (1984). *Dinosaurs beware*. Boston: Little, Brown.

Brown, M. (1985). *Arthur's Christmas*. Boston: Little, Brown.

Brown, M. (1985). *Bionic bunny show*. Boston: Little, Brown.

Brown, M. (1986). *Arthur's eyes*. Boston: Little, Brown.

Brown, M. (1986). *Arthur's nose*. Boston: Little, Brown.

Brown, M. (1986). *Arthur's tooth*. Boston: Little, Brown.

Brown, M. (1987). *Arthur's valentine*. Boston: Little, Brown.

Brown, M. (1989). *Arthur's birthday*. Boston: Little, Brown.

Brown, M. (1989). *Arthur's teacher trouble*. Boston: Little, Brown.

Brown, M. (1990). *Arthur's baby*. Boston: Little, Brown.

Brown, M. (1990). *Arthur's pet business*. Boston: Little, Brown

Brown, M. (1991). *Arthur meets the president*. Boston: Little, Brown.

Brown, M. (1991). *D.W. all wet*. Boston: Little, Brown.

Brown, M. (1992). *Arthur babysits*. Boston: Little, Brown.

Brown, M. (1993). *Arthur's family vacation*. Boston: Little, Brown.

Brown, M. (1993). *Arthur's new puppy*. Boston: Little, Brown.

Brown, M. (1994). *Arthur's first sleepover*. Boston: Little, Brown.

Brown, M. (1995). *Arthur goes to school*. New York: Random House.

Brown, M. (1996). *Arthur's reading race*. New York: Random House.

Brown, M. (1996). *Arthur writes a story*. New York: Little, Brown.

Brown, M. (1997). *Arthur's computer disaster*. New York: Little, Brown.

Brown, M. (2000). *Arthur and the race to read*. Boston: Little, Brown.

Brown, M. (2000). *Arthur's lost puppy*. New York: Random House.

Brown, M. (2002). *Arthur's back-to-school surprise*. New York: Random House.

Chapter Books

Brown, M. (1998). *Arthur's mystery envelope* (#1). New York: Little, Brown.

Brown, M. (1998). *Arthur and the scare-your-pants-off club* (#2). New York: Little, Brown.

Brown, M. (1998). *Arthur makes the team* (#3). New York: Little, Brown.

Brown, M. (1998). *Arthur and the crunch cereal contest* (#4). New York: Little, Brown.

Brown, M. (1998). *Arthur accused!* (#5). New York: Little, Brown.

Brown, M. (1998). *Locked in the library!* (#6). New York: Little, Brown.

Brown, M. (1998). *Buster's dino dilemma* (#7). New York: Little, Brown.

Brown, M. (1998). *The mystery of the stolen bike* (#8). New York: Little, Brown.

Brown, M. (1998). *Arthur and the lost diary* (#9). New York: Little, Brown.

Brown, M. (1998). *Who's in love with Arthur?* (#10). New York: Little, Brown.

Brown, M. (1998). *Arthur rocks with Binky* (#11). New York: Little, Brown.

Brown, M. (1998). *Arthur and the popularity test* (#12). New York: Little, Brown.

Brown, M. (1999). *King Arthur* (#13). New York: Little, Brown.

Brown, M. (1999). *Francine, believe it or not* (#14). New York: Little, Brown.

Brown, M. (1999). *Arthur and the cootie-catcher* (#15). New York: Little, Brown.

Brown, M. (1999). *Buster makes the grade* (#16). New York: Little, Brown.

Brown, M. (1999). *Muffy's secret admirer* (#17). New York: Little, Brown.

Brown, M. (1999). *Arthur and the poetry contest* (#18). New York: Little, Brown.

Brown, M. (2000). *Arthur chapter books #1–3*. New York: Little, Brown.

Brown, M. (2000). *Buster Baxter, cat saver* (#19). New York: Little, Brown.

Brown, M. (2000). *Arthur and the big blow-up* (#20). New York: Little, Brown.

Brown, M. (2000). *Arthur and the perfect brother* (#21). New York: Little, Brown.

Brown, M. (2000). *Francine the superstar* (#22). New York: Little, Brown.

Brown, M. (2000). *Buster's new friend* (#23). New York: Little, Brown.

Brown, M. (2000). *Binky rules* (#24). New York: Little, Brown.

Brown, M. (2001). *Arthur and the race to read* (Good Sports #1). New York: Little, Brown.

Brown, M. (2001). *Arthur and the seventh-inning stretcher* (Good Sports #2). New York: Little, Brown.

Brown, M. (2001). *Arthur and the recess rookie* (Good Sports #3). New York: Little, Brown.

Brown, M. (2001). *Arthur and the best coach ever* (Good Sports #4). New York: Little, Brown.

Brown, M. (2001). *Arthur and the goalie ghost* (Good Sports #5). New York: Little, Brown.

Brown, M. (2001). *Arthur and the pen-pal playoff* (Good Sports #6). New York: Little, Brown.

Brown, M. (2002). *Arthur chapter books #4–6*. New York: Little, Brown.

Brown, M. (2002). *Arthur and the double dare (#25)*. New York: Little, Brown.

Brown, M. (2002). *Arthur and the no-brainer (#26)* . New York: Little, Brown.

Brown, M. (2002). *Arthur and comet crisis (#27)*. New York: Little, Brown.

Websites

The Aardvark—Description (Geo Zoo)
　　www.geobop.com/mammals

Forest Friends: Sloth, Anteater, and Aardvark
　　www.jeannieshouse.com

PBS Kids: Arthur Teacher Guides
　　pbskids.org/arthur/grownups/teacherguides

Scholastic Authors Online: Marc Brown
　　www.teacherscholastic.com/authorsandbooks/authors/brown/bio.html

Time Warner Bookmark
　　www.twbookmark.com

Cassettes and Compact Discs

Brown, M. (1998). Marc Brown's Arthur chapter books: *Arthur and the brunch cereal contest, Arthur accused*, and *Locked in the library* [Cassettes]. New York: Listening Library.

Brown, M. (2001). *Marc Brown's Arthur anniversary collection* [CD]. New York: Listening Library.

Brown, M. (2001). *Marc Brown's Arthur chapter books* [CD]. New York: Listening Library.

Videos

Arthur and the square knights of the round table. (1984). New York: Sony Wonder.

Arthur's pet business. (1997). New York: Sony Wonder.

Arthur's birthday. (1998). New York: Sony Wonder.

Arthur's computer adventure. (1998). New York: Sony Wonder.

Arthur's family vacation. (1998). New York: Sony Wonder.

Arthur's treasure hunt. (1998). New York: Sony Wonder.

Arthur's TV-free week. (1998). New York: Sony Wonder.

Arthur gets lost. (1999). New York: Sony Wonder.

Arthur's famous friends. (2000). New York: Sony Wonder.

Arthur goes to Hollywood. (2000). New York: Sony Wonder.

Arthur's perfect Christmas. (2000). New York: Sony Wonder.

Arthur's scary stories. (2000). New York: Sony Wonder.

Arthur's best school days. (2001). New York: Sony Wonder.

Arthur goes on a field trip. (2001). New York: Sony Wonder.

Arthur makes a movie. (2001). New York: Sony Wonder.

Arthur's mystery files. (2001). New York: Sony Wonder.

Arthur goes to the doctor. (2001). New York: Sony Wonder.

Arthur's storybook. (2001). New York: Sony Wonder.

Arthur—It's only rock & roll (starring the Back Street Boys). (2002). New York: Sony Wonder.

Software

Arthur's first grade. (2001). Fremont, CA: The Learning Company.

Arthur's kindergarten. (2001). Fremont, CA: The Learning Company.

Arthur's reading games. (2001). Fremont, CA: The Learning Company.

Arthur's second grade. (2001). Fremont, CA: The Learning Company.

Performance Extensions Across the Curriculum

Art/Music/Drama

• Create Arthur characters or real aardvarks in a variety of mediums, including puppets and masks.

• Create an Arthur the Aardvark mural and illustrate favorite scenes from different Arthur books.

• Create and perform Lyric Summaries about Arthur books or real aardvarks.

• Create and perform an aardvark dance to celebrate the theme.

• Engage in dramatizing Marc Brown stories or Marc Brown's life story.

Math

• Survey peers to determine favorite Marc Brown books. Graph the results to determine the most popular titles.

• Create and solve mathematical problems based on Arthur characters and stories.

Science

• Use the Internet to access information about aardvarks and create an Aardvarks Are… poster to display in the theme gallery.

• Research and investigate the characteristics of the aardvark—its lifestyle, features, habitat, and geographical locations.

• Use technology to create a class aardvark alphabet book.

• Read the section of *Arthur Writes a Story* about outer space and invent, describe, and create a new planet.

• Create a new version of *Arthur's Computer Disaster* in which you play the lead character.

Social Studies

• Use settings for Arthur books to study the community (home, school, etc.). Compare and contrast Arthur's community with yours. Illustrate similarities and differences (Arthur's school, your school; Arthur's house, your house).

Culminating Activity

An Arthur Author Celebration! Extend student-authored invitations to parents and family members, requesting their attendance at an Arthur Author Celebration. Students will dress as their favorite character from a Marc Brown book. Display theme-related projects. Create a library of student-authored books and have an autographing session. Share information about Arthur books and Marc Brown through PowerPoint computer projection. Have the students present their work through a variety of modalities (singing, acting, art, PowerPoint) and escort their families on classroom theme tours. Provide refreshments that include aardvark cookies, Buster banana cake, and D.W. desserts. Provide interactive activities, such as an "I like Arthur because…" mural and opportunities for students and guests to contribute their thoughts about the Arthur celebration to the class homepage on the school's website.

CHAPTER 8

Animals, Animals!

Animals fascinate us. It seems to be the nature of the animal—its appearance, its habitat, and its behavior—that keeps us engaged. In this Guided Comprehension theme we meet all different kinds of animals from roosters, cows, and pigs to polar bears, bats, and wolves. Some of the theme texts tell stories in which the characters are animals; others offer factual information.

The sample Theme-Based Plan for Guided Comprehension: Animals, Animals! (see Figure 19) offers an overview of the thinking and resources that support this theme. It presents a sampling of goals, state standards, assessments, texts, technology resources, comprehension strategies, teaching ideas, comprehension centers, and comprehension routines. The plan begins by delineating examples of student goals and related state standards. The student goals for this theme include the following:

- use appropriate comprehension skills and strategies
- interpret and respond to literature
- write a variety of types of text
- communicate effectively

These goals support the following state standards:

- learning to read independently
- reading, analyzing, and interpreting literature
- types and quality of writing
- speaking and listening

Sample assessments include observation, running records and retellings, skill and strategy applications, and student self-assessments. The Guided Comprehension lessons, which were designed and taught by primary-grade teachers, are based on the following strategies and corresponding teaching ideas:

- Visualizing: Draw and Label Visualizations
- Knowing How Words Work: Concept of Definition Map
- Monitoring: Say Something

Figure 19. Theme-Based Plan for Guided Comprehension: Animals, Animals!

Goals and Connections to State Standards

Students will

- use appropriate comprehension skills and strategies. Standard: learning to read independently
- interpret and respond to literature. Standard: reading, analyzing, and interpreting literature
- write a variety of types of text. Standard: types and quality of writing
- communicate effectively. Standards: types and quality of writing; speaking and listening

Assessment

The following measures can be used for a variety of purposes, including diagnostic, formative, and summative assessment:

Concept of Definition Map	Running Records
Draw and Label	Say Something
Visualizations	Student Self-Assessments
Observation	Student Writing
Retelling	

Text	Title	Theme	Level
1.	*Cook-a-Doodle-Doo!*	Animals	2
2.	*Do Penquins Get Frostbite? Questions and Answers About Polar Animals*	Animals	2
3.	*Bats*	Animals	3

Technology Resources

Animal Pictures Archive
www.animalpicturesarchive.com

Animal Planet
animal.discovery.com

Animal Resources from the Electronic Zoo (NetVet)
netvet.wustl.edu/ssi.htm

Comprehension Strategies

1. Visualizing
2. Knowing How Words Work
3. Monitoring

Teaching Ideas

1. Draw and Label Visualizations
2. Concept of Definition Map
3. Say Something

Comprehension Centers

Students will apply the comprehension strategies and related teaching ideas in the following comprehension centers:

Art Center
Making Words Center
Theme Center
Writing Center

Comprehension Routines

Students will apply the comprehension strategies and related teaching ideas in the following comprehension routines:

Literature Circles
Reciprocal Teaching
Cross-Age Reading Experiences

Cook-a-Doodle-Doo! (Stevens & Crummel, 1999), *Do Penguins Get Frostbite? Questions and Answers About Polar Animals* (Berger & Berger, 2000), and *Bats* (Gibbons, 2000) are the texts used in Stage One for teacher-directed whole-group instruction. Numerous additional theme-related resources—including texts, websites, performance extensions across the curriculum, and a culminating activity—are presented in the Theme Resources at the end of the chapter.

Examples of comprehension centers students use during Stage Two of Guided Comprehension include art, making words, theme, and writing. Students also engage in strategy application in comprehension routines such as Literature Circles, Reciprocal Teaching, and Cross-Age Reading Experiences. Sample websites complete the overview.

The three Guided Comprehension lessons that follow are presented through first-person teacher commentaries. Examples of student work are featured throughout the lessons.

GUIDED COMPREHENSION LESSONS

Animals, Animals!
Guided Comprehension Strategy: Visualizing
Teaching Idea: Draw and Label Visualizations

STAGE ONE: Teacher-Directed Whole-Group Instruction

Text: *Cook-a-Doodle-Doo!* (Stevens & Crummel, 1999)

Explain: I explained that visualization, one of the comprehension strategies good readers use, involves creating mental pictures based on verbal or written cues. Next, I introduced and explained the teaching idea called Draw and Label Visualizations. I explained to the students that we would be using simple sketching to draw the images that we were creating in our minds as I read aloud. I modeled some simple lines and shapes and reminded the students that it was important to sketch the images and that we did not need to be great artists to do that.

Demonstrate: I demonstrated Draw and Label Visualizations using a read-aloud of *Cook-a-Doodle-Doo!*, a think-aloud, and large chart paper (see Appendix C, page 249). I introduced the book by sharing the title and reading the first page aloud. (I didn't share the cover because I didn't want that picture to influence the images students would be creating.) I thought aloud about the mental images I was creating based on the information I shared. Referring to the title, I said, "I know the sound that roosters make. It's 'cock-a-doodle doo.' I notice that the title of this book is *Cook-a-doodle-doo!* and that it says on the first page that the rooster is tired of eating chicken feed every day. So I wonder if this rooster is going to cook during this story. After reading the title and the first few pages, the picture I have in my mind is of the rooster cooking food that isn't chicken feed." Then I started sketching on the first of several pieces of large poster paper I had adhered to the chalkboard. I was careful to remind students that when we draw visualizations, our focus should be conveying the pictures we have inside our minds, not worrying about how well we can draw. When I finished sketching, I wrote this sentence as the label: *Rooster is cooking food that is not chicken feed.* We briefly discussed my drawing and label. Then I read the next four pages and sketched the rooster reading a cookbook. I labeled it *The rooster is reading a cookbook, so he can cook some good food.* After that, we briefly discussed my sketch. One student noticed that the book I had sketched didn't have the title on it. He said that he had also visualized the rooster reading the book, but in his visualization the cover of the book said *Great-Grandma's Cookbook.* Because the Little Red Hen was the rooster's great-grandmother, this prompted a discussion of the original story of *The Little Red Hen* (Galdone, 1979).

Guide: I read aloud the next four pages and guided pairs of students to create pictures in their minds and sketch what they were thinking about the story while listening to the read-aloud. I monitored this activity, prompting as necessary. The students used paper and pencils I had provided. They used Think-Alouds to share their reasoning with their partners as they individually sketched the images they pictured in their minds and wrote their labels. When they finished, I thought aloud and sketched the mental image I had created as I was reading. I waited to do my sketch because I wanted the students to focus on their visualizations, not copy mine. Then the students and I each shared our sketch and our thinking with a partner. Although each sketch was

GUIDED COMPREHENSION: ANIMALS, ANIMALS!
VISUALIZING: DRAW AND LABEL VISUALIZATIONS

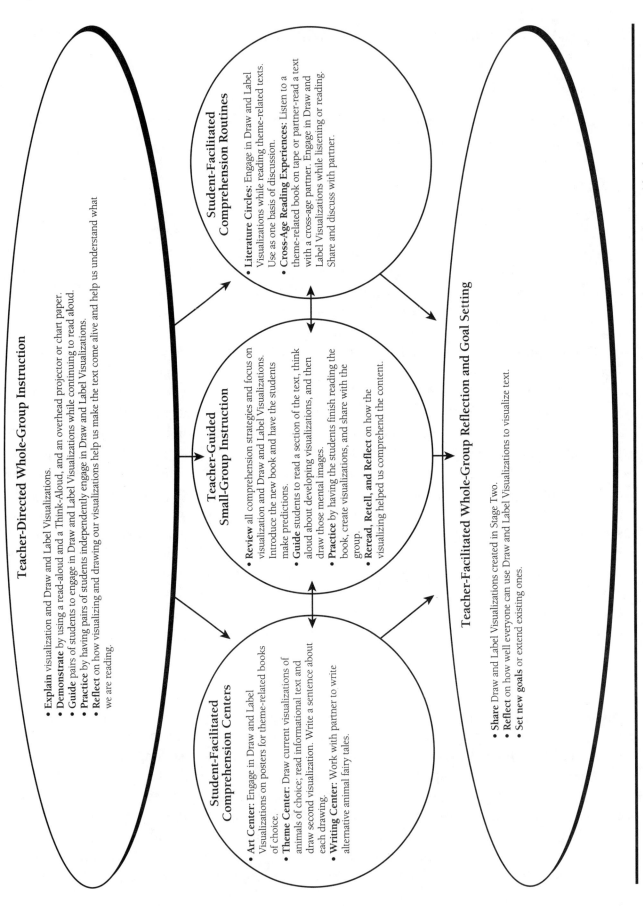

Teacher-Directed Whole-Group Instruction

- **Explain** visualization and Draw and Label Visualizations.
- **Demonstrate** by using a read-aloud and a Think-Aloud, and an overhead projector or chart paper.
- **Guide** pairs of students to engage in Draw and Label Visualizations while continuing to read aloud.
- **Practice** by having pairs of students independently engage in Draw and Label Visualizations.
- **Reflect** on how visualizing and drawing our visualizations help us make the text come alive and help us understand what we are reading.

Student-Facilitated Comprehension Routines

- **Literature Circles:** Engage in Draw and Label Visualizations while reading theme-related texts. Use as one basis of discussion.
- **Cross-Age Reading Experiences:** Listen to a theme-related book on tape or partner-read a text with a cross-age partner. Engage in Draw and Label Visualizations while listening or reading. Share and discuss with partner.

Teacher-Guided Small-Group Instruction

- **Review** all comprehension strategies and focus on visualization and Draw and Label Visualizations. Introduce the new book and have the students make predictions.
- **Guide** students to read a section of the text, think aloud about developing visualizations, and then draw those mental images.
- **Practice** by having the students finish reading the book, create visualizations, and share with the group.
- **Reread, Retell, and Reflect** on how the visualizing helped us comprehend the content.

Student-Facilitated Comprehension Centers

- **Art Center:** Engage in Draw and Label Visualizations on posters for theme-related books of choice.
- **Theme Center:** Draw current visualizations of animals of choice; read informational text and draw second visualization. Write a sentence about each drawing.
- **Writing Center:** Work with partner to write alternative animal fairy tales.

Teacher-Facilitated Whole-Group Reflection and Goal Setting

- **Share** Draw and Label Visualizations created in Stage Two.
- **Reflect** on how well everyone can use Draw and Label Visualizations to visualize text.
- **Set new goals** or extend existing ones.

Guided Comprehension in the Primary Grades by Maureen McLaughlin ©2003. Newark, DE: International Reading Association. May be copied for classroom use.

unique, most of us had visualized a team of bakers working together (see Amitra's Draw and Label Visualization in Figure 20). One of the students drew two images: one of the group of bakers from the book and one of a group of people from her family engaging in holiday baking. This led to a discussion of making connections. I drew attention to the individual nature of the visualizations and reinforced the roles that text and prior knowledge play in the personal construction of meaning. I repeated this process with pages 10 and 11.

Practice: The students practiced by continuing to create Draw and Label Visualizations and share with partners, as I continued to read aloud the remaining sections of the book. Because the cooking team in the story actually followed a recipe and used real baking utensils and measurements, I used props to develop an interactive read-aloud during the reading of this section of the story. I spoke with selected students before the lesson and enlisted their assistance in sharing the props at the appropriate points in the cake-baking segment. I labeled each prop and signaled the appropriate student as each prop was needed. The author also included homophones in this section of the text, so I was careful to include items such as a flower and flour in my prop selection. I also did a minilesson on this topic after reading. Other props included a large bowl, a measuring cup, a tablespoon, a teaspoon, a teapot, a ruler, a stick, a stick of butter, a knife, and an eggbeater. When I had finished reading the book, the students shared their final application of Draw and Label Visualizations with the class. Then we discussed the story. We talked about how well the cooking team worked together and why it

Figure 20. Draw and Label Visualization for *Cook-a-Doodle-Doo!*

was important for everyone on the team to help. We also noted that the cooking team followed the steps of the recipe in sequence. We had a very interesting discussion about how the author's inclusion of homophones during the making of the cake made the story funny. One student said that he was imagining what the cake would have looked like and how it would have tasted if the bakers had used a flower instead of flour and if they had used the baseball bat to beat the eggs. His observation prompted great discussion. We revisited the text, reread that section, and talked about what the cake would have looked like if the reader didn't know about homophones. We all enjoyed that. Then we discussed how important it was to try again if our plans didn't work out the first time and made personal connections to times that had happened in our lives.

Reflect: We discussed how Draw and Label Visualizations helped us to think about the story and understand what we were reading. Then we talked about how we could use visualizing when reading different types of text.

STAGE TWO: Teacher-Guided Small-Group Instruction

Text: *The Little Red Hen Makes a Pizza* (Sturges, 1999) (Texts varied according to students' abilities.)

Review: I briefly reviewed the reading comprehension strategies good readers use and focused on visualizing and Draw and Label Visualizations. Next, I introduced the new text and asked the students to sketch and label what they were picturing in their minds as they listened to me share the title and read the first page. I also sketched and labeled my mental image. Then we shared and discussed.

Guide: The students whisper-read the next section of the book and stopped to sketch and label the pictures in their minds. I guided their reading and sketching, prompting as necessary. We followed the same procedure with the next section of the text.

Practice: The students practiced by independently reading the remaining sections of the book. They stopped twice at designated points to sketch and discuss the pictures they created in their minds. I monitored their discussion, prompting when necessary.

Reread, Retell, and Reflect: The students engaged in a second reading of the text, and I used that as an opportunity to complete a running record with one of the students. Then we engaged in an oral retelling of the story. Finally, we discussed how the visualized images belonged to each reader, and how they were sometimes similar and sometimes very different from the images of others in our group. We also talked about how drawing and labeling our visualizations helped us comprehend the content. It was quite an interesting discussion. Maria said, "I like having pictures of the story in my head. It helps me to remember the story," and Carey observed, "Authors and illustrators must visualize, too. That must be how they decide what pictures to put in their books." This prompted the other group members to make connections to books we had written and illustrated as a class and ones the students had created on their own. As an extending activity, students created pizza recipes and sketched the resulting pizzas (see Lindsay's recipe in Figure 21). We shared and discussed the students' efforts and then displayed their completed Draw and Label Visualizations in our theme gallery.

Student-Facilitated Comprehension Centers

Art Center: Students worked with a partner to read theme-related books and create a Draw and Label Visualizations poster. Figure 22 shows the poster Betsy and Andres created based on their reading of *Miss Hen's Feast* (McVeigh, 2003).

Figure 21. Pizza Recipe

Figure 22. Draw and Label Visualization for *Miss Hen's Feast*

Theme Center: Students sketched images that represented farm animals they would like to study. Then they read an informational text about that animal and drew a second visualization based on their reading. They used the In My Head…What I Read organizer (see Appendix C, page 250) to draw and label their ideas. Finally, students shared and discussed their images.

Writing Center: Students worked with partners to write and illustrate alternative fairy tales about *The Little Red Hen*.

Student-Facilitated Comprehension Routines

Literature Circles: While reading, students stopped at designated points and drew and labeled visualizations in their Guided Comprehension Journals. When the group members had finished reading, they met in a circle and used their drawings as the basis of discussion. At the conclusion of the discussion, students used the Literature Circle Self-Evaluation (see Appendix D, page 290) to comment on their participation and how well the group worked.

Cross-Age Reading Experiences: Students either listened to a theme-related audio book or partner-read a text with a cross-age partner. While listening or reading, students engaged in Draw and Label Visualizations and shared their applications with their partners.

STAGE THREE: Teacher-Facilitated Whole-Group Reflection and Goal Setting

Share: The students shared and discussed their applications of Draw and Label Visualizations from Stage Two in small groups. This included visiting our theme gallery and visualizations drawn in students' Guided Comprehension Journals. Then students shared and discussed selected applications with the whole group.

Reflect: We reflected on the quality of the applications of Draw and Label Visualizations we had shared from Stage Two and how well we thought we could use this technique. Then we built on that to broaden our discussion and examine how using visualization can help us understand what we read. David observed, "When we picture the story in our heads, it's like seeing a movie." Diane said, "When we picture the story in our heads, I feel like I am part of the story. It helps me know what is going on." We also reviewed and explored the importance of prior knowledge and text clues in creating visualizations.

Set New Goals: We decided that we could all use Draw and Label Visualizations effectively and that we would expand our understanding by using them to help us visualize while we were reading different types of texts. We also decided we would extend our understanding of visualization by learning how to use Open-Mind Portraits (Tompkins, 2001).

Assessment Options

I used observation in various stages of the lesson to assess students' understanding of visualization. I also reviewed and commented on students' applications of Draw and Label Visualizations and completed running records and retellings with several students.

Animals, Animals!
Guided Comprehension Strategy:
Knowing How Words Work
Teaching Idea: Concept of Definition Map

STAGE ONE: Teacher-Directed Whole-Group Instruction

Text: *Do Penguins Get Frostbite? Questions and Answers About Polar Animals* (Berger & Berger, 2000)

Explain: I explained Knowing How Words Work and focused on the Concept of Definition Map. I explained that we use Concept of Definition Maps to make connections between words and ideas we already know and information we discover in texts. I also noted that we could record what we already know about the topic on the Concept of Definition Map before reading, and after reading we could add new information we learned from the text. Next, I explained that we would use our completed maps to write a brief summary of the focus topic.

Demonstrate: I demonstrated by using a Think-Aloud, a poster board, and a read-aloud of the section about polar bears in *Do Penguins Get Frostbite? Questions and Answers About Polar Animals*. I began by introducing the Concept of Definition Map, which I had drawn on the poster board the previous day (see Appendix C, page 256). I read aloud the various categories of information we would need to complete it. I wrote *polar bear*, the topic for our Concept of Definition Map, in the center oval and explained that I would need to provide information for each category on the map. I read aloud the next category of information, "What is it?" I thought aloud and said, "I know that polar bears are animals because all bears are animals. I have also seen polar bears at zoos, so I know they are animals." Then I wrote *animal* in the space provided on the poster board. I continued my demonstration by writing what I already knew about polar bears in each section of the organizer. I examined the section labeled *How would you describe it?* and thought aloud about what I see when I visualize a polar bear, and then I wrote three words to describe polar bears in the boxes: *big, white,* and *furry.* I prompted students to complete the next part of the Concept of Definition Map by thinking aloud about three things a polar bear does. (I had adapted this section from the part of the map usually labeled "three examples.") Students suggested writing *lives where it is very cold* in a space provided at the bottom of the graphic organizer. We decided that we would complete the other two sections as we learned more about polar bears. Then we discussed all the information we knew about polar bears at that point.

Guide: I began by reminding students that as I read aloud we should be listening for new information about polar bears. I noted that I would record new information on the poster board and we would add some of that information to our Concept of Definition Map. I explained that when I recorded the information we had learned from the text on the map, I would use a different color marker. That way we would be able to easily distinguish between what we knew before reading and what we learned from reading the text. I introduced *Do Penguins Get Frostbite?* to the students by sharing the cover, providing a brief overview of text, and sharing the title of the section on polar bears: "Polar Bears and Other Land Animals." We summarized what we had already written about polar bears on the Concept of Definition Map, and I noted that the section title in the text had already confirmed that polar bears are animals. When I finished reading the first section of the

GUIDED COMPREHENSION: ANIMALS, ANIMALS, ANIMALS!
KNOWING HOW WORDS WORK: CONCEPT OF DEFINITION MAP

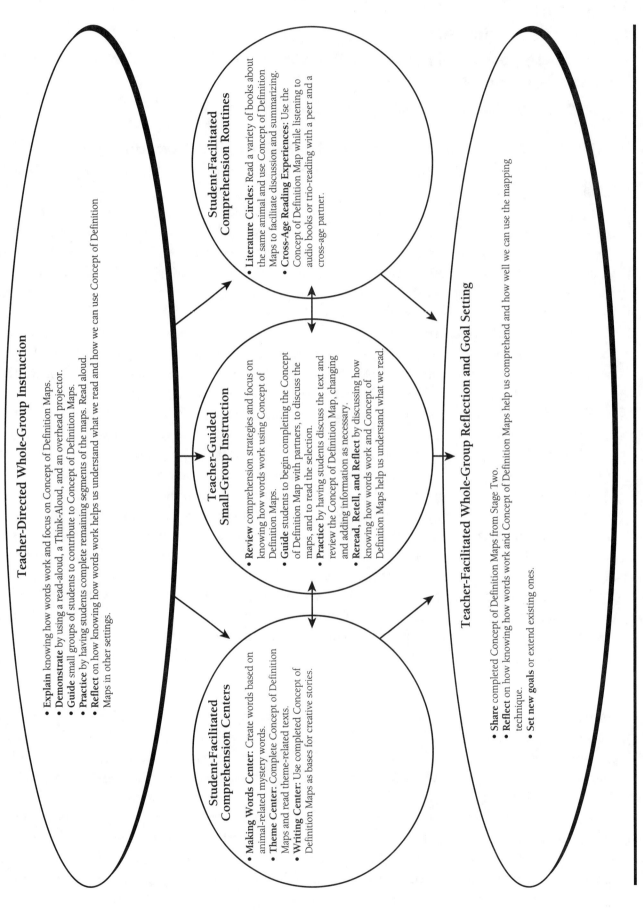

Teacher-Directed Whole-Group Instruction

- **Explain** knowing how words work and focus on Concept of Definition Maps.
- **Demonstrate** by using a read-aloud, a Think-Aloud, and an overhead projector.
- **Guide** small groups of students to contribute to Concept of Definition Maps.
- **Practice** by having students complete remaining segments of the maps. Read aloud.
- **Reflect** on how knowing how words work helps us understand what we read and how we can use Concept of Definition Maps in other settings.

Student-Facilitated Comprehension Routines

- **Literature Circles:** Read a variety of books about the same animal and use Concept of Definition Maps to facilitate discussion and summarizing.
- **Cross-Age Reading Experiences:** Use the Concept of Definition Map while listening to audio books or trio-reading with a peer and a cross-age partner.

Teacher-Guided Small-Group Instruction

- **Review** comprehension strategies and focus on knowing how words work using Concept of Definition Maps.
- **Guide** students to begin completing the Concept of Definition Map with partners, to discuss the maps, and to read the selection.
- **Practice** by having students discuss the text and review the Concept of Definition Map, changing and adding information as necessary.
- **Reread, Retell, and Reflect** by discussing how knowing how words work and Concept of Definition Maps help us understand what we read.

Student-Facilitated Comprehension Centers

- **Making Words Center:** Create words based on animal-related mystery words.
- **Theme Center:** Complete Concept of Definition Maps and read theme-related texts.
- **Writing Center:** Use completed Concept of Definition Maps as bases for creative stories.

Teacher-Facilitated Whole-Group Reflection and Goal Setting

- **Share** completed Concept of Definition Maps from Stage Two.
- **Reflect** on how knowing how words work and Concept of Definition Maps help us comprehend and how well we can use the mapping technique.
- **Set new goals** or extend existing ones.

Guided Comprehension in the Primary Grades by Maureen McLaughlin ©2003. Newark, DE: International Reading Association. May be copied for classroom use.

text, I prompted the students to share new information about polar bears. First, they suggested we add *eats seals* and *swims* to our list of things a polar bear does on our Concept of Definition Map. Then they offered the following information, which I recorded on the bottom section of the poster board:

- Polar bears travel alone.
- There is fat underneath their fur that keeps them warm.
- Polar bears live about 33 years.
- A running polar bear is faster than a swimming polar bear.

Stuart asked about the word *Arctic* because the text said that is where polar bears live. We went to our wall map to see where the Arctic was located and had a discussion about what we knew about the Arctic. Then we decided that it gave more specific information about where polar bears live. So, we changed *lives where it is very cold* to *lives in the Arctic* on our map.

Practice: I continued to read aloud the rest of the text as students worked with partners to jot down new information about polar bears. This time students suggested the following:

- Only one polar bear cub is born at a time.
- Newborn polar bear cubs are tiny enough to stay between their mothers' toes.
- Polar bear mothers teach the cubs to hunt and search for berries and plants.

I recorded these suggestions on the poster board, and we decided that we didn't need to include any of this information on our Concept of Definition Map. Because our map was complete, the students and I wrote a summary of what we knew about polar bears. Our completed Concept of Definition Map, Concept Map Summary, and list of other things we learned appear in Figure 23.

Reflect: We reflected on how we used the Concept of Definition Map to help us understand how words work and comprehend what we read. The students were excited about learning information about real animals. We also talked about how we could use the completed Concept of Definition Map and Concept Map Summary to review what we know about different animals. Finally, we talked about how we could use the maps with other texts in other settings.

STAGE TWO: Teacher-Directed Small-Group Instruction

Text: *Wolves* (Simon, 1993) (Texts varied according to students' abilities.)

Review: I reminded students about comprehension strategies active readers use and focused on knowing how words work and on using Concept of Definition Maps.

Guide: I gave the small group of students Concept of Definition Map graphic organizers and explained that our focus word was *wolves*. We briefly discussed some things we knew about wolves and then I guided the students to work with a partner to provide information about wolves for the first two categories. We discussed each group's responses, which included that wolves were animals and that they were similar to dogs. Judy, a student who had an Akita for a pet, said, "Some of them look a lot like my dog." She promised to bring in a photo of her dog so we could see the similarities. I continued to guide the students as they completed the map. When they had recorded what they already knew about wolves, we had a brief discussion. They had described wolves with

Figure 23. Polar Bear Concept of Definition Map

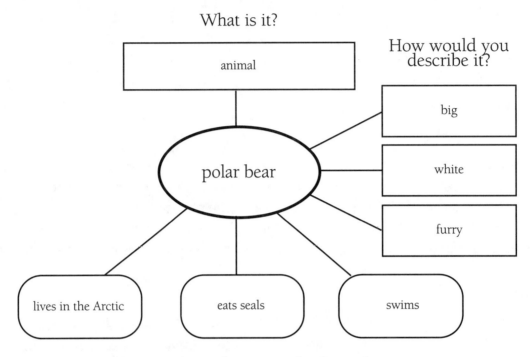

What is it?

animal

How would you describe it?

big

white

furry

polar bear

lives in the Arctic

eats seals

swims

What are three things a polar bear does?

Concept Map Summary:

A polar bear is an animal that is big, white, and furry. A polar bear lives in the Arctic, eats seals, and swims.

We also learned:

- Polar bears travel alone.
- There is fat underneath their fur that keeps them warm.
- Polar bears live about 33 years.
- A running polar bear is faster than a swimming polar bear.
- Only one polar bear cub is born at a time.
- Newborn polar bear cubs are tiny enough to stay between their mothers' toes.
- Polar bear mothers teach the cubs to hunt and search for berries and plants.

adjectives such as *furry*, *mean*, and *fast*, and the phrase *have big teeth*. *Gray wolf* was the only response offered in the section labeled *different kinds*, so I reminded the students that we would add information we learned from the book to that and other sections of our maps. Next, I introduced the book *Wolves* and guided the students' reading of the first few sections. We stopped briefly so they could record new information about wolves in their Guided Comprehension Journals. Then they added information to their Concept of Definition Maps.

Practice: Students practiced by continuing to read to the end of the text and by revisiting their maps as necessary. For example, in the section of the map labeled *different kinds*, they recorded a variety of responses that included arctic wolves, red wolves, Mexican wolves, and Rocky Mountain wolves. When the students finished reading and revising, we discussed the maps and other information we had learned from the text. Then the students completed their Concept Map Summaries.

Reread, Retell, and Reflect: Because our text was informational, the students read their summaries to a partner rather than reread and retell. Next, we reflected on how Concept of Definition Maps help us to understand how words work and to make connections between what we know and what we have read. Todd said, "Before today, most of what I knew about wolves happened in stories." Cristiana said, "The pictures of wolves in this book were beautiful. They don't look that way in a lot of stories." Finally, we discussed how we could use Concept of Definition Maps and Concept Map Summaries to help us understand other texts in other settings.

Student-Facilitated Comprehension Centers

Making Words Center: Students used Making and Writing Words using mystery words such as *elephant* from our Animals, Animals! theme. The students used magnetic letters to spell the words and then wrote them in their Guided Comprehension Journals.

Theme Center: I placed a variety of informational books and related Concept of Definition Maps at this center. I had also provided the focus word for each map. Students worked with partners to complete the maps and read the texts. After reading, students revisited the maps and added information they thought to be important. Next, they wrote Concept Map Summaries based on their completed maps. Some students then took their completed maps to the writing center.

Writing Center: Pairs of students used their completed Concept Map Summaries to write paragraphs, poems, or stories about the animals they had learned about. Some of the students used paragraph, poem, or story frames; others did not. Titles of their poems and stories included "Wally the Whale," "The Wolf Goes to School," and "Ellie the Elefant Lives in the Jungel."

Student-Facilitated Comprehension Routines

Literature Circles: Students completed Concept of Definition Maps and Concept Map Summaries as they read a variety of books about the same animal. They worked with partners to record initial information and then individually read and completed the maps. They shared their map information and summaries during group discussion.

Cross-Age Reading Experiences: Students completed Concept of Definition Maps with a partner while listening to audio books or trio-reading about the animal of their choice with a peer and a cross-age partner. After revisiting and revising their maps, students wrote a Concept Map Summary.

STAGE THREE: Teacher-Facilitated Whole-Group Reflection and Goal Setting

Share: Students shared their Concept of Definition Maps and Concept Map Summaries from Stage Two in small groups. Then we discussed selected examples as a whole class.

Reflect: We reflected on how knowing how words work and using Concept of Definition Maps helped us to understand what we read. We also talked about how well we could use the maps and that they seemed to work best with informational texts.

Set New Goals: We decided to continue working on knowing how words work by learning about Semantic Feature Analysis.

Assessment Options

I used observation, completed Concept of Definition Maps and Concept Map Summaries, discussion, and students' self-assessments during this lesson. I also completed a number of running records and retellings with individual students. The assessments were a natural part of each stage of the process.

Animals, Animals!
Guided Comprehension Strategy: Monitoring
Teaching Idea: Say Something

STAGE ONE: Teacher-Directed Whole-Group Instruction

Text: *Bats* (Gibbons, 2000)

Explain: I began by explaining to the students the importance of monitoring our understanding while we are reading. I reminded them that our ultimate goal was to make sense of the text and that while we were reading we should be asking ourselves if what we are reading is making sense. I described Say Something as a technique we can use to help us examine what we were reading to see if it does make sense. I noted that Say Something would help us think about our reading and share our ideas. I explained that we could use Say Something when working with a partner or in a trio. I explained that when using this technique, we would read a section of the text, stop and Say Something based on what we have read, and then continue reading, stopping periodically to Say Something.

Demonstrate: I demonstrated Say Something by using a read-aloud and a Think-Aloud. I also modeled the technique with two of my students. Billy, James, and I planned the demonstration a few days before the lesson. I began by introducing the text. I shared the cover and title and read the first three pages. I focused on the factual information about bats, and then Billy, James, and I engaged in Say Something. I said, "I didn't know that bats are shy and gentle animals. I think that's interesting because I always thought they were harmful." Billy said, "I didn't know that *nocturnal* meant that they were awake at night and asleep during the day." James said, "There are almost a thousand kinds of bats. I thought there was only one." I read the next two pages and said, "I didn't know that bats were the only mammals that could fly." Billy said, "I didn't know that baby bats are born—not hatched from eggs." James said, "I didn't know that bats are 50 million years old. That's really, really old."

Guide: Students worked with partners as I read the next four pages and stopped to guide the students to Say Something to their partners about what I had read. I suggested focusing on restating facts they already knew, revising ideas they had that now appeared to be incorrect, and learning new information. As I monitored, I heard a variety of responses including, "Bats have arms and fingers," "Bats can change direction quickly," "Bats can fly high and fast," and "I knew bats hung upside down, but I didn't know they held on by their toe claws."

Practice: I read the next section and stopped to provide the pairs of students time to Say Something. I circulated around the room to monitor what students were saying and offer support as necessary. We continued this process throughout the reading of the book. Then we summarized what we had learned about bats. The book had in-depth information about bats, and the students enjoyed learning so many new things about them.

Reflect: We reflected on the importance of thinking about what we are reading and how using techniques like Say Something helped us engage with text and monitor our understanding. Richard said, "I need to think about what I will say when we're using Say Something." Gabrielle said, "I like Say Something because we can pick what we want to say."

GUIDED COMPREHENSION: ANIMALS, ANIMALS! MONITORING: SAY SOMETHING

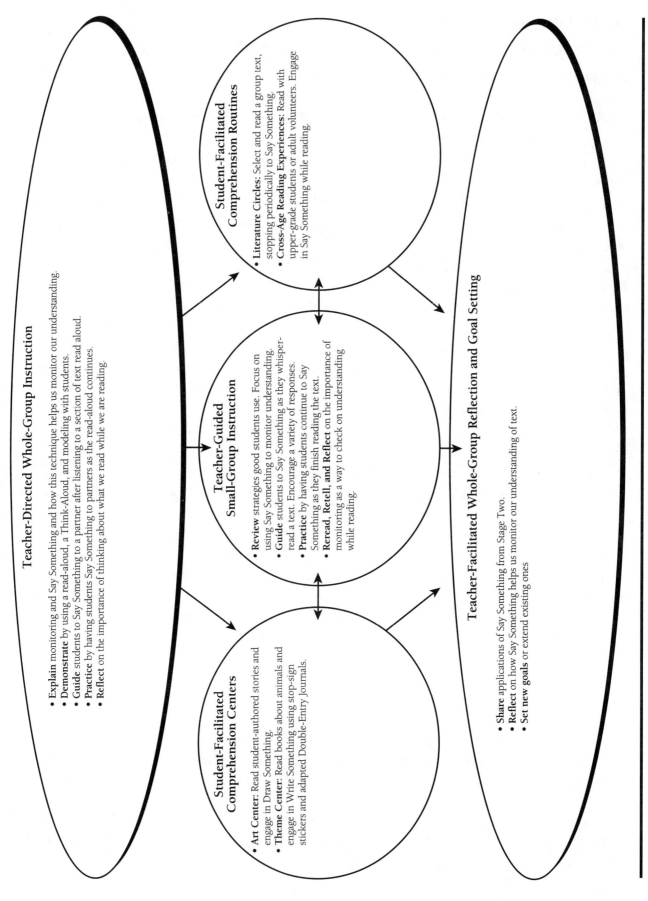

Teacher-Directed Whole-Group Instruction

- **Explain** monitoring and Say Something and how this technique helps us monitor our understanding.
- **Demonstrate** by using a read-aloud, a Think-Aloud, and modeling with students.
- **Guide** students to Say Something to a partner after listening to a section of text read aloud.
- **Practice** by having students Say Something to partners as the read-aloud continues.
- **Reflect** on the importance of thinking about what we read while we are reading.

Student-Facilitated Comprehension Routines

- **Literature Circles:** Select and read a group text, stopping periodically to Say Something.
- **Cross-Age Reading Experiences:** Read with upper-grade students or adult volunteers. Engage in Say Something while reading.

Teacher-Guided Small-Group Instruction

- **Review** strategies good students use. Focus on using Say Something to monitor understanding.
- **Guide** students to Say Something as they whisper-read a text. Encourage a variety of responses.
- **Practice** by having students continue to Say Something as they finish reading the text.
- **Reread, Retell, and Reflect** on the importance of monitoring as a way to check on understanding while reading.

Student-Facilitated Comprehension Centers

- **Art Center:** Read student-authored stories and engage in Draw Something.
- **Theme Center:** Read books about animals and engage in Write Something using stop-sign stickers and adapted Double-Entry Journals.

Teacher-Facilitated Whole-Group Reflection and Goal Setting

- **Share** applications of Say Something from Stage Two.
- **Reflect** on how Say Something helps us monitor our understanding of text.
- **Set new goals** or extend existing ones

Guided Comprehension in the Primary Grades by Maureen McLaughlin ©2003. Newark, DE: International Reading Association. May be copied for classroom use.

STAGE TWO: Teacher-Guided Small-Group Instruction

Text: *Sea Turtles* (Gibbons, 1998) (Texts varied according to students' abilities.)

Review: First I reviewed with the students the strategies good readers use to make sense of text, and then I focused them on monitoring by using Say Something.

Guide: We briefly discussed what we knew about turtles in general and about sea turtles in particular. Next, I introduced the text by sharing the cover and reading the first few pages. Then I guided the students to read the text, stopping at designated points to Say Something. (I had placed stop-sign stickers in the texts to indicate where the students should stop.) Then they started to whisper-read the book. I listened to each student whisper-read a portion of the text to check for fluency. The students read two sections of text and stopped at designated points to Say Something to their partners. I encouraged a variety of responses, including predictions, connections, and questions. Students' comments included, "I didn't know that a bunch of sea turtle eggs were called a clutch," "I think it is interesting that sea turtles can lay 100 eggs at a time," and "I think it's sad that some people steal the sea turtles' eggs."

Practice: Students finished whisper-reading *Sea Turtles*, stopping at designated points to Say Something to a partner. I continued to monitor throughout this process. When the students had finished reading, we discussed many new things we had learned about sea turtles.

Reread, Retell, and Reflect: We did a choral rereading of the text and summarized what we had learned. Next, we discussed that what we say during Say Something can differ when we read different kinds of text. Then we reflected on how Say Something helped us make sense of what we were reading. Joaquin observed, "When we use Say Something, we get to say what we think is important about what we read."

Student-Facilitated Comprehension Centers

Art Center: Students read student-authored animal stories and engaged in Draw Something (see Appendix C, page 261). The completed organizers were displayed in our theme gallery.

Theme Center: I placed a variety of animal books at this center and inserted stop-sign stickers at several points in each text. Pairs of students selected books to partner-read. They used the partner-reading pattern Read-Pause-Say Something. They paused to Say Something each time they encountered a stop-sign sticker. Students recorded their responses on adapted Double-Entry Journal forms on which the column headings were replaced by the two students' names.

Student-Facilitated Comprehension Routines

Literature Circles: Groups of students partner-read animal books of their choice. One of the roles in our adapted Literature Circles was "the stopper." That student held up a stop sign and said, "Stop reading and Say Something at the end of page ___." At that point each student said something to the group. The stopper did this at points I had specified in the text she was reading. When the students finished reading the text, they engaged in discussion.

Cross-Age Reading Experiences: Upper-grade students and adult volunteers visited the class and paired with students from our class. The students read an animal book either to or with the cross-age literacy volunteer and engaged in Say Something. Then the students orally summarized what they had read.

STAGE THREE: Teacher-Facilitated Whole-Group Reflection and Goal Setting

Share: Students shared and discussed their applications of Say Something in small groups. This included responses recorded in students' Guided Comprehension Journals and the Draw Something organizers displayed in our theme gallery. Then each group shared with the whole class.

Reflect: We reflected on how using Say Something helped us monitor our understanding of what we were reading. Students seemed to enjoy using this technique.

Set New Goals: Students thought that they did a good job of using Say Something to help monitor their understanding. We revisited the idea of how what we say in Say Something is influenced by the type of text we are reading. We decided to extend our goal and use Say Something when reading different types of text, including poetry.

Assessment Options

I observed students during all stages of Guided Comprehension and reviewed and commented on their responses in their Guided Comprehension Journals, their completed Double-Entry Journal forms, and their completed Draw Something graphic organizers. I also completed running records and retellings with selected students.

FINAL THOUGHTS ABOUT THE ANIMALS, ANIMALS! THEME

Whether reading about house pets or residents of the local zoo, students engaged in this theme reveled in learning about animals. They were equally captivated by narrative texts such as *Cook-a-Doodle-Do!* and any informational texts written by Gail Gibbons or Seymour Simon.

As noted in previous chapters, lessons on a variety of skills that underpin comprehension strategies were also taught during this theme. For example, aspects of language development, such as phonemic awareness and phonics, and skills such as sequencing, generating questions, and distinguishing important from less important ideas were embedded in the theme. (For ideas about how to use literature to teach phonemic awareness, phonics, and fluency, see Appendix B.) Books that involved using recipes, such as *The Little Red Hen Makes a Pizza* were used to teach sequencing, and a number of informational texts were used to teach text structures and how to generate questions at a variety of levels. In addition, students engaged in repeated readings and Readers Theatre to improve fluency. Because students found this theme so interesting, they were highly motivated to learn and readily engaged in applying the comprehension strategies. In addition, teachers adapted lessons for prereaders and prewriters by engaging in read-alouds and encouraging response through a variety of modes—including discussion, drawing, painting, singing, dancing, and dramatizing.

THEME RESOURCES

Texts

Ada, A.F. (1998). *Yours truly, Goldilocks*. New York: Aladdin.

Adams, J. (2000). *Clarence goes out West and meets a purple horse*. Flagstaff, AZ: Rising Moon.

Andreae, G. (2001). *Giraffes can't dance*. New York: Scholastic.

Andrews, J.L. (1990). *Poisonous creatures*. New York: Trumpet Club.

Arnosky, J. (1994). *All about alligators*. New York: Scholastic.

Arnosky, J. (1995). *All about owls*. New York: Scholastic.

Barrett, J. (1974). *Animals should definitely not wear clothing*. New York: Aladdin.

Base, G. (2001). *The water hole*. New York: Harry N. Abrams.

Berger, M., & Berger, G. (2000). *Do penguins get frostbite? Questions and answers about polar animals*. New York: Scholastic.

Bloom, B. (1999). *Wolf!* New York: Orchard Books.

Brenner, B., & Chardiet, B. (1993). *Where's that reptile?* New York: Scholastic.

Brown, K. (2001). *The scarecrow's hat*. Atlanta, GA: Peachtree.

Brown, K. (2001). *What's the time, Grandma Wolf?* Atlanta, GA: Peachtree.

Calmenson, S. (1998). *Shaggy, waggy dogs and others*. New York: Scholastic.

Cannon, J. (1993). *Stellaluna*. New York: Scholastic.

Carle, E. (1989). *Eric Carle's animals, animals*. New York: Philomel.

Carlisle, M.W. (1993). *Slippery, splendid sea creatures*. Hauppauge, NY: Barrons.

Carlson, N. (2001). *How about a hug?* New York: Viking.

Cherry, L. (1990). *The great kapok tree*. New York: Harcourt Brace.

Churchill, V. (2001). *Sometimes I like to curl up in a ball*. New York: Sterling.

Cimaruti, M.T. (1998). *Peek-a-moo!* New York: Penguin Putnam.

Clement-Davies, D. (2002). *Spirit*. New York: Penguin Putnam.

Clements, A. (2001). *Brave Norman: A true story*. New York: Simon & Schuster.

Cowcher, H. (1990). *Antarctica*. New York: Scholastic.

Creech, S. (2001). *Love that dog*. New York: HarperCollins.

Cronin, D. (2000). *Click, clack, moo: Cows that type*. Simon & Schuster.

Cronin, D. (2002). *Giggle, giggle, quack*. New York: Simon & Schuster.

Dale, J. (1999). *Spot the sporty puppy*. New York: Aladdin.

Day, D. (1992). *Alaska's birds*. New York: Doubleday.

Earle, A. (1995). *Zipping, zapping, zooming bats*. New York: HarperCollins.

Elya, S. (2002). *Eight animals bake a cake*. New York: Penguin.

Falconer, I. (2000). *Olivia*. New York: Simon & Schuster.

Falconer, I. (2001). *Olivia saves the circus*. New York: Simon & Schuster.

Faulkner, K. (2001). *Ten little monkeys*. New York: Scholastic.

Fischer, A. (1994). *A to z animals*. New York: Grossett & Dunlap.

Florian, D. (2000). *Mammalabilia: Poems and paintings*. New York: Scholastic.

Frasier, M.A. (2002). *I.Q. goes to school*. New York: Walker.

Freedman, C. (2001). *Where's your smile, crocodile?* Atlanta, GA: Peachtree.

French, V. (1998). *Whale journey*. New York: Zero to Ten.

Fuge, C. (2002). *I know a rhino*. New York: Sterling.

Galdone, P. (1979). *The little red hen*. Boston: Houghton Mifflin.

Garland, M. (2000). *Icarus Swinebuckle*. Morton Grove, IL: Albert Whitman.

George, J.C. (1997). *Look to the north: A wolf pup diary*. New York: Scholastic.

Gibbons, G. (1991). *Whales*. New York: Holiday House.

Gibbons, G. (1992). *Sharks*. New York: Holiday House.

Gibbons, G. (1996). *Cats*. New York: Scholastic.

Gibbons, G. (1996). *Dogs*. New York: Scholastic.

Gibbons, G. (1998). *Sea turtles*. New York: Holiday House.

Gibbons, G. (2000). *Bats*. New York: Holiday House.

Gibbons, G. (2000). *Rabbits, rabbits, & more rabbits*. New York: Scholastic.

Gibbons, G. (2002). *Polar bears*. New York: Holiday House.

Gibbs, B. (1992). *Mommy & baby in the wild*. New York: Aladdin.

Haas, J. (2002). *Appaloosa zebra: A horse lover's alphabet*. New York: Greenwillow.

Heller, R. (1986). *How to hide a crocodile & other reptiles*. New York: Grosset & Dunlap.

Hirschmann, K. (2001). *Bats: The Magic School Bus fact finder*. New York: Scholastic.

James, D., & Lynn, S. (1995). *Underwater: A first look at animals*. New York: Scholastic.

Kitchen, B. (1994). *When hunger calls*. Cambridge, MA: Candlewick.

Lillegard, D. (1994). *Frog's lunch*. New York: Scholastic.

Lionni, L. (1988). *Six crows*. New York: Scholastic.

Lobel, A. (1970). *Frog and Toad are friends*. New York: Scholastic.

Lobel, A. (1977). *Mouse soup*. New York: Scholastic.

Luke, M. (2001). *Helping paws: Dogs that serve*. New York: Scholastic.

Maestro, B. (1990). *A sea full of sharks*. New York: Scholastic.

Markes, J. (2001). *Good thing you're not an octopus!* New York: HarperCollins.

Martin, B. Jr. (1967). *Brown bear, brown bear, what do you see?* New York: Henry Holt.

Martin, B. Jr. (1991). *Polar bear, polar bear, what do you hear?* New York: Henry Holt.

Martin, J. (1991). *Chameleons: Dragons in the trees*. New York: Drown.

Masson, J. (2000). *Dogs have the strangest friends: And other true stories of animal feelings*. New York: Penguin Putnam.

Masurel, C. (2002). *Big bad wolf*. New York: Scholastic.

McKissack, P.C. (1986). *Flossie and the fox*. New York: Scholastic.

McMillan, B. (1995). *Nights of the pufflings*. New York: Houghton Mifflin.

McVeigh, L. (2003). *Miss Hen's feast*. Boston: Houghton Mifflin.

National Geographic Society. (2000). *National Geographic animal encyclopedia*. Washington, DC: Author.

Noble, T.H. (1980). *The day Jimmy's boa ate the wash*. New York: Scholastic.

Numeroff, L. (1991). *If you give a moose a muffin*. New York: HarperCollins.

Numeroff, L. (1998). *If you give a pig a pancake*. New York: HarperCollins.

Numeroff, L. (2002). *If you take a mouse to school*. New York: HarperCollins.

Numeroff, L. (2002). *Laura Numeroff's 10-step guide to living with your monster*. New York: HarperCollins.

Osborne, M.P. (1997). *Magic tree house: Dolphins at daybreak*. New York: Scholastic.

Osborne, M.P. (1998). *Magic tree house: Polar bears past bedtime*. New York: Scholastic.

Osborne, M.P. (1999). *Magic tree house: Buffalo before breakfast*. New York: Scholastic.

Palatini, M. (1997). *Moostache*. New York: Scholastic.

Park, B. (2000). *Junie B. Jones has a peep in her pocket*. New York: Scholastic.

Patent, D.H. (1997). *Flashy fantastic rainforest frogs*. New York: Scholastic.

Patent, D.H. (1998). *Bold and bright black and white animals*. New York: Scholastic.

Patent, D.H. (2000). *Slinky scaly slithery snakes*. New York: Scholastic.

Peet, B. (1972). *The ant and the elephant*. New York: Scholastic.

Pratt, K.J. (1994). *A swim through the sea*. Nevada City, CA: Dawn.

Pringle, L. (2000). *Bats! Strange and wonderful*. Honesdale, PA: Boyds Mills Press.

Pringle, L. (2001). *Scholastic encyclopedia of animals*. New York: Scholastic.

Puttock, S., & Chapman, L. (2002). *Big bad wolf is good*. New York: Scholastic.

Rey, M. *The Curious George series*. Boston: Houghton Mifflin.

Rowland, D. (1991). *Explorer books: Whales & dolphins*. New York: Trumpet Club.

Royston, A. (1992). *Night-time animals*. New York: Aladdin.

Ryden, H. (1988). *Wild animals of America*. New York: E.P. Dutton.

Schoenherr, J. (1991). *Bear*. New York: Crown.

Shahan, S. (2000). *Feeding time at the zoo*. New York: Random House.

Simon, S. (1992). *Sharks*. New York: Scholastic.

Simon, S. (1993). *Wolves*. New York: Scholastic.

Simon, S. (1995). *Snakes*. New York: Scholastic.

Spinelli, E. (1991). *Whales: Children's nature library*. Lincolnwood, IL: Publications International.

Steig, W. (1971). *Amos & Boris*. New York: Scholastic.

Steig, W. (1982). *Doctor DeSoto*. New York: Scholastic.

Stevens, J., & Crummel, S.S. (1999). *Cook-a-doodle-doo!* New York: Harcourt Brace.

Sturges, P. (1999). *The little red hen makes a pizza.* New York: Dutton.

Trapani, I. (1997). *How much is that doggie in the window?* New York: Scholastic.

Weston, M. (1999). *Cats are like that.* New York: Scholastic.

Wiesner, D. (2001). *The three pigs.* New York: Clarion.

Wild, M., & Argent, K. (2000). *Nighty night!* Atlanta, GA: Peachtree.

Winthrop, E. (2001). *Dumpy LaRue.* New York: Henry Holt.

Yolen, J. (1993). *Welcome to the greenhouse.* New York: Scholastic.

Websites

Animal Pictures Archive
> www.animalpicturesarchive.com

Animal Planet
> animal.discovery.com

Animal Resources from the Electronic Zoo (NetVet)
> netvet.wustl.edu/ssi.htm

ASPCA Animal Land
> www.animaland.org

Care 2 Make a Difference
> www.care2.com/channels/ecoinfo/kids

EE-Link Endangered Species
> eelink.net/EndSpp

The Kids Room
> www.chirpingbird.com/netpets/html

Searching the Animal Diversity Web
> www-personal.umich.edu/~cberger/syllabusfolder/animaldiversity/Searching.start

SeaWorld/Busch Gardens Animal Information Database
> www.seaworld.org/infobook.html

South Washington County Schools: Animals
> www.sowashco.k12.mn.us/virtualmedia/elementary/animals.htm

Sounds of the World's Animals
> www.georgetown.edu/cball/animals

Zoobooks
> www.zoobooks.com

Performance Extensions Across the Curriculum

Art/Music/Drama

• Create animals using various mediums including construction paper, paints, markers, crayons, clay, etc. Students should use information they researched in science to help construct animals accurately.

• Create animal masks, representing self-selected favorite animals.

- Explore wildlife artists and create wildlife paintings.
- Write and perform Lyric Summaries or original songs based on factual information learned about animals.
- Listen to songs about animals and create and perform interpretive dances.
- Create puppets and use them to perform a retelling of a book, share factual information about animals, or dramatize an original animal story.

Mathematics

- Create and solve number sentences using animal manipulatives and mathematical operations currently being studied.
- Survey students and teachers about their favorite animals and graph the results.

Science

- Visit any of the various animal websites and research animals of choice. Information can be placed on a mobile to be displayed in the theme gallery.
- Classify animals by their groups (mammals, reptiles, amphibians, birds, fish, etc.).

Social Studies

- Map animals according to the continents in which they live and create an interactive display.
- Explore animals in different habitats around the world (desert, rainforest, etc.).

Culminating Activity

Animal Adventure Day: Invite parents to participate in an Animal Adventure Day. Display students' projects and exhibit students' art. Have the students perform songs they have written with instruments they have made. Display the books and poems the students have written. Have students serve as tour guides for the many displays. Students will wear the masks of their favorite animals, which they created in art class. A representative of the local zoo will share some exotic animals with the audience. Serve a variety of refreshments in the shapes of animals including animal crackers, cougar cupcakes, bat brownies, and other fun foods. Conclude the evening by having students present their Family Animal Trees, which will include photos of each family member's favorite animals. This event will be a time of adventure and celebration!

CHAPTER 9

Dinosaur Discoveries

Dinosaurs roamed the earth millions of years ago. Some were meat eaters that often stalked other dinosaurs, while others were more docile plant eaters. Although dinosaurs ceased to exist 65 million years ago, we are still learning about them today. Every time dinosaur fossils are unearthed, it is a time of discovery. Paleontologists use the bones to learn about the dinosaurs' size and other characteristics. This often leads to the discovery of new kinds of dinosaurs, which captures the interest and imaginations of children and adults alike.

In this Guided Comprehension theme, students read stories that feature dinosaurs as characters, as well as informational texts that provide factual information about dinosaurs. The sample Theme-Based Plan for Guided Comprehension: Dinosaur Discoveries (see Figure 24) offers an overview of the thinking and resources that support the theme. It presents a sampling of goals, state standards, assessments, texts, technology resources, comprehension strategies, teaching ideas, comprehension centers, and comprehension routines. The plan begins by delineating examples of student goals and related state standards. The student goals for this theme include the following:

- use appropriate comprehension skills and strategies
- interpret and respond to literature
- write a variety of types of text
- communicate effectively

These goals support the following state standards:

- learning to read independently
- reading, analyzing, and interpreting literature
- types and quality of writing
- speaking and listening

Examples of assessments used in the theme-based Guided Comprehension lessons include observation, running records and retellings, skill and strategy applications, and student self-assessments. The Guided Comprehension lessons, which were designed and taught by primary-grade teachers, are based on the following strategies and corresponding teaching ideas:

- Previewing: Semantic Question Map

Figure 24. Theme-Based Plan for Guided Comprehension: Dinosaur Discoveries

Goals and Connections to State Standards | Students will

- use appropriate comprehension skills and strategies. Standard: learning to read independently
- interpret and respond to literature. Standard: reading, analyzing, and interpreting literature
- write a variety of types of text. Standard: types and quality of writing
- communicate effectively. Standards: types and quality of writing; speaking and listening

Assessment

The following measures can be used for a variety of purposes, including diagnostic, formative, and summative assessment:

Lyric Retelling	Semantic Question Map
Observation	Student Self-Assessments
Retelling	Student Writing
Running Records	Thick and Thin Questions

Text	Title	Theme	Level
1.	*The Encyclopedia of Awesome Dinosaurs*	Dinosaur	2
2.	*Tyrannosaurus Was a Beast: Dinosaur Poems*	Dinosaur	3
3.	*Did Dinosaurs Live in Your Backyard?*	Dinosaur	2
4.	*The Three Little Dinosaurs*	Dinosaur	2

Comprehension Strategies

1. Previewing
2. Self-Questioning
3. Summarizing

Teaching Ideas

1. Semantic Question Map
2. Thick and Thin Questions
3. Lyric Retelling

Comprehension Centers

Students will apply the comprehension strategies and related teaching ideas in the following comprehension centers:

ABC Center	Project Center
Art Center	Theme Center
Making Words Center	Writing Center
Poetry Center	

Comprehension Routines

Students will apply the comprehension strategies and related teaching ideas in the following comprehension routines:

Literature Circles
Reciprocal Teaching
Cross-Age Reading Experiences

Technology Resources

Dinorama
www.nationalgeographic.com/dinorama/frame.html
Dinosaur Guide—Discovery Channel—dino, prehistoric
dsc.discovery.com/guides/dinosaur/dinosaur.html
Sue at The Field Museum of Natural History
www.fmnh.org/sue

- Self-Questioning: Thick and Thin Questions
- Summarizing: Lyric Retelling

The texts used in teacher-directed whole-group instruction include "Brachiosaurus" from *Tyrannosaurus Was a Beast: Dinosaur Poems* (Prelutsky, 1992) and *The Encyclopedia of Awesome Dinosaurs* (Benton, 2000), *Did Dinosaurs Live in Your Backyard?* (Berger & Berger, 1998), and *The Three Little Dinosaurs* (Harris, 1999). Numerous additional theme-related resources—including texts, websites, performance extensions across the curriculum, and a culminating activity—are presented in the Theme Resources at the end of the chapter.

In this theme, students' independent strategy applications occur in the comprehension centers and comprehension routines. The centers include ABC, art, making words, poetry, project, theme, and writing. The routines include Literature Circles, Reciprocal Teaching, and Cross-Age Reading Experiences. Sample websites complete the overview.

The three Guided Comprehension lessons that follow are presented through first-person teacher commentaries. Examples of student work are featured throughout the lessons.

GUIDED COMPREHENSION LESSONS

Dinosaur Discoveries

Guided Comprehension Strategy: Previewing

Teaching Idea: Semantic Question Maps

STAGE ONE: Teacher-Directed Whole-Group Instruction

Texts: "Brachiosaurus" from *Tyrannosaurus Was a Beast* (Prelutsky, 1992) and *The Encyclopedia of Awesome Dinosaurs* (Benton, 2000)

Explain: I began by explaining previewing and reminding students about the graphophonic, syntactic, and semantic cue systems. Then I focused on Semantic Question Maps and how they can help us to organize and learn information about words.

Demonstrate: I demonstrated by using a read-aloud, a Think-Aloud, and large poster board. I introduced the text by reading the title and explaining that one of our books was a collection of poems about different types of dinosaurs and the other was an encyclopedia that also provided information about dinosaurs. I approached a Semantic Question Map form that I had drawn on the poster board before class (see Appendix C, page 234). There was a centered oval for the focus word and webbed question categories including *How did it look? How long and tall was it? How much did it weigh? How did it move?* and *What did it eat?* I said, "I will write *Brachiosaurus* inside the oval because that is the focus word for this Semantic Question Map." Then I said, "Now I need to think about what I already know about Brachiosauruses." I read the first category, *How did it look?* and I said, "I think that Brachiosauruses had long necks, so I will write *long neck* underneath this category." Then I thought aloud about what I knew about each of the remaining categories and wrote the following underneath each one: *tall, heavy, very slowly,* and *plants.* I explained to the students that I would read information about the Brachiosaurus and revisit the Semantic Map to verify or revise the ideas I had written on the map and to include additional information we might learn from the text. Then I read aloud "Brachiosaurus." When I finished, I returned to the Semantic Question Map and noted that the information I had included in the map was correct. Then I reviewed each category to see if I had new information to add. The students also contributed suggestions based on the reading.

Guide: I guided pairs of students to think about the categories of our Semantic Question Map as they listened to me read aloud a brief selection about Brachiosauruses from *The Encyclopedia of Awesome Dinosaurs.* This text provided more detailed information, so when I asked the students what they would like to add to our Semantic Question Map, they offered suggestions such as the following: "75 feet long," "50 to 70 tons," "legs like tree trunks," and "hardly able to move." The students wrote their ideas on our map under the appropriate categories.

Practice: Students practiced by listing additional details to add to our Semantic Question Map as I read another section of text. When I finished, they added "teeth with shaped edges" to our map and noted that some information we had written on our map was verified by the ideas in this text. Then we used our map to create an oral summary. Our completed Semantic Question Map about Brachiosauruses appears in Figure 25.

Reflect: We reflected on what we had learned about Brachiosauruses and how the Semantic Question Map helped us to organize our thinking. We decided that we would leave our map on

GUIDED COMPREHENSION: DINOSAUR DISCOVERIES
PREVIEWING: SEMANTIC QUESTION MAP

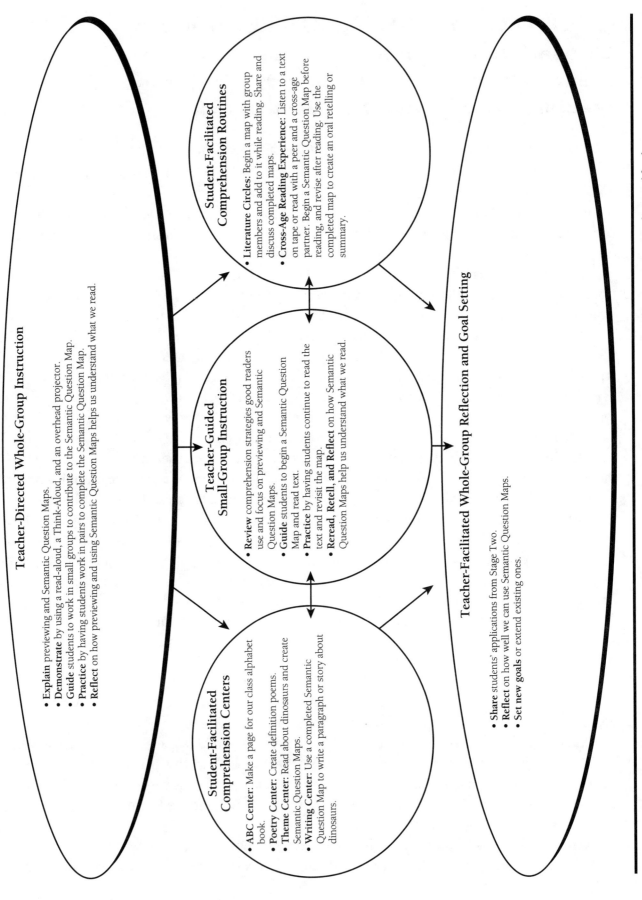

Teacher-Directed Whole-Group Instruction

- **Explain** previewing and Semantic Question Maps.
- **Demonstrate** by using a read-aloud, a Think-Aloud, and an overhead projector.
- **Guide** students to work in small groups to contribute to the Semantic Question Map.
- **Practice** by having students work in pairs to complete the Semantic Question Map.
- **Reflect** on how previewing and using Semantic Question Maps helps us understand what we read.

Student-Facilitated Comprehension Routines

- **Literature Circles:** Begin a map with group members and add to it while reading. Share and discuss completed maps.
- **Cross-Age Reading Experience:** Listen to a text on tape or read with a peer and a cross-age partner. Begin a Semantic Question Map before reading, and revise after reading. Use the completed map to create an oral retelling or summary.

Teacher-Guided Small-Group Instruction

- **Review** comprehension strategies good readers use and focus on previewing and Semantic Question Maps.
- **Guide** students to begin a Semantic Question Map and read text.
- **Practice** by having students continue to read the text and revisit the map.
- **Reread, Retell, and Reflect** on how Semantic Question Maps help us understand what we read.

Student-Facilitated Comprehension Centers

- **ABC Center:** Make a page for our class alphabet book.
- **Poetry Center:** Create definition poems.
- **Theme Center:** Read about dinosaurs and create Semantic Question Maps.
- **Writing Center:** Use a completed Semantic Question Map to write a paragraph or story about dinosaurs.

Teacher-Facilitated Whole-Group Reflection and Goal Setting

- **Share** students' applications from Stage Two.
- **Reflect** on how well we can use Semantic Question Maps.
- **Set new goals** or extend existing ones.

Guided Comprehension in the Primary Grades by Maureen McLaughlin ©2003. Newark, DE: International Reading Association. May be copied for classroom use.

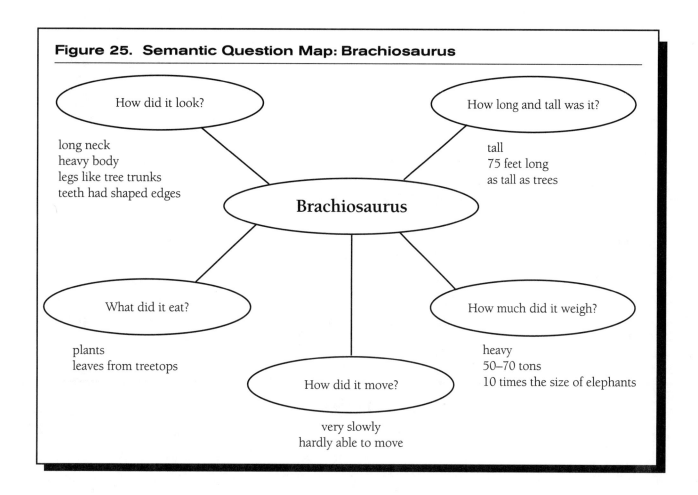

Figure 25. Semantic Question Map: Brachiosaurus

How did it look?

long neck
heavy body
legs like tree trunks
teeth had shaped edges

How long and tall was it?

tall
75 feet long
as tall as trees

Brachiosaurus

What did it eat?

plants
leaves from treetops

How much did it weigh?

heavy
50–70 tons
10 times the size of elephants

How did it move?

very slowly
hardly able to move

display and add new information to the categories as we learned more about this kind of dinosaur. The students asked if we could create poster board Semantic Question Maps for other kinds of dinosaurs and I noted we would be doing that in Stage Two. We also talked about how the organization of the map helped us to remember the information. Finally, we discussed how we would use Semantic Question Maps in other settings.

STAGE TWO: Teacher-Guided Small-Group Instruction

Text: *Dinosaur Bones* (Barner, 2001) (Texts varied according to students' abilities.)

Review: I began by reviewing the comprehension strategies good readers use and focused on previewing and Semantic Question Maps. I introduced *Dinosaur Bones* and explained that this book contained both a poem and facts about dinosaurs. I shared the cover, showed the format of the book through a picture walk, and read the poem aloud. Then I briefly discussed the book with the students and asked which dinosaur they would like to use as the focus of our question map. They chose Tyrannosaurus Rex and I wrote that in the center oval of the poster board Semantic Question Map I had prepared before our lesson. It contained the same questions we had addressed during direct instruction.

Guide: We briefly discussed what we already knew about this type of dinosaur. Students' responses generally focused on Tyrannosaurus Rex being huge and eating meat. We wrote those descriptors on our map and decided to read to verify this information and find out more detailed information about this and other kinds of dinosaurs. Students read silently and I offered support as requested. Because the book offered information about a variety of dinosaurs, we decided to read it in sections and record information as we read it. Students noted that Tyrannosaurus Rex means "King of Tyrant Lizards," so we added that to the center of our map. They also suggested that we include information about the weight of its skull. We added that to the *What did it look like?* category.

Practice: Students practiced by continuing to read the text. They were pleased that the author had included more information about Tyrannosaurus Rex at the end of the book. We learned that we were correct about Tyrannosaurus Rex being a meat eater. We also added its length and weight to the map.

Reread, Retell, and Reflect: Rather than reread this text, students suggested we check texts we had already read for more information about Tyrannosaurus Rex. So students reread segments of *Dinosaurs* by Gail Gibbons (1987) and other theme-related texts (see the Theme Resources at the end of this chapter), and then we added additional descriptors to our map. Our Semantic Question Map about Tyrannosaurus Rex, as it appeared at the end our guided small-group lesson, appears in Figure 26.

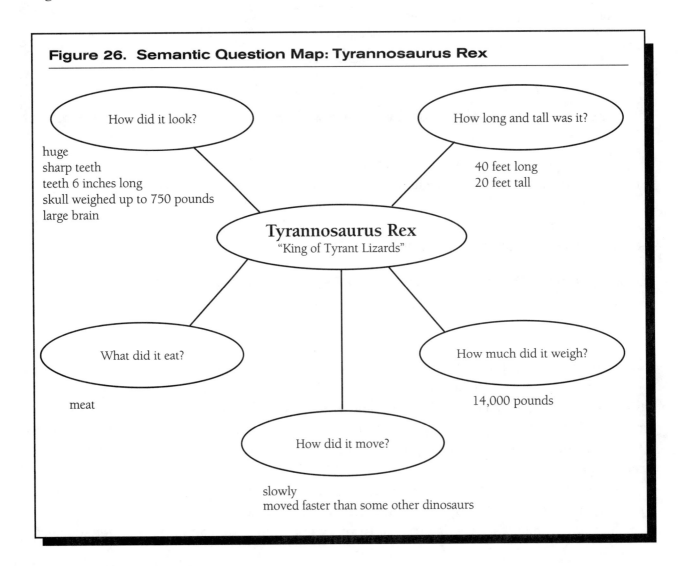

Figure 26. Semantic Question Map: Tyrannosaurus Rex

How did it look?

huge
sharp teeth
teeth 6 inches long
skull weighed up to 750 pounds
large brain

How long and tall was it?

40 feet long
20 feet tall

Tyrannosaurus Rex
"King of Tyrant Lizards"

What did it eat?

meat

How much did it weigh?

14,000 pounds

How did it move?

slowly
moved faster than some other dinosaurs

Student-Facilitated Comprehension Centers

ABC Center: Students worked in pairs on the computer to create a page for our class dinosaur alphabet book. We completed a Sequential Roundtable Alphabet about dinosaurs as a class (see Figure 27) and left it at the center. Students used this to select a topic for their pages. When this project was complete, we shared the alphabet book in class, exhibited it during our theme celebration, and then placed it in our classroom library.

Poetry Center: Students used completed Semantic Question Maps to write and illustrate definition poems (see Appendix D, page 302) either about dinosaurs in general or about a particular type. Here is a definition poem written by Alicia and Bobby:

What is a dinosaur?

Huge.

Lived long ago.

Ate meat or plants.

Died 65 million years ago.

That is a dinosaur!

Theme Center: Students self-selected texts from a large selection I had left at the theme center and worked either individually or with a partner to complete a Semantic Question Map.

Writing Center: Students used a Semantic Question Map they had completed previously to write and illustrate a paragraph or story about dinosaurs.

Figure 27. Sequential Roundtable Alphabet About Dinosaurs

A is for asteroid. It may have been an asteroid hitting the Earth that caused the dinosaurs to become extinct.	**B** is for biped. This word describes a creature that walks on two legs.	**C** is for carnivore. This word describes animals that only eat meat.
D is for different. There were many kinds of dinosaurs.	**E** is for egg. Most dinosaurs hatched from an egg.	**F** is for female. This is another word to describe a girl.
G is for gigantic. This word describes many dinosaurs. It is another way to say big.	**H** is for herbivore. This word describes animals that only eat plants.	**I** is for immense. This is another way to say big and describe many of the dinosaurs.
J is for Jurassic Period. It is a time when many dinosaurs lived.	**K** is for kingdom. Dinosaurs are members of the animal kingdom.	**L** is for locomotion. This word means how the dinosaurs traveled from place to place. Some walked, some flew, some swam.
M is for male. This is another word to describe a boy.	**N** is for nesting ground. This is a special place where some dinosaurs came to lay their eggs.	**O** is for omnivore. This word describes animals that eat plants and meat.
P is for paleontologist. It is a person who digs for fossils and studies them to get information about dinosaurs.	**Q** is for quadruped. This is a creature that walks on 4 legs.	**R** is for reptile. The dinosaurs are related to some reptiles that are alive today.
S is for skeleton. It is the bony framework of an animal.	**T** is for troop. This is another word for a group. Some dinosaurs lived together in a troop.	**U** is for unknown. There is still a lot we do not know about dinosaurs.
V is for volcano. There were many volcanos when the dinosaurs were alive.	**W** is for warmer and wetter. These two words describe the earth when the dinosaurs were alive.	**X** is for extinct. This word means the dinosaurs are no longer alive.
Y is for young. This word describes baby dinosaurs. Many dinosaurs took care of their young.	**Z** is for zero. This is the number of dinosaurs we will see alive.	

Student-Facilitated Comprehension Routines

Literature Circles: Students used the Semantic Question Map to take notes as they read the text(s) the group had selected. After reading the text and completing the maps, students used them to facilitate discussion.

Cross-Age Reading Experience: Students listened to a text on tape or read with a peer and a cross-age partner. They began completing the Semantic Question Map prior to reading, and added information as necessary during and after reading. Then they used the completed map to create an oral summary.

STAGE THREE: Teacher-Facilitated Whole-Group Reflection and Goal Setting

Share: Students shared their completed Semantic Question Maps from Stage Two in small groups and then shared selected maps, poems, paragraphs, and stories with the whole group.

Reflect: We reflected on how completing Semantic Question Maps helped to guide our reading and how well we could use them. The students seemed to take great pride in the super-sized Semantic Question Maps we had created for each type of dinosaur.

Set New Goals: We all felt very comfortable using the Semantic Question Map. The students were especially pleased that the completed maps could be used as the basis of discussion and writing. We decided to extend our goal of previewing and self-questioning by learning how to use "I Wonder" Statements.

Assessment Options

I used a variety of assessments, including observation, running records, students' strategy applications, student writing, and student self-assessments during this lesson.

Dinosaur Discoveries
Guided Comprehension Strategy: Self-Questioning
Teaching Idea: Thick and Thin Questions

STAGE ONE: Teacher-Directed Whole-Group Instruction

Text: *Did Dinosaurs Live in Your Backyard?* (Berger & Berger, 1998)

Explain: I explained that when we self-question we create questions to guide our reading and that in order to ask effective questions, we needed to learn how to ask different kinds of questions. Next, I explained Thick and Thin Questions (Lewin, 1998). I noted that thin questions usually address the content of the text and their answers are short and close-ended. As an example, I asked the students who was trying to hurt the three little dinosaurs in a story we had read recently. When the students responded with "T-rex," I showed the students that the answer to that thin question was short and it was contained in the story we had read. Then I explained thick questions and noted that these questions usually dealt with large concepts and that their answers were usually longer, more complex, and open-ended. I added that the answers to thick questions were often not found in the text or may require information in the text plus additional knowledge. To demonstrate thick questions I asked the students to imagine what they would have done if they had been one of the three little dinosaurs and T-rex came knocking on their door. The students offered a variety of problem-solving responses that were not found in the book we had read. I noted how they had used their knowledge of the book and their own thinking to answer the thick question. I was careful to explain that we could use Thick and Thin Questions when we were reading stories or informational text and that our focus would be learning how to create and respond to Thick and Thin Questions.

Demonstrate: I demonstrated Thick and Thin Questions (see Appendix C, page 241) by using a read-aloud, a Think-Aloud, and large and small wall-size sticky notes. I introduced *Did Dinosaurs Live in Your Backyard?* and read aloud about the origin of the word *dinosaur*. I noted the subheading and created a thin question and wrote it on the smaller sticky note: *What does the word* dinosaur *mean?* Then I recalled the answer from the text: *Dinosaur* means "terrible lizard." I reminded students that thick questions usually address larger concepts and have longer responses. Next, I created a thick question and wrote it on the larger sticky note: *How did different kinds of dinosaurs get their names?* Then I responded by explaining that dinosaurs got their names in several different ways. Sometimes the person who discovered the dinosaur gave it a name that described what the dinosaur looked like, and sometimes the dinosaur was named after the place where it was found. Finally, it could also be named for the person who first found the fossil. I reminded students that Sue, the dinosaur on display at The Field Museum, was named after the person who discovered the fossil.

Guide: I guided pairs of students to create Thick and Thin Questions while I continued to read aloud. Marissa and Mimi suggested this thin question: "How long ago did the first dinosaurs live?" (The answer was 225 million years ago.) Dan and Terri suggested this thick question: "Why would you want to have a dinosaur for a pet?" Dan and Terri responded to this and then several other students shared. It was clear that dinosaurs would have been very popular pets with my students.

Practice: I continued to read aloud and the pairs of students created Thick and Thin Questions for each segment that I read. I provided them with sticky notes in two sizes and after they had recorded their questions, we responded to them.

GUIDED COMPREHENSION: DINOSAUR DISCOVERIES
SELF-QUESTIONING: THICK AND THIN QUESTIONS

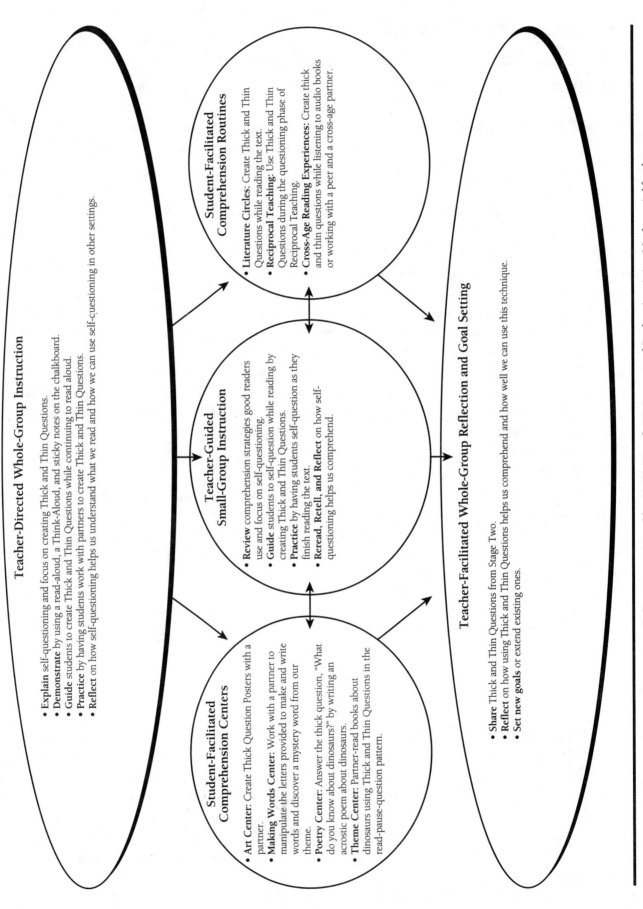

Teacher-Directed Whole-Group Instruction

- **Explain** self-questioning and focus on creating Thick and Thin Questions.
- **Demonstrate** by using a read-aloud, a Think-Aloud, and sticky notes on the chalkboard.
- **Guide** students to create Thick and Thin Questions while continuing to read aloud.
- **Practice** by having students work with partners to create Thick and Thin Questions.
- **Reflect** on how self-questioning helps us understand what we read and how we can use self-questioning in other settings.

Student-Facilitated Comprehension Routines

- **Literature Circles:** Create Thick and Thin Questions while reading the text.
- **Reciprocal Teaching:** Use Thick and Thin Questions during the questioning phase of Reciprocal Teaching.
- **Cross-Age Reading Experiences:** Create thick and thin questions while listening to audio books or working with a peer and a cross-age partner.

Teacher-Guided Small-Group Instruction

- **Review** comprehension strategies good readers use and focus on self-questioning.
- **Guide** students to self-question while reading by creating Thick and Thin Questions.
- **Practice** by having students self-question as they finish reading the text.
- **Reread, Retell, and Reflect** on how self-questioning helps us comprehend.

Student-Facilitated Comprehension Centers

- **Art Center:** Create Thick Question Posters with a partner.
- **Making Words Center:** Work with a partner to manipulate the letters provided to make and write words and discover a mystery word from our theme.
- **Poetry Center:** Answer the thick question, "What do you know about dinosaurs?" by writing an acrostic poem about dinosaurs.
- **Theme Center:** Partner-read books about dinosaurs using Thick and Thin Questions in the read-pause-question pattern.

Teacher-Facilitated Whole-Group Reflection and Goal Setting

- **Share** Thick and Thin Questions from Stage Two.
- **Reflect** on how using Thick and Thin Questions helps us comprehend and how well we can use this technique.
- **Set new goals** or extend existing ones.

Guided Comprehension in the Primary Grades by Maureen McLaughlin ©2003. Newark, DE: International Reading Association. May be copied for classroom use.

Reflect: We reflected on how self-questioning helps to guide our reading. Miguel said, "Making questions when we read is like having a map." Julianna commented, "I ask a lot of questions, but I never thought about doing it while I was reading. I like it. It helps me think."

STAGE TWO: Teacher-Guided Small-Group Instruction

Text: *The Encyclopedia of Awesome Dinosaurs* (Benton, 2000) (Texts varied according to students' abilities.)

Review: I reviewed the comprehension strategies good readers use and revisited Thick and Thin Questions. I reminded students of the qualities of the question types and referred to the prompts I had used in Stage One. Then I introduced "Dinosaurs Today," Chapter 10 of the text.

Guide: I guided the students as they read the first page and stopped to create one thin and one thick question on the different sized sticky notes I had provided. Students placed the sticky-note questions they wrote on that page. Then we discussed their Thick and Thin Questions and possible responses. Mayling's thin question was "What are two dinosaur relatives that are still alive today?" The answer, which we found in the text, was "reptiles and birds." Her thick question was, "What would happen if dinosaurs were still alive today?" To provide an answer to this question, we thought about what we knew about dinosaurs, including the size of dinosaurs. Then we thought about the world we live in. This question prompted quite a discussion. We talked about other big animals like elephants and noted that the elephants we had seen were either in a zoo or in a circus. Then we thought about the variety of sizes of dinosaurs—some were huge, but some were the size of chickens—and imagined how dinosaurs might be a part of our lives. Students suggested that it would be difficult to have the really large ones as pets, but that they might provide some help in transportation or be kept in zoos. Then students talked about the smaller dinosaurs and said that they might live on farms, because some were the same size as farm animals. This led to some interesting descriptions of farms. Then we took a few minutes for pairs of students to sketch some aspect of their life that they thought would be different if dinosaurs were still alive. The sketches were very creative and showed contributions dinosaurs could make to our lives, including dinosaur trains, dinosaur crossing guards, and dinosaur firefighters. Next, we listened to Jim's thin question: "When did the dinosaurs die?" The answer, which we located in the text was "65 million years ago." His thick question was similar to Mayling's, which he noted as he shared it.

Practice: Students practiced by reading the remainder of Chapter 10 and creating at least two additional Thick and Thin Questions. Thin questions focused on dinosaur relatives: "Where do tortoises and turtles live?" (on land and in the sea) "How big are marine turtles?" (six feet long) "Which reptile today most closely resembles the dinosaur?" (crocodile) "What is the dinosaur's closest living relative?" (birds) An example of a thick question was, "What do we still have to learn about dinosaurs?" (Many things: 20 new species are named every year…some species are yet to be discovered…computers can help us study dinosaurs—make accurate models…Sue.)

Reread, Retell, and Reflect: Students reread selected sections of text and we created a group oral summary. We reflected on how Thick and Thin Questions helped to keep us focused on what we were reading. Jeremy said, "The questions gave me a reason to think." Then we talked about how we could use Thick and Thin Questions in the other settings in Stage Two.

Student-Facilitated Comprehension Centers

Art Center: Students worked with partners and selected a text about their favorite dinosaur. Then they created a Thick Question Poster that included the question, the response, and an illustration of what they had learned about the dinosaur.

Making Words Center: Students engaged in making and writing words by manipulating magnetic letters I had provided to spell words of varying lengths. The theme-based mystery word was *Tyrannosaurus Rex*, so students had many word options.

Poetry Center: Students worked with partners and responded to the thick question, "What do you know about dinosaurs?" by writing acrostic poems based on the word *dinosaur*. This is Cristin and Caitlin's acrostic poem:

Digging up fossils

Iguanodon

New dinosaurs still being found

Over 65 million years ago the dinosaurs died

Stegosaurus

Allosaurus

Use plants or meat for food

Really huge or as small as chickens

Sue is in the Field Museum

Theme Center: Students partner-read a variety of books about dinosaurs using the read-pause-question pattern. They used a blackline master and created Thick and Thin Questions during the questioning phase of the pattern.

Student-Facilitated Comprehension Routines

Literature Circles: Students partner-read the text and created Thick and Thin Questions to serve as the basis of the group discussion.

Reciprocal Teaching: Students created Thick and Thin Questions while reading, and the "teacher" used them during the questioning phase of the routine.

Cross-Age Reading Experiences: Students worked with a peer and either listened to an audio book or read with a cross-age partner. While reading, the students alternated creating Thick and Thin Questions.

STAGE THREE: Teacher-Facilitated Whole-Group Reflection and Goal Setting

Share: Students shared their Thick and Thin Questions from Stage Two in small groups and then shared a few examples with the whole class.

Reflect: We reflected on how Thick and Thin Questions helped to guide our reading and why we would use both types when reading.

Set New Goals: The students felt good about their ability to use Thick and Thin Questions, so we decided to use self-questioning while we were reading and learn more about it by exploring Question-Answer Relationships (QAR).

Assessment Options

I observed students during all stages of Guided Comprehension. I read and commented on their poems and posters and also used their completed Thick and Thin Question blacklines as assessments. In addition, I reviewed students' self-assessments and completed several running records.

Dinosaur Discoveries
Guided Comprehension Strategy: Summarizing
Teaching Idea: Lyric Retelling

STAGE ONE: Teacher-Directed Whole-Group Instruction

Text: *The Three Little Dinosaurs* (Harris, 1999)

Explain: I began by reminding students about what we had already learned about summarizing—that we needed to include the important information from the text and that we summarized different kinds of text in different ways. Next, I focused on retelling and reviewed the narrative elements. I shared the Lyric Retelling/Lyric Summary blackline (see Appendix C, page 263) and noted that the important points from the story—the characters, the setting, what happened, and how the story ended—would appear in our retellings. I also reminded students that we would need to retell what happened in the story in the correct sequence. Next, I explained that the Lyric Retelling would be a bit different from other retellings we had done because we would be choosing background music—a song that everyone knew—and writing our retellings as lyrics—or words—for that song.

Demonstrate: I demonstrated by using a Think-Aloud, the chalkboard, and a story I had read aloud earlier that morning. I wrote an outline on the board that addressed the story elements *Who? Where? What happened? How did it end?* and used it to record the narrative elements from *The Three Little Dinosaurs*. I thought aloud as I wrote. I began by saying, "To start my retelling I need to think about where the story takes place and who the characters are." I read the title, showed the cover and reread the first page. I said, "This story takes place in the jungle and the three little dinosaurs and the Tyrannosaurus Rex are the main characters. That's important information that I need to include in the retelling." I wrote the information on the board. Next, I said, "Now I need to figure out the problem in this story." I revisited the next few pages of the book and said, "The Tyrannosaurus Rex tries to blow down the three little dinosaurs' houses." Then I added the problem to our retelling.

Guide: I guided pairs of students to contribute to the retelling. I reviewed the list of story elements and said, "The next important information we need to include is how the characters attempted to resolve the problem. Let's remember the problem and think about how they tried to solve it." Marilee and David suggested, "When the T-rex blew down the first house and melted the second house, the dinosaurs ran to their brother's house." I asked the students if they agreed with that suggestion. They did, so I added that idea to our retelling. Next, Susan and Alicia said, "When T-rex tried to blow down the last house, the little dinosaurs had gotten really big and T-rex got scared and ran away." Everyone agreed that we should add that idea. Next, Michael and Jeannine suggested we end our retelling by adding, "Then the three dinosaurs built new houses and were happy and T-rex went fishing." We used their idea as the last sentence. Next, we read the retelling aloud and discussed whether we had included all the important information from the story. We decided that we had.

Practice: The students practiced by working in small groups to create Lyric Retellings. To facilitate this process, I needed to revisit some of the earlier steps in the direct instruction process to explain Lyric Retellings and demonstrate how they worked. I began by explaining to the students that we would be using the information we had just recorded to write our Lyric Retelling about

GUIDED COMPREHENSION: DINOSAUR DISCOVERIES
SUMMARIZING: LYRIC RETELLING

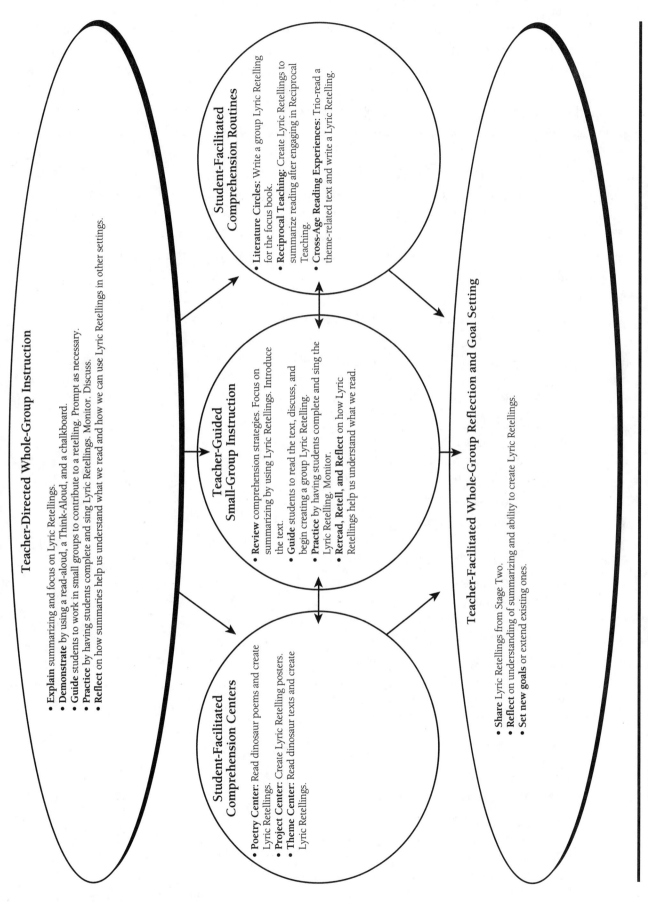

Teacher-Directed Whole-Group Instruction

- **Explain** summarizing and focus on Lyric Retellings.
- **Demonstrate** by using a read-aloud, a Think-Aloud, and a chalkboard.
- **Guide** students to work in small groups to contribute to a retelling. Prompt as necessary.
- **Practice** by having students complete and sing Lyric Retellings. Monitor. Discuss.
- **Reflect** on how summaries help us understand what we read and how we can use Lyric Retellings in other settings.

Student-Facilitated Comprehension Centers

- **Poetry Center:** Read dinosaur poems and create Lyric Retellings.
- **Project Center:** Create Lyric Retelling posters.
- **Theme Center:** Read dinosaur texts and create Lyric Retellings.

Teacher-Guided Small-Group Instruction

- **Review** comprehension strategies. Focus on summarizing by using Lyric Retellings. Introduce the text.
- **Guide** students to read the text, discuss, and begin creating a group Lyric Retelling.
- **Practice** by having students complete and sing the Lyric Retelling. Monitor.
- **Reread, Retell, and Reflect** on how Lyric Retellings help us understand what we read.

Student-Facilitated Comprehension Routines

- **Literature Circles:** Write a group Lyric Retelling for the focus book.
- **Reciprocal Teaching:** Create Lyric Retellings to summarize reading after engaging in Reciprocal Teaching.
- **Cross-Age Reading Experiences:** Trio-read a theme-related text and write a Lyric Retelling.

Teacher-Facilitated Whole-Group Reflection and Goal Setting

- **Share** Lyric Retellings from Stage Two.
- **Reflect** on understanding of summarizing and ability to create Lyric Retellings.
- **Set new goals** or extend existing ones.

Guided Comprehension in the Primary Grades by Maureen McLaughlin ©2003. Newark, DE: International Reading Association. May be copied for classroom use.

The Three Little Dinosaurs. I reiterated that we would need to choose a song that everyone knew as the music for their Lyric Retelling because they would be writing their retelling of the book as lyrics to the song. I explained that I would start out being the recorder—the one who would write the Lyric Retelling on the board—but that we would need other volunteers to help with that. I explained that after we finished our Lyric Retelling, we would share it by singing it. To demonstrate this idea, I put a Lyric Retelling of the original story of "The Three Little Pigs," which I had written to the tune of "Jingle Bells," on the overhead projector and sang it for the students. Then we began writing our Lyric Retelling using the holiday song "Up on the House Top" and the information we had recorded earlier. I wrote the first stanza as a demonstration. Next, I guided small groups of students in writing the chorus and second verse. Then the students practiced by finishing the Lyric Retelling with their groups. I monitored as they did this. When we had finished, we all sang it together. It was great fun. This is the Lyric Retelling I began writing that was completed by Anne, Bobby, Valerie, and Diego:

The Three Little Dinosaurs: A Lyric Retelling to the Tune of "Up on the House Top"

Three little dinosaurs built houses in a jungle,
They were made of grass, mud bricks, and rocks.
Along came T-rex to blow them down,
He huffed and he puffed and the first one was gone.

Oh, oh, oh, go, dino, go
Oh, oh, oh, go, dino, go
On to the next house before T-rex gets you
You'll be safe in your brother's house.

Dino One ran to his brother's
And they sat down and watched TV
Then T-rex came to blow the house down,
This time he used water and then it was gone.

Oh, oh, oh, go, dinos, go
Oh, oh, oh, go, dinos, go
On to the next house before T-rex gets you
You'll be safe in your brother's house.

Dinos One and Two ran to their brother's
And they were not afraid
Then T-Rex came to blow the house down,
But this house was made of stone.

Oh, oh, oh, try, T-rex, try
Oh, oh, oh, try, T-rex, try
To figure out how to knock the house down,
And get the dinos before they're gone.

It took T-rex a long, long time,
But he knocked the house down with a big rock,
When the three dinos asked him why,
He saw how big they were and ran away.

Oh, oh, oh, go, T-rex, go
Oh, oh, oh, go, T-rex, go
On to your new job of fishing
You should watch out for what you are catching!

Reflect: We reflected on how writing retellings helped us understand what we were reading and how much fun it was to use Lyric Retellings. We all had a great deal of fun using this comprehension idea. We all enjoyed singing the Lyric Retelling.

STAGE TWO: Teacher-Guided Small-Group Instruction

Text: *Mama Rex & T: Homework Trouble* (Vail, 2001) (Texts varied according to students' abilities.)

Review: I began by reviewing the strategies good readers use and focusing on summarizing. Then I reviewed the process for creating Lyric Retellings and distributed the organizer to the students.

Guide: I introduced the text by sharing the cover and title and reading aloud the first three pages of Chapter 1. We discussed the dinosaurs as characters in the story and what homework trouble might mean. Then I guided the students in reading the text, prompting as necessary. They paused when they finished reading each of the very brief chapters, so we could discuss the story, note the important information from that section, and record it.

Practice: The students practiced by creating a Lyric Retelling. The song they chose was "Are You Sleeping?" What follows is the Lyric Retelling of *Mama Rex & T: Homework Trouble* that the students wrote and sang:

Little T,
Little T,
Where's your homework?
Did you forget?
You need a diorama,
One that is about pigs,
But you haven't done it,
You haven't done it.

To the library
To the museum
You and your mom went
You and your mom went.
Then you made the diorama
You put a pink pig in mud
In a cottage cheese tub
Now your homework's done.

Reread, Retell, and Reflect: We did a choral rereading of the text and revisited our retelling. Then we reflected on how to create Lyric Retellings and how they helped us understand what we read. Alysia said, "Writing a Lyric Retelling is like writing a story in a song." Everyone agreed that writing Lyric Retellings was fun.

Student-Facilitated Comprehension Centers

Poetry Center: Students worked with a partner to read dinosaur poetry from a variety of books, including *Dinosaur Dances* by Jane Yolen (1990) and *Tyrannosaurus Was a Beast: Dinosaur Poems* by Jack Prelutsky. Then the students wrote a Lyric Retelling of a poem of their choice.

Project Center: Students worked in trios to create Lyric Retelling posters. They selected a book, wrote the title and author, discussed the story elements, and chose the music. Then they wrote the Lyric Retelling on a poster-size sticky note and illustrated it. Finally, they practiced singing it so they would be ready to perform it in Stage Three.

Theme Center: Students made selections from a variety of titles I had placed at the center and worked with a partner to create Lyric Retellings. They partner-read the book, using the read-pause-discuss pattern, and recorded information about the story elements. Then they chose their music and wrote their Lyric Retellings.

Student-Facilitated Comprehension Routines

Literature Circles: Students had just finished discussing a book, so they used their Lyric Retelling as an extension activity. They began by discussing the elements of the story. They used notes about the book that they had recorded in their Guided Comprehension Journals to facilitate this process. Then they created a group Lyric Retelling of the book.

Reciprocal Teaching: Students engaged in Reciprocal Teaching and recorded information about the story elements after they summarized each section. After reading, they created a Lyric Retelling of the book.

Cross-Age Reading Experiences: Students listened to a theme-related audio book or trio-read with a cross-age partner. The students recorded information about the story elements as they read. Then they selected the music and wrote a Lyric Retelling.

STAGE THREE: Teacher-Facilitated Whole-Group Reflection and Goal Setting

Share: Students sang their Lyric Retellings from Stage Two to the class. It was a fun sharing session because the students enjoyed singing as well as being audience members.

Reflect: We reflected on our understanding of summarizing and our ability to create Lyric Retellings.

Set New Goals or extend current ones. We decided that we all felt very comfortable creating Lyric Retellings for stories. So we extended our goal to learn how to summarize and write Lyric Summaries for informational texts about dinosaurs.

Assessment Options

I observed students throughout the Guided Comprehension process and reviewed and commented on their Lyric Retellings. I also used the students' self-assessments as information sources and competed running records with several students.

FINAL THOUGHTS ABOUT THE DINOSAUR THEME

Dinosaurs are generally viewed as the favorite animals of primary-grade students. Students' engagement in this theme supports that thinking. Whether students are in kindergarten or third grade, any news about dinosaurs garnered their interest.

As noted in previous chapters, it is important to acknowledge that lessons about a variety of skills that underpin comprehension strategies were taught during this theme. For example, aspects of language development, such as phonemic awareness and phonics, and skills such as sequencing, generating questions, and distinguishing important from less important ideas were embedded in the theme. (For ideas about how to use literature to teach phonemic awareness, phonics, and fluency, see Appendix B.) A variety of informational texts such as *Did Dinosaurs Live in Your Backyard?* and *The Ultimate Book of Dinosaurs: Everything You Always Wanted to Know About Dinosaurs—But Were Too Terrified to Ask* (Doswell, Malam, Mason, & Parker, 2002) were used to teach text frames and generating questions at a variety of levels. Time lines of dinosaur discoveries were used to teach sequencing. Students also used Readers Theatre, Poetry Theater, and repeated readings to improve fluency. Students' fascination with the dinosaur theme motivated them to read and promoted their engagement in learning. In addition, teachers adapted lessons for prereaders and prewriters by engaging in read-alouds and encouraging response through a variety of modes—including discussion, drawing, singing, dancing, and dramatizing.

THEME RESOURCES

Texts

Aliki. (1985). *My visit to the dinosaurs*. New York: Harper Trophy.

Aliki. (1988). *Digging up dinosaurs*. New York: HarperCollins.

Aliki (1990). *Fossils tell of long ago*. New York: Harper Trophy.

Aliki. (1996). *Dinosaurs are different*. New York: Harper Trophy.

Barner, B. (2001). *Dinosaur bones*. San Francisco: Chronicle Books.

Barton, B. (1994). *Dinosaurs, dinosaurs*. New York: HarperCollins.

Benton, M. (2000). *The encyclopedia of awesome dinosaurs*. Brookfield, CT: Copper Beech Books.

Berger, M., & Berger, G. (1998). *Did dinosaurs live in your backyard?* New York: Scholastic.

Boynton, S. (2000). *Dinos to go: 7 nifty dinosaurs in 1 swell book*. New York: Simon & Schuster.

Branley, F.M. (1991). *What happened to the dinosaurs*. New York: HarperCollins.

Carrick, C. (1985). *Patrick's dinosaurs*. Boston: Houghton Mifflin.

Carrick, C. (1988). *What happened to Patrick's dinosaurs?* Boston: Houghton Mifflin.

Cole, J. (1995). *The magic school bus in the time of the dinosaurs*. New York: Scholastic.

Crotty. K. (2000). *Dinosongs: Poems to celebrate a T-rex named Sue*. New York: Scholastic.

Crozat, F. (1990). *I am a big dinosaur*. Hauppauge, NY: Barron's Educational Series.

Davis, L., & Taylor, B. *Dorling Kindersley Readers: Dinosaur dinners* (Level 2: Beginning to read alone). New York: Dorling Kindersley.

Dowswell, P., Malam, J., Mason, P., & Parker, S. (2002). *The ultimate book of dinosaurs: Everything you always wanted to know about dinosaurs—But were too terrified to ask.* London: Parragon.

Gibbons, G. (1987). *Dinosaurs.* New York: Scholastic.

Gurney, J. (1998). *A dinotopia: The land apart from time.* New York: HarperCollins.

Harris, J. (1999). *The three little dinosaurs.* Gretna, LA: Pelican.

Hennessy, B.G. (1990). *The dinosaur who lived in my backyard.* New York: Penguin Putnam.

Hoban, L. (1996). *Joe and Betsy the dinosaur* (I Can Read book series: Level 1). New York: HarperCollins.

Hoff, S. (1978). *Danny and the dinosaur* (I Can Read book series: Level 1). New York: HarperCollins.

Hoff, S. (1997). *Happy birthday, Danny and the dinosaur!* (I Can Read book series: Level 1). New York: HarperCollins.

Joyce, W. (1995). *Dinosaur Bob and his adventures with the family Lazardo.* New York: HarperCollins.

Kerley, B. (2001). *The dinosaurs of Waterhouse Hawkins: An illuminating history of Mr. Waterhouse Hawkins, artist and lecturer.* New York: Scholastic.

Lambert, D., & Hutt, S. (2000). *Dorling Kindersley guide to dinosaurs: A thrilling journey through prehistoric times.* New York: Dorling Kindersley.

Lauber, P. (1994). *The news about dinosaurs.* New York: Aladdin.

McGough, K. (2001). *Fossils.* Washington, DC: National Geographic Society.

McMullan, K.H., & Jones, J.R. (1989). *Dinosaur hunters* (Step Into Reading books series: A step 4 book). New York: Random House.

Milton, J. (1985). *Dinosaur days* (Step Into Reading books series: A step 2 book). New York: Random House.

Most, B. (1978). *If the dinosaurs came back.* New York: Harcourt Brace.

Most, B. (1987). *Dinosaur cousins?* New York: Harcourt Brace.

Most, B. (1995). *How big were the dinosaurs?* New York: Harcourt Brace.

Osborne, M.P. (1992). *Dinosaurs before dark* (Magic Tree House series #1). New York: Random House.

Osborne, W., & Osborne, M.P. (2000). *Dinosaurs: A nonfiction companion to* Dinosaurs Before Dark (Magic Tree House research guide series). New York: Random House.

Pallotta, J. (1990). *The dinosaur alphabet book.* Watertown, MA: Charlesbridge.

Parish, P. (1983). *Dinosaur time* (I Can Read book series: Level 1). New York: HarperCollins.

Penner, L.R. (1991). *Dinosaur babies* (Step Into Reading books series: A step 1 book). New York: Random House.

Petty, K. (1997). *Dinosaurs laid eggs: And other amazing facts about prehistoric reptiles.* Brookfield, CT: Millbrook.

Prelutsky, J. (1992). *Tyrannosaurus was a beast: Dinosaur poems.* New York: William Morrow.

Prelutsky, J. (1999). *The 20th century children's poetry treasury.* New York: Alfred A. Knopf.

Relf, P. (2000). *A dinosaur named Sue: The story of the colossal fossil.* New York: Scholastic.

Rey, M. (1989). *Curious George and the dinosaur.* Boston: Houghton Mifflin.

Robinson, F. (1999). *A dinosaur named Sue: The find of the century.* New York: Scholastic.

Schnetzler, P.L. (1996). *Ten little dinosaurs.* Denver, CO: Accord Publishing.

Sereno, P.C. (1989). *How tough was a tyrannosaurus? More fascinating facts about dinosaurs.* New York: Putnam.

Shields, C. (1997). *Saturday night at the dinosaur stomp.* Cambridge, MA: Candlewick.

Sierra, J. (2002). *Good night, dinosaurs.* Boston: Houghton Mifflin.

Skofield, J. (1998). *Detective Dinosaur* (I Can Read book series: Level 2). New York: HarperCollins.

Soderberg, E. (2000). *Dinosaur dig: Picture clue book.* New York: Scholastic.

Steer, D. (2001). *Snappy little dinosaurs.* Brookfield, CT: Millbrook.

Tanaka, S., Hallett, M., & Barnard, A. (1998). *Graveyards of the dinosaurs.* New York: Hyperion.

Thomson, R. (2000). *Dinosaur's day.* New York: Dorling Kindersley.

Vail, R. (2001). *Mama Rex & T: Homework trouble.* New York: Scholastic.

Wahl, J. (1997). *I met a dinosaur.* New York: Harcourt.

Wahl, J. (2000). *The field mouse and the dinosaur named Sue.* New York: Scholastic.

Whybrow, I. (1999). *Sammy and the dinosaurs.* New York: Scholastic.

Whybrow, I. (2001). *Sammy and the dinosaurs deluxe gift set.* New York: Scholastic.

Wilkes, A. (1994). *The big book of dinosaurs: A first book for young children.* New York: Dorling Kindersley.

Worth, B. (1999). *Oh, say can you say di-no-saur? All about dinosaurs.* New York: Random House.

Yolen, J. (1990). *Dinosaur dances.* New York: Putnam.

Yolen, J. (2000). *How do dinosaurs say good night?* New York: Scholastic.

Zimmerman, H., & Olshevsky, G. (2000). *Dinosaurs: The biggest, baddest, strangest, fastest.* New York: Simon & Schuster.

Websites

The Academy of Natural Sciences—Dinosaur Hall
www.acnatsci.org/museum/dinohall/index.html

The Academy of Natural Sciences—Just for Kids
www.acnatsci.org/kids

American Museum of Natural History
ology.amnh.org/index.html

Billy Bear's Land O' Dinosaurs
www.billybear4kids.com/dinosaurs/long-long-ago.html

Dinobase
palaeo.gly.bris.ac.uk/dinobase/dinopage.html

DinoDictionary
www.dinodictionary.com/imain.html

Dinorama
www.nationalgeographic.com/dinorama/frame.html

Dinosaur Fun and Games
www.enchantedlearning.com/subjects/dinosaurs/fun/Games.html

Dinosaur Illustrations
www.search4dinosaurs.com/pictures.html

Dinosaur Links
www.ucmp.berkeley.edu/diapsids/dinolinks.html

The Dinosauria
   www.dinosauria.com

Dinosaurs
   www.bonus.com/bonus/list/n_digthese.right.html

Dinosaurs for Kids
   easyweb.easynet.co.uk/~skafi/DINO.HTM

Discovery Channel Dinosaur Guide
   dsc.discovery.com/guides/dinosaur/dinosaur.html

The Fossil and Dinosaurs Page
   www.eyesoftime.com/teacher/dino.htm

Kids Domain Dinosaurs Links
   www.kidsdomain.com/kids/links/Dinosaurs.html

My Dinomite Site!! Dinosaurs for Kids!!
   members.aol.com/cahaston

Peabody Museum of Natural History, Yale University
   www.nhm.ac.uk/education/online/dinosaur_data_files.html

Sue at The Field Museum
   www.fmnh.org/sue

Zoom Dinosaurs
   www.enchantedlearning.com/subjects/dinosaurs/toc.shtml

Performance Extensions Across the Curriculum

Art/Drama/Music

- Visit the local museum of natural history or visit virtual museums online to observe the appearance of different kinds of dinosaurs. Use the information gleaned from this experience and texts to create different kinds of dinosaurs in a variety of mediums from sketching to Eric Carle-style collage.

- Create dino-puppets in a variety of mediums, including paper bags and socks. Stage puppet shows that demonstrate what students have learned about dinosaurs throughout the theme or what our world would be like if dinosaurs were still alive.

- Work in small groups to create dinosaur dances based on Jane Yolen's poems "Twinkle Toes Triceratops," "When the Allosaurus," "Tyrannosaurus," "Kick Line," and "Dinosaur Waltz." Perform the dances for the class as one group member reads the poem.

- Write and perform a variety of songs about dinosaurs. As an alternative, create Lyric Summaries about dinosaurs by adapting classic melodies such as "Oh, Susanna!" to "Sue, the Fossil." Create posters to advertise your song.

Mathematics

- Create and solve dino-problems using the measurements and weights of a variety of dinosaurs. Base the problems on the mathematical operations currently being studied. Design dino-math cards by writing the problem on one side of the card and a solution on the other. Play "math cards" with peers.

- Use the Write and Draw math strategy (McLaughlin, Corbett, & Stevenson, 2000) to use both words and symbols to make students' thinking about problem solving visible to themselves and others. Begin by posing a problem. Have the students read or listen to the problem and paraphrase if desired. Next, have the students record their thinking about how to solve the problem on a paper that has been divided in half vertically. On one side of the paper, students draw a picture to show how they would solve the problem. On the other side, they use words to describe how they solved the problem. Have the students share their Write and Draw applications with a partner.

Science

- Explore how fossils are created and endure through such prolonged periods of time. Visit the local museum to examine plant or animal fossils that have been found in the community. Discuss what we can learn from fossils. Create fossil-like imprints in class (see Badlands National Park Lesson Plans: Fossils—Making Plaster Casts—http:// www.nps.gov/badl/teacher/fossils.htm and You are a paleontologist! Day 1, Part 1, Discovery—http://www.artdiscovery.org/lesson-plans).
- Investigate the work of paleontologists. Create an illustrated, interactive time line of the process from fossil discovery to fossil exhibition by examining dinosaur discoveries such as Sue. (Sue is on display at the Field Museum of Natural History, http://www.fmnh.org/sue)

Social Studies

- Create an interactive wall map of dino-discovery sites. Research each site to learn more about the type of dinosaur discovered there as well as information about the country and the people who live there. Display this information about each site around the map, connecting it to the site with a piece of yarn. At the end of the information, include questions on flaps and place responses so students can access them by lifting the flap. Include an "I Learned Something New" area for students to record ideas and sign their names.

Culminating Activity

Dinosaurs Alive! Students will create and deliver invitations to Dinosaurs Alive! Students' dinosaur performances across the curriculum will be displayed in the hallways approaching the classroom. The classroom itself will feature student performances such as self-authored books, a class alphabet book, Lyric Summaries, mobiles, and strategy applications. Students and guests will wear nametags shaped liked dinosaurs. Students will wear dino-masks that they created in art class and serve as dino-guides, sharing their knowledge of dinosaurs as they escort their guests on tours of the classroom. An expert from a local university or museum will speak briefly about dinosaurs and make connections to the students' performances. As dino-desserts are served, a PowerPoint slideshow featuring the highlights of theme performances and field trips will be shared. During the course of the celebration, everyone will be invited to visit an interactive display titled "We Are Dino-Fans!" where students and guests will write their reactions to and comments about the Dinosaur Discoveries theme.

CHAPTER 10

Situating Guided Comprehension in Other Themes

I n Chapters 6 through 9, I situated Guided Comprehension within a variety of themes and provided planning ideas, lessons, examples of student work, and numerous resources. The themes addressed included Favorite Author Eric Carle; The Neverending Adventures of Arthur the Aardvark; Animals, Animals!; and Dinosaur Discoveries. Now it is your turn to situate Guided Comprehension in four other themes.

In this chapter, I have included the resources necessary to plan theme-based Guided Comprehension lessons on the following topics:

- The Ocean
- Poetry
- Transportation
- Weather

To facilitate your planning process, blank forms for developing themes and creating Guided Comprehension lessons are provided (see pages 169 and 170). A sample Guided Comprehension schedule is also included (see page 171). Booklists, websites, performance extensions across the curriculum, and a culminating activity for each theme complete the planning resources. Simply set the goals for your lessons, make connections to your state standards, select the comprehension strategies and teaching ideas you want to teach, and use the resources provided to complete your plans. Remember that detailed explanations of the teaching ideas used in this book and a variety of blackline masters to facilitate their use are included in Appendix C.

SAMPLE THEME-BASED PLAN FOR GUIDED COMPREHENSION

Goals and Connections to State Standards	Students will

• • •

Assessment

The following measures can be used for a variety of purposes, including diagnostic, formative, and summative assessment:

Comprehension Strategies	Teaching Ideas
1.	
2.	
3.	
4.	

Comprehension Centers

Students will apply the comprehension strategies and related teaching ideas in the following comprehension centers:

Text	Title	Theme	Level
1.			
2.			
3.			
4.			

Comprehension Routines

Students will apply the comprehension strategies and related teaching ideas in the following comprehension routines:

Technology Resources

GUIDED COMPREHENSION PLANNING FORM

Strategy: _____

Teaching Idea: _____

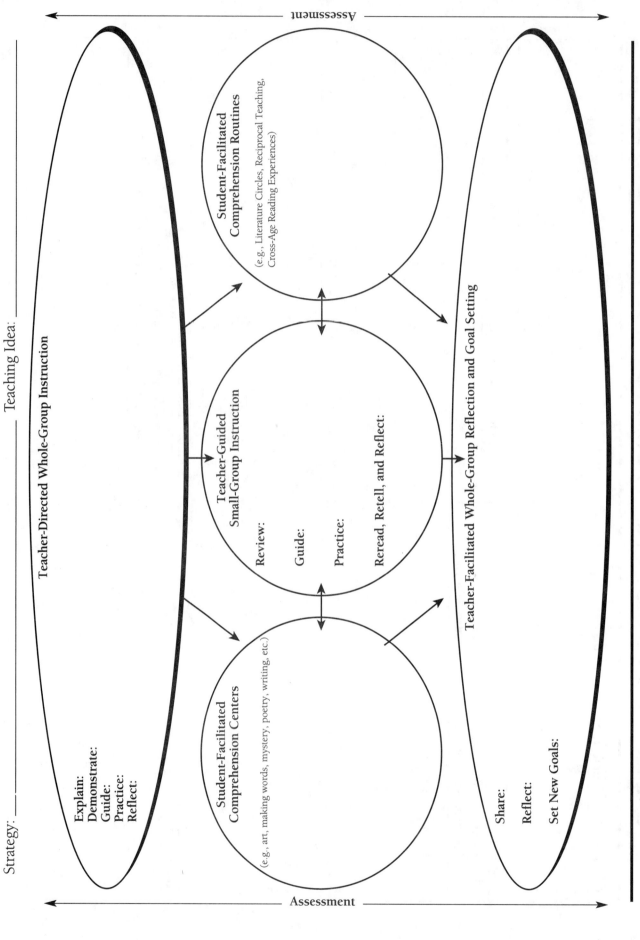

Teacher-Directed Whole-Group Instruction

Explain:
Demonstrate:
Guide:
Practice:
Reflect:

Student-Facilitated Comprehension Routines

(e.g., Literature Circles, Reciprocal Teaching, Cross-Age Reading Experiences)

Teacher-Guided Small-Group Instruction

Review:

Guide:

Practice:

Reread, Retell, and Reflect:

Student-Facilitated Comprehension Centers

(e.g., art, making words, mystery, poetry, writing, etc.)

Teacher-Facilitated Whole-Group Reflection and Goal Setting

Share:

Reflect:

Set New Goals:

Assessment

Guided Comprehension in the Primary Grades by Maureen McLaughlin ©2003. Newark, DE: International Reading Association. May be copied for classroom use.

SAMPLE SCHEDULES FOR GUIDED COMPREHENSION IN THE PRIMARY GRADES

90-Minute Schedule		My Schedule

| 20 minutes | ——————— Stage 1 ———————
 Teacher-Directed Whole-Group Instruction | _____ minutes |

| 60 minutes | ——————— Stage 2 ——————— | _____ minutes |

| 20 minutes (three groups) | Teacher-Guided Small-Group Instruction | _____ minutes (_____ groups) |

| Students not meeting with the teacher are working in centers and routines. | Comprehension Centers
 Comprehension Routines | Students not meeting with the teacher are working in centers and routines. |

| 10 minutes | ——————— Stage 3 ———————
 Teacher-Facilitated Whole-Group Reflection and Goal Setting | _____ minutes |

Guided Comprehension in the Primary Grades by Maureen McLaughlin ©2003.
Newark, DE: International Reading Association. May be copied for classroom use.

THEME RESOURCES

The Ocean

Texts

Andreae, G. (2002). *Commotion in the ocean.* Alpharetta, GA: Tiger Tales.

Berger, M., & Berger, G. (2001). *What makes an ocean wave? Questions and answers about the ocean and ocean life.* New York: Scholastic.

Bramwell, M. (2001). *Ocean watch.* New York: Dorling Kindersley

Bright, M. (2002). *The encyclopedia of awesome oceans.* Brookfield, CT: Copper Beech Books.

Bright, M. (2002). *People and the sea.* Brookfield, CT: Millbrook.

Bryan, A. (2000). *Salting the ocean: 100 poems by young poets.* New York: HarperCollins.

Burns, K. (1996). *In the ocean.* New York: Little, Brown.

Clarke, P. (1997). *Beneath the oceans.* New York: Scholastic.

Cole, J. (1996). *The Magic School Bus on the ocean floor.* New York: Scholastic.

Condra, E. (2002). *See the ocean.* Nashville, TN: Hambleton-Hill.

Craig, J. (1990). *What's under the ocean?* New York: Troll Communications.

Crema, L. (1998). *Look inside the ocean.* New York: Putnam.

Dawson, S. (2001). *Sea and land animals.* Washington, DC: National Geographic Society.

Denne, B. (2001). *First encyclopedia of seas and oceans.* Tulsa, OK: EDC.

Fowler, A., & Hillerich, R.L. (1995). *The earth is mostly ocean.* New York: Scholastic.

Frasier, D. (1998). *Out of the ocean.* New York: Harcourt.

Ganeri, A. (1995). *I wonder why the sea is salty.* New York: Kingfisher.

Gibbons, G. (1991). *Whales.* New York: Holiday House.

Gibbons, G. (1992). *Sharks.* New York: Holiday House.

Gibbons, G. (1998). *Sea turtles.* New York: Holiday House.

Gibbons, G. (2002). *Exploring the deep, dark sea.* New York: Little, Brown.

Guiberson, B.Z. (2002). *Ocean life.* New York: Scholastic.

Heinrichs, S. (1986). *The Atlantic Ocean.* New York: Scholastic.

Heller, R. (1992). *How to hide an octopus and other sea creatures.* New York: Putnam.

Lauber, P. (1996). *Octopus is amazing.* New York: HarperCollins.

Littlefield, C. (2002). *Awesome ocean science! Investigating the secrets of the underwater world.* Charlotte, VT: Williamson.

Markle, S. (1999). *Down, down, down in the ocean.* New York: Walker.

Morris, N. (1995). *Oceans.* New York: Crabtree.

Morris, N., & Card, V. (1997). *Oceans and seas.* Austin, TX: Steck-Vaughn.

Nye, B., Dykes, J., & Saunders, I. (1999). *Bill Nye the science guy's big blue ocean.* New York: Disney Press.

Nyquist, K.B. (2002). *The oceans around us.* Washington, DC: National Geographic Society.

O'Mara, A. (1996). *Oceans.* Mankato, MN: Capstone.

Pallotta, J. (1991). *Ocean alphabet book.* Watertown, MA: Charlesbridge.

Palmer, J. (1992). *Oceans.* Austin, TX: Steck-Vaughn.

Parker, S. (1998). *Seas and oceans*. New York: Scholastic.

Petersen, D., & Petersen, C.A. (2001). *The Atlantic Ocean*. New York: Scholastic.

Raymer, D. (2002). *Samantha's ocean liner adventure*. Middleton, WI: Pleasant.

Riordan, J. (1996). *Stories from the sea*. New York: Abbeville.

Rothaus, J. (1997). *Oceans*. Chanhassen, MN: Child's World.

Ryan, P. (2001). *Hello ocean*. Watertown, MA: Charlesbridge.

Savage, S. (1997). *Animals of the oceans*. Austin, TX: Raintree.

Seuss, Dr. (1976). *One fish, two fish, red fish, blue fish*. New York: Random House.

Seymour, S. (1990). *Oceans*. New York: William Morrow.

Stille, D. (2000). *Oceans*. New York: Scholastic.

Taylor, B. (2002). *Oceans and rivers*. New York: Kingfisher.

Ward, K. (1995). *Oceans*. New York: Rosen.

Websites

American Oceans Campaign—Beach Water Quality for Kids
    www.americanoceans.org/beach/kids.htm

The Big Blue Bus: Kid's Corner!
    www.dfo-mpo.gc.ca/canwaters-eauxcan/bbb-lgb/index_e.asp

International Year of the Ocean—Kid's and Teacher's Resources
    www.yoto98.noaa.gov/kids.htm

Kids' Corner: Oceans—Greenpeace USA
    www.greenpeaceusa.org/oceans/kids/kidstext.htm

Ocean Collection for Kids
    www.calstatela.edu/faculty/eviau/edit557/oceans

Oceanography for Kids
    oncampus.richmond.edu/academics/as/education/projects/hunts/oceans.html

Oceans and Coastal Protection: Kids' Page
    www.epa.gov/owow/oceans/kids.html

Oceans for Youth: Educational Website for Kids of All Ages
    www.oceansforyouth.com

Ocean Songs and Fingerplays
    www.angelfire.com/la/kinderthemes/ofingerplays.html

Welcome to WhaleNet Student Page
    whale.wheelock.edu/Students.html

Performance Extensions Across the Curriculum

Art/Music/Drama

• Create a class mural of undersea life and cover it with aqua cellophane to enhance its underwater appearance.

• Invent new kinds of fish or other ocean inhabitants. Design them and suspend them from the ceiling.

- Write Lyric Summaries of informational books such as *Sea Turtles*, *Sharks*, and *Whales* by Gale Gibbons and perform them for the class.
- Create ocean life dances like "The Octopus Rock," "The Turtle Twist," and "The Whale Wiggle." Perform the dances for classmates and teach them how to do the dances.
- Dramatize selected scenes from Debra Frasier's *Out of the Ocean*.

Mathematics
- Create and solve theme-based problems involving the mathematical operations currently being studied.
- Create a math book about the ocean. Use books such as *One Fish, Two Fish, Red Fish, Blue Fish* as models and include information such as the length of sharks and the weight of whales.

Science
- Explore how the sea affects our lives. Share what you learn through the medium of your choice.
- Investigate undersea plant life and create posters to represent the various types of plants.
- Explore the uses of fresh water and salt water. Present your findings through a fact or fiction book or a Venn Diagram (see Appendix C, page 252).

Social Studies
- Create a wall map that illustrates the locations of oceans around the world. Choose an ocean and use the theme books to research it. Share at least three new facts about it with the class.
- Explore communities, such as fishing villages, that rely on the ocean for their livelihood. Report on the many ways the ocean supports the community and jobs community members have that are connected to the sea.
- Think about someplace you would like to visit that is across a sea. Create a travel brochure that describes the trip you would like to take and offers information about the place you would like to visit.

Culminating Activity

Somewhere Under the Sea Celebration: Have students create underwater masks in art class and wear them as they greet their guests at our Somewhere Under the Sea Celebration. Hang sheared blue cellophane from the hall and classroom ceilings to create an underwater effect. Display students' performances in the corridors and in the classroom. Have students engage in a variety of performances, which will include singing original ocean songs, dramatizing a play the class wrote about ocean life, playing the fact or fiction ocean game show, and discussing the ocean as a habitat for animals and plants. Serve refreshments, including a wide variety of theme desserts. Invite participants to write family ocean rhymes on poster board sailboats, and display them on the ocean mural. Give autographed copies of the class ocean alphabet book to the guests as the evening concludes.

Poetry

Texts

Bryan, A. (2000). *Salting the ocean: 100 poems by young poets*. New York: HarperCollins.
Carle, E. (1989). *Eric Carle's animals, animals*. New York: Philomel.

Cullinan, B.E. (Ed.). (1996). *A jar of tiny stars: Poems by NCTE award-winning poets*. Honesdale, PA: Boyds Mills Press.

Dakos, K. (1995). *If you're not here, raise your hand*. New York: Aladdin.

Dakos, K. (2002). *The bug in teacher's coffee and other school poems*. New York: HarperCollins.

DePaola, T. (1988). *Book of poems*. New York: G.P. Putnam's Sons.

Fleischman, P. (1992). *Joyful noises: Poems for two voices*. New York: HarperCollins.

Fleischman, P. (2000). *Big talk: Poems for four voices*. Cambridge, MA: Candlewick.

Florian, D. (1998). *Insectlopedia*. New York: Scholastic

Florian, D. (1999). *Laugh-eteria*. New York: Scholastic.

Frost, R. (1982). *A swinger of birches: Poems of Robert Frost for young people*. Owings Mills, MD: Stemmer House.

Hoberman, M.A. (2001). *Fathers, mother, sisters, brothers: A collection of family poems*. New York: Little, Brown.

Holbrook, S., & Yolen, J. (2002). *Wham! It's a poetry jam! Discovering performance poetry*. Honesdale, PA: Boyds Mills Press.

Hopkins, L. (1999). *LIVES: Poems about famous Americans*. New York: HarperCollins.

Hudson, W. (1993). *Pass it on: African American poetry for young children*. New York: Scholastic.

Lansky, B. (1991). *Kids pick the funniest poems*. Minnetonka, MN: Meadowbrook.

Lansky, B. (1994). *A bad case of the giggles: Kids pick the funniest poems, Book 2*. Minnetonka, MN: Meadowbrook.

Lansky, B. (1997). *No more homework! No more tests! Kids' favorite funny school poems*. New York: Scholastic.

Martin, B. (2000). *Chicka chicka boom boom*. New York: Aladdin.

Moroney, T. (2001). *A classic treasury of nursery songs & rhymes*. New York: Barnes and Noble.

Numeroff, L. (1999). *Sometimes I wonder if poodles like noodles*. New York: Simon & Schuster.

Prelutsky, J. (1983). *The Random House book of poetry for children: A treasury of 572 poems for today's child*. New York: Random House.

Prelutsky, J. (1986). *Read-aloud rhymes for the very young*. New York: Alfred E. Knopf.

Prelutsky, J. (1990). *New kid on the block*. New York: Greenwillow.

Prelutsky, J. (1990). *Something big has been here*. New York: Greenwillow.

Prelutsky, J. (1991). *For laughing out loud: Poems to tickle your funnybone*. New York: Alfred A. Knopf.

Prelutsky, J. (1992). *The headless horseman rides tonight: More poems to trouble your sleep*. New York: William Morrow.

Prelutsky, J. (1992). *Tyrannosaurus was a beast: Dinosaur poems*. New York: William Morrow.

Prelutsky, J. (1995). *My parents think I'm sleeping*. New York: William Morrow.

Prelutsky, J. (1996). *It's Halloween*. New York: William Morrow.

Prelutsky, J. (1996). *It's Thanksgiving*. New York: William Morrow.

Prelutsky, J. (1996). *A pizza the size of the sun*. New York: Greenwillow.

Prelutsky, J. (1997). *Ride a purple pelican*. New York: William Morrow.

Prelutsky, J. (1998). *The dragons are singing tonight*. New York: William Morrow.

Prelutsky, J. (1999). *Dog days: Rhymes around the year*. New York: Alfred A. Knopf.

Prelutsky, J. (1999). *The 20th century children's poetry treasury*. New York: Alfred A. Knopf.

Prelutsky, J. (2000). *It's raining pigs and noodles*. New York: HarperCollins.

Prelutsky, J. (2002). *The frogs wore red suspenders*. New York: William Morrow.

Seuss, Dr. (1976). *One fish, two fish, red fish, blue fish*. New York: Random House.

Seuss, Dr. (1996). *Dr. Seuss's ABC*. New York: Random House.

Seuss, Dr. (1996). *Mr. Brown can moo! Can you? Dr. Seuss's book of wonderful noises*. New York: Random House.

Seuss, Dr. (2000). *There's a wocket in my pocket: Dr. Seuss's book of ridiculous rhymes*. New York: Random House.

Silverstein, S. (1973). *Where the sidewalk ends: Poems and drawings by Shel Silverstein*. New York: HarperCollins.

Silverstein, S. (1981). *A light in the attic*. New York: HarperCollins.

Silverstein, S. (1996). *Falling up: Poems and drawings*. New York: HarperCollins.

Stevenson, R.L. (1999). *Child's garden of verses*. New York: Simon & Schuster.

Taback, S. (1997). *There was an old lady who swallowed a fly*. New York: Viking.

Viorst, J. (1984). *If I were in charge of the world and other worries: Poems for children and their parents*. New York: Aladdin.

Websites

Barking Spiders, (and Other Such Stuff), Poetry for Children
www.barkingspiderspoetry.com

The Chuckle Corner Kid's Stuff
www.lyfe.freeserve.co.uk/kidspage.htm

FizzyFunnyFuzzy—Fun Poetry for Kids
www.fizzyfunnyfuzzy.com

Funny Children's Poetry
robertpottle.com

Funny Poetry for Children
www.gigglepoetry.com

Imagine Songs—Every Kind of Magic
www.imaginesongs.com/index2.html

Kidzpage! Poetry and Verse for Children of All Ages
www.veeceet.com/index.html

Ogden Nash
www.westegg.com/nash

Poetry for Kids by Kenn Nesbitt
www.poetry4kids.com

The Rhyme Zone
www.rhymezone.com

Performance Extensions Across the Curriculum

Art/Music/Drama

- Use a variety of art techniques to respond to poetry. Display your work as a mobile, with the poem on one side and the artistic interpretation on the other.
- Set poetry to music and sing the poems.
- Respond to poetry through interpretive dance.
- Write poetry and illustrate it in the medium of your choice.

Mathematics

- Write a variety of poems about mathematics. Poetry forms such as acrostics and definition poems may be used (see Appendix D). Illustrate and display the poems.

Science

- Create an invention and write a poem telling what it is and what it does.
- Write definition poems about plants, insects, weather, inventions, or any science-related topic and illustrate them.

Social Studies

- Read Jack Prelutsky's "New York Is in North Carolina" and use it as a pattern to write a mixed-up geography poem. Draw a map to complement the poem.
- Write poems about the community, the city, the state, or the country. (Forms for acrostics, cinquains, and diamantes can be found in Appendix D.)

Culminating Activity

We Are Poets! Invite parents and community members to participate in a celebration of poets and their poetry. Prior to the celebration, invite students' families to submit a rhyme or poem for publication in the class poetry book. Display students' poetry and projects and feature live performances in which the students read, sing, or dramatize their poetry. Have students wear nametags that say, "Ask me about my favorite poet!" Serve refreshments named for poets, such as Prelutsky pretzels and Dakos doughnuts. Have the students present autographed copies of the class poetry book to their families. Make the poetry book available on the school website, so families and community members can access it easily.

Transportation

Texts

Awdry, W. (1997). *Thomas the tank engine: The complete collection.* New York: Random House.

Baer, E. (1992). *This is the way we go to school.* New York: Scholastic.

Barton, B. (1998). *Planes.* New York: HarperCollins.

Barton, B. (1998). *Trains.* New York: HarperCollins.

Barton, B. (2001). *My car.* New York: HarperCollins.

Cameron, A. (1987). *Julian's glorious summer.* New York: Random House.

Cleary, B. *The mouse and the motorcycle.* New York: William Morrow.

Coerr, E. (1984). *The big balloon race.* New York: HarperCollins.

Crews, D. (2002). *School bus.* New York: HarperCollins.

Heap, C. (1998). *The Dorling Kindersley big book of trains*. New York: Dorling Kindersley.

Holling, H.C. (1976). *Paddle-to-the-sea*. Boston: Houghton Mifflin.

Inches, A. (2001). *Bob the builder: Wendy helps out*. New York: Simon & Schuster Children's.

Lewis, K. (2001). *Chugga-chugga choo-choo*. New York: Hyperion.

McDonnell, B.P. (1992). *Junie B. Jones and the stupid smelly bus*. New York: Random House.

Nicholas, C. (2002). *Follow that fire truck!* New York: Random House.

Piper, W. (1996). *The little engine that could*. New York: Grosset & Dunlap.

Pomerantz, C. (1997). *How many trucks can a tow truck tow?* New York: Random House.

Rey, M. (1973). *Curious George rides a bike*. Boston: Houghton Mifflin.

Rey, M. (1998). *Curious George and the hot air balloon*. Boston: Houghton Mifflin.

Rey, M. (1999). *Curious George and the dump truck*. Boston: Houghton Mifflin.

Rey, M. (2002). *Curious George takes a train*. Boston: Houghton Mifflin.

Scarry, R. (1974). *Cars and trucks and things that go*. New York: Golden Books.

Scarry, R. (1990). *Richard Scarry's cars and trucks: From a to z*. New York: Random House.

Scarry, R. (2001). *Richard Scarry's a day at the airport*. New York: Random House.

Shannon, D. (2002). *Duck on a bike*. New York: Scholastic.

Steen, S., & Steen, S. (2001). *Car wash*. New York: G.P. Putnam's Sons.

Steers, B. (1999). *Tractor Mac*. New York: Golden Books.

Thompson, K. (1990). *Eloise*. New York: Simon & Schuster.

Zelinsky, P.O. (2000). *The wheels on the bus: 10th anniversary special edition*. New York: Penguin Putnam.

Websites

Air Transportation: Exhibition Home Page
www.nasm.si.edu/galleries/gal102/gal102.html

How Stuff Works: How Airplanes Work
www.howstuffworks.com/airplane.htm

How Stuff Works: Transportation
www.howstuffworks.com/category.htm?cat=Trans

Museum Stuff
www.museumstuff.com/museums/types/transportation/index2.html

NASA Kids
kids.msfc.nasa.gov

National Geographic
nationalgeographic.com

Science Fun With Airplanes
www.ag.ohio-state.edu/~flight

Smithsonian
www.si.edu/kids

Smithsonian National Air and Space Museum
www.nasm.si.edu/nasm/arch

Transportation: FirstGov for Kids
  www.kids.gov/k_transport.htm

Transportation Technology
  www.gsu.edu/other/timeline/trans.html

Performance Extensions Across the Curriculum

Art/Music/Drama
- Create models of a variety of types of transportation and explain how each is used.
- Create advertisements for different types of transportation to persuade businesses to use them.
- Write transportation songs to sing while riding in airplanes, trains, and buses.
- Write and dramatize original scenes involving transportation settings (airports, train stations, bus stations).

Mathematics
- Create poster-board schedules for transportation centers such as airports and train stations.
- Create math problems related to transportation (distance traveled, amount of gas and time needed, etc.) and have other students solve them.

Science
- Investigate air transportation. Create focus questions about how planes stay in the air and how our lives would be different if planes did not exist.
- Investigate transportation as a source of noise pollution. Take a field trip to community sites such as the airport to gather information.

Social Studies
- Imagine what it would be like to operate a plane, train, or truck along a trade route in the United States. Examine maps of major U.S. transportation networks and explain how specific products might get from one place to another (see http://www.nationalgeographic.com/xpeditions/lessons/11/gk2/belongings.html).

Culminating Activity

Planes, Trains, and Automobiles: A Transportation Extravaganza! Create and deliver invitations featuring a variety of modes of transportation. Have student pilots, truck drivers, train conductors, and ship captains serve as tour guides for the visitors. Display students' theme-related performances and arrange the classroom chairs in rows, so visitors will feel as if they are seated on a train or plane. Present a PowerPoint slideshow to share the highlights of the theme, including community field trips. Sing theme-related songs such as "Up, Up, and Away," "The Wheels on the Bus," "I Believe I Can Fly," "On the Road Again," and student-authored original songs. Serve theme-related refreshments and invite the guests to write comments about the theme in the class visitors' book.

Weather

Texts

Aardema, V. (1983). *Bringing the rain to Kapiti Plain: A Nandi tale*. New York: Penguin.
Barrett, J. (1982). *Cloudy with a chance of meatballs*. New York: Simon & Schuster.
Bennett-Hopkins, L. (1995). *Weather: Poems for all seasons*. New York: HarperCollins.
Berger, M., & Berger, G. (1999). *Can it rain cats and dogs?* New York: Scholastic.

Brandt, K. (1990). *What makes it rain? The story of a raindrop*. Mahway, NJ: Troll.

Branley, F.M. (1989). *Sunshine makes the seasons*. New York: HarperCollins.

Branley, F.M. (1997). *Down comes the rain: Stage 2*. New York: HarperCollins.

Branley, F.M. (1999). *Flash, crash, rumble, and roll*. New York: HarperCollins.

Branley, F.M. (1999). *Snow is falling: Stage 1*. New York: HarperCollins.

Bridwell, N. (1998). *Clifford's first snow day*. New York: Scholastic.

Carle, E. (1996). *Little cloud*. New York: Putnam.

DePaola, T. (1984). *The cloud book*. New York: Holiday House.

DeWitt, L. (1993). *What will the weather be?* New York: Harper Collins.

Dorros, A. (1990). *Feel the wind*. New York: HarperCollins.

Ets, M.H. (1978). *Gilberto and the wind*. New York: Penguin Putnam.

Gibbons, G. (1993). *Weather forecasting*. New York: Simon & Schuster.

Gibbons, G. (1996). *The reasons for seasons*. New York: Holiday House.

Gibbons, G. (1996). *Weather words and what they mean*. New York: Holiday House.

Hader, B., & Hader, E. (1976). *The big snow*. New York: Simon & Schuster.

Hines, A.G. (1999). *What can you do in the snow?* New York: Greenwillow.

Inkpen, M. (1999). *Kipper's snowy day*. New York: Harcourt.

Inkpen, M. (1999). *Splosh!* New York: Harcourt.

Keats, E.J. (1976). *The snowy day*. New York: Penguin Putnam.

Koscielniak, B. (1998). *Geoffrey Groundhog predicts the weather*. Boston: Houghton Mifflin.

Landstrom, O., Landstrom, L., & Sandin, J. (1996). *Boo and baa in windy weather*. New York: Farrar, Straus & Giroux.

Locker, T. (2000). *Cloud dance*. New York: Harcourt.

Malone, P. (2001). *Desert rain*. Washington, DC: National Geographic Society.

Martin, J. (1998). *Snowflake Bentley*. Boston: Houghton Mifflin.

Marzollo, J. (1999). *I am snow*. New York: Scholastic.

McGough, K. (2001). *When a storm comes*. Washington, DC: National Geographic Society.

Mitra, A. (1998). *Chloe's rainy day*. New York: Sterling.

Mitra, A. (1998). *Chloe's snowy day*. New York: Sterling.

Morgan, A. (1986). *Sadie and the snowman*. New York: Scholastic.

Palazzo-Craig, J. (1990). *What makes the weather*. Mahway, NJ: Troll.

Palmer, J.A. (1992). *Sunshine*. Austin, TX: Steck-Vaughn.

Rey, M. (1998). *Curious George in the snow*. Boston: Houghton Mifflin.

Rockwell, A., & Rockwell, H. (1992). *The first snowfall*. New York: Simon & Schuster.

Saunders-Smith, G. (1998). *Sunshine*. Mankato, MN: Capstone.

Simon, S. (2000). *Weather*. New York: HarperCollins.

Singer, M. (2001). *On the same day in March: A tour of the world's weather*. New York: HarperCollins.

Stoeke, J. (1994). *A hat for Minerva Louise*. New York: Penguin.

Stojic, M. (2000). *Rain*. New York: Crown.

Wada, J. (2000). *Eevee's weather report*. San Francisco: Viz Communications.

Wallace, K. (1999). *Dorling Kindersley readers: Whatever the weather*. New York: Dorling Kindersley.

Wellington, M. (1999). *Bunny's rainbow day*. New York: Dutton.

White, N. (2000). *The Magic School Bus kicks up a storm*. New York: Scholastic.

Wiesner, D. (1997). *Sector 7*. New York: Clarion.

Yolen, J. (1998). *Snow, snow! Winter poems for children*. Honesdale, PA: Boyds Mills Press.

Websites

Dan's Wild Wild Weather Page
    www.wildwildweather.com

Kids Web: Weather
    www.npac.syr.edu/textbook/kidsweb/weather.html

National Geographic Book Club for Kids
    www.nationalgeographic.com/bookclub

National Weather Service
    weather.gov/om/reachout/kidspage.shtml

The Weather Channel
    www.weather.com

Weather Dude: Meteorology Made Simple for Kids, Parents, and Teachers
    www.wxdude.com

Web Weather for Kids
    www.ucar.edu/40th/webweather

Performance Extensions Across the Curriculum

Art/Music/Drama

- Create a variety of types of weather using different mediums.
- Create sounds to represent different kinds of weather and use them while acting out scenes from a book or an original play.
- Sing classic weather songs such as "Let It Snow" and "The Itsy Bitsy Spider" and create motions to represent the song lyrics while singing.
- Write and perform original songs about weather.

Mathematics

- Record weather statistics for a week. Create math problems to compare and contrast items such as amounts of rainfall and wind speeds.

Science

- Demonstrate how one type of severe weather occurs by creating a tornado in a bottle. To learn how to create a tornado in a bottle, consult these websites:

    Exploratorium: Science Snacks: Vortex
        www.exploratorium.edu/snacks/vortex.ht

    Funology.com—Laboratory —Tornado in a Bottle
        www.funology.com/laboratory/lab052.cfm

    Tornado in a Bottle
        www.galaxy.net/~k12/weather/tornado.sh

    Twister in a Bottle!
        whyfiles.org/013tornado/recipe.html

- Visit websites such as the Weather Channel's weather.com. Print the weather forecast and maintain a class journal to compare and contrast the weather that was forecast and the weather that actually occurred.

Social Studies

- Compare and contrast weather in geographical locations such as deserts, mountains, or the seashore with weather in your community.
- Explore different types of extreme weather, such as hurricanes and tornados, and map where they most frequently occur.

Culminating Activity

Welcome to Weather Central! Invite parents and friends to join in a celebration of weather. The students will share a variety of weather-related projects at different stations around the room. They will demonstrate their weather-predicting inventions and discuss their original weather poems and songs. Visitors will move from station to station to learn about the students' work. Then a local meteorologist will speak briefly and award the students "Honorary Meteorologist" badges. Conclude the celebration by serving weather-related desserts, such as cream-cloud cookies and snow-sprinkle cake.

APPENDIXES

Guided Comprehension Resources

Focus: Resources that underpin the Guided Comprehension Model and facilitate its use in the primary grades.

Developmental Continuum: Appendix A contains the Continuum of Children's Development in Early Reading and Writing, from *Learning to Read and Write: Developmentally Appropriate Practices for Young Children* (IRA/NAEYC, 1998), which suggests skills students should be able to use at various points in the primary grades.

Key Topics: Appendix B contains teaching ideas and booklists focused on phonemic awareness, phonics, fluency, vocabulary, and comprehension—the emphases of the National Reading Panel report (NICHD, 2000) and other recent U.S. government publications and legislation. The topics are presented in terms of their definitions, what research can tell us about them, and how we can teach them. A list of suggested readings appears at the close of each section. An extensive bibliography of trade books to use when teaching phonemic awareness, phonics, and fluency completes this appendix.

Comprehension Strategies, Teaching Ideas, and Blacklines: Appendix C offers a wide variety of ideas for teaching comprehension strategies that can be used before, during, and after reading. Organized by comprehension strategy, the teaching ideas are presented in a step-by-step instructional format. Teaching examples and reproducible blackline masters complete this appendix.

Resources for Organizing and Managing Comprehension Centers and Routines: A wide variety of reproducible blackline masters to facilitate classroom organization and management, as well as graphic organizers that support a number of comprehension centers and comprehension routines, are presented in Appendix D.

Informal Assessments and Sources of Leveled Texts: Informal assessments, ranging from attitude and motivation surveys to observation guides, are featured in Appendix E. Sources of leveled texts, including websites and publishers' materials, are presented in Appendix F.

Ideas for Creating Home-School Connections: A variety of activities that are easily adaptable to the themes presented in Chapters 6–10 are described in Appendix G.

Primary-Level Developmental Continuum for Reading and Writing

Note: This list is intended to be illustrative, not exhaustive. Children at any grade level will function at a variety of phases along the reading/writing continuum.

Phase 1: Awareness and exploration (goals for preschool)

Children explore their environment and build the foundations for learning to read and write.

Children can

- enjoy listening to and discussing storybooks
- understand that print carries a message
- engage in reading and writing attempts
- identify labels and signs in their environment
- participate in rhyming games
- identify some letters and make some letter-sound matches
- use known letters or approximations of letters to represent written language (especially meaningful words like their name and phrases such as "I love you")

What teachers do

- share books with children, including Big Books, and model reading behaviors
- talk about letters by name and sounds
- establish a literacy-rich environment
- reread favorite stories
- engage children in language games
- promote literacy-related play activities
- encourage children to experiment with writing

Source: Reprinted from International Reading Association & National Association for the Education of Young Children. (1998). *Learning to read and write: Developmentally appropriate practices for young children* (position statement).

What parents and family members can do

- talk with children, engage them in conversation, give names of things, show interest in what a child says
- read and reread stories with predictable texts to children
- encourage children to recount experiences and describe ideas and events that are important to them
- visit the library regularly
- provide opportunities for children to draw and print, using markers, crayons, and pencils

Phase 2: Experimental reading and writing (goals for kindergarten)

Children develop basic concepts of print and begin to engage in and experiment with reading and writing.

Kindergartners can

- enjoy being read to and retelling simple narrative stories or informational texts
- use descriptive language to explain and explore
- recognize letters and letter-sound matches
- show familiarity with rhyming and beginning sounds
- understand left-to-right and top-to-bottom orientation and familiar concepts of print
- match spoken words with written ones
- begin to write letters of the alphabet and some high-frequency words

What teachers do

- encourage children to talk about reading and writing experiences
- provide many opportunities for children to explore and identify sound-symbol relationships in meaningful contexts
- help children to segment spoken words into individual sounds and blend the sounds into whole words (for example, by slowly writing a word and saying its sound)
- frequently read interesting and conceptually rich stories to children
- provide daily opportunities for children to write
- help children build a sight vocabulary
- create a literacy-rich environment for children to engage independently in reading and writing

What parents and family members can do

- daily read and reread narrative and informational stories to children
- encourage children's attempts at reading and writing
- allow children to participate in activities that involve writing and reading (for example, cooking, making grocery lists)
- play games that involve specific directions (such as "Simon Says")
- have conversations with children during mealtimes and throughout the day

---

Guided Comprehension in the Primary Grades by Maureen McLaughlin ©2003.
Newark, DE: International Reading Association.

Phase 3: Early reading and writing (goals for first grade)

Children begin to read simple stories and can write about a topic that is meaningful to them.

First graders can

- read and retell familiar stories
- use strategies (rereading, predicting, questioning, contextualizing) when comprehension breaks down
- use reading and writing for various purposes on their own initiative
- orally read with reasonable fluency
- use letter-sound associations, word parts, and context to identify new words
- identify an increasing number of words by sight
- sound out and represent all substantial sounds in spelling a word
- write about topics that are personally meaningful
- attempt to use some punctuation and capitalization

What teachers do

- support the development of vocabulary by reading daily to the children, transcribing their language, and selecting materials that expand children's knowledge and language development
- model strategies and provide practice for identifying unknown words
- give children opportunities for independent reading and writing practice
- read, write, and discuss a range of different text types (poems, informational books)
- introduce new words and teach strategies for learning to spell new words
- demonstrate and model strategies to use when comprehension breaks down
- help children build lists of commonly used words from their writing

What parents and family members can do

- talk about favorite storybooks
- read to children and encourage them to read to you
- suggest that children write to friends and relatives
- bring to a parent-teacher conference evidence of what your child can do in writing and reading
- encourage children to share what they have learned about their writing and reading

Phase 4: Transitional reading and writing (goals for second grade)

Children begin to read more fluently and write various text forms using simple and more complex sentences.

Second graders can

- read with greater fluency
- use strategies more efficiently (rereading, questioning, and so on) when comprehension breaks down

---

Guided Comprehension in the Primary Grades by Maureen McLaughlin ©2003.
Newark, DE: International Reading Association.

- use word identification strategies with greater facility to unlock unknown words
- identify an increasing number of words by sight
- write about a range of topics to suit different audiences
- use common letter patterns and critical features to spell words
- punctuate simple sentences correctly and proofread their own work
- spend time reading daily and use reading to research topics

What teachers do

- create a climate that fosters analytic, evaluative, and reflective thinking
- teach children to write in multiple forms (stories, information, poems)
- ensure that children read a range of texts for a variety of purposes
- teach revising, editing, and proofreading skills
- teach strategies for spelling new and difficult words
- model enjoyment of reading

What parents and family members can do

- continue to read to children and encourage them to read to you
- engage children in activities that require reading and writing
- become involved in school activities
- show children your interest in their learning by displaying their written work
- visit the library regularly
- support your child's specific hobby or interest with reading materials and references

Phase 5: Independent and productive reading and writing (goals for third grade)

Children continue to extend and refine their reading and writing to suit varying purposes and audiences.

Third graders can

- read fluently and enjoy reading
- use a range of strategies when drawing meaning from the text
- use word identification strategies appropriately and automatically when encountering unknown words
- recognize and discuss elements of different text structures
- make critical connections between texts
- write expressively in many different forms (stories, poems, reports)
- use a rich variety of vocabulary and sentences appropriate to text forms
- revise and edit their own writing during and after composing
- spell words correctly in final writing drafts

Guided Comprehension in the Primary Grades by Maureen McLaughlin ©2003.
Newark, DE: International Reading Association.

What teachers do

- provide opportunities daily for children to read, examine, and critically evaluate narrative and expository texts
- continue to create a climate that fosters critical reading and personal response
- teach children to examine ideas in texts
- encourage children to use writing as a tool for thinking and learning
- extend children's knowledge of the correct use of writing conventions
- emphasize the importance of correct spelling in finished written products
- create a climate that engages all children as a community of literacy learners

What parents and family members can do

- continue to support children's learning and interest by visiting the library and bookstores with them
- find ways to highlight children's progress in reading and writing
- stay in regular contact with your children's teachers about activities and progress in reading and writing
- encourage children to use and enjoy print for many purposes (such as recipes, directions, games, and sports)
- build a love of language in all its forms and engage children in conversation

Guided Comprehension in the Primary Grades by Maureen McLaughlin ©2003.
Newark, DE: International Reading Association.

Research-Based Resources for Teaching Phonemic Awareness, Phonics, Fluency, Vocabulary, and Comprehension

Research-based ideas for teaching phonemic awareness, phonics, fluency, vocabulary, and comprehension are presented in this appendix. Each term's definition is followed by a summary of its research base, practical ideas for teaching it, and suggestions for further reading. A list of books to use when teaching phonemic awareness, phonics, and fluency—titles that emphasize particular sounds or contain repeated patterns—completes the appendix.

PHONEMIC AWARENESS

What is it?

"Phonemic awareness is the awareness of the sounds (phonemes) that make up spoken words" (Harris & Hodges, 1995, p. 185). Note the distinction between phonemic awareness and phonics: Phonics correlates phonemes (the smallest units of sound) with graphemes (written letters). Ehri and Nunes (2002) elaborate on this distinction by observing, "Whereas phonemic awareness is a specific skill that involves manipulating sounds in speech, phonics is a method of teaching reading" (p. 113).

What does the research tell us?

Researchers agree that phonemic awareness is a powerful predictor of reading and spelling acquisition (Ball & Blachman, 1991; Ehri & Nunes, 2002; IRA, 1998). We also know that phonemic awareness can be taught, but Yopp and Yopp (2000) caution that its instruction needs to be situated in a broader reading program to be effective. The National Reading Panel (NICHD, 2000) presents

---

similar conclusions, noting that teaching children to manipulate phonemes in words was highly effective under a variety of teaching conditions with a variety of learners.

What are some practical ideas for teaching phonemic awareness?

There are numerous practical, motivational, and fun ways to teach different aspects of phonemic awareness. Frequently hearing, saying, and creating rhymes; manipulating sounds; and singing songs adapted to promote phonemic awareness are among many found to be effective. According to Ehri and Nunes (2002), phonemic awareness tasks include the following:

1. Phoneme isolation, which requires recognizing individual sounds in words, for example, "Tell me the first sound in *paste*." (/p/)

2. Phoneme identity, which requires recognizing the common sound in different words, for example, "Tell me the sound that is the same in *bike*, *boy*, and *bell*." (/b/)

3. Phoneme categorization, which requires recognizing the word with the odd sound in a sequence of three or four words, for example, "Which word does not belong? *Bus*, *bun*, or *rug*." (*rug*)

4. Phonemic blending, which requires listening to a sequence of separately spoken sounds and combining them to form a recognizable word, for example, "What word is /s/ /k/ /u/ /l/?" (*school*)

5. Phoneme segmentation, which requires breaking a word into its sounds by tapping out or counting the sounds, or by pronouncing and positioning a marker for each sound, for example, "How many phonemes in *ship*?" (three: /š/ /l/ /p/)

6. Phoneme deletion, which requires stating the word that remains when a specified phoneme is removed, for example, "What is smile without the /s/?" (*mile*) (pp. 111–112)

What follows is a sampling of ideas for teaching phonemic awareness. For a more extensive list of teaching ideas, see the articles cited at the conclusion of this section. For fun and engaging literature to use when teaching phonemic awareness, see the booklist at the conclusion of this appendix.

Rhyme. Read a variety of rhymes to students and encourage them to say or sing them along with you. *Read-Aloud Rhymes for the Very Young*, compiled by Jack Prelutsky (1986) and illustrated by Marc Brown, is one example of a book that provides a wide variety of rhymes to share. The students will also enjoy developing their understanding of rhyme by frequently saying classic nursery rhymes such as "Jack and Jill" and "Humpty Dumpty."

Read books with rhyming texts to the students. After the students become familiar with the rhyme scheme, pause and encourage them to predict the next rhyming word. Nancy Shaw's sheep books—*Sheep in a Jeep* (1986), *Sheep in a Shop* (1991), *Sheep Out to Eat* (1995), *Sheep Trick or Treat* (1997)—are examples of texts that would work well. See the booklist at the end of this appendix for other suggestions. To access a wide variety of rhyming words to use in phonemic awareness activities, visit the Rhyme Zone at http://www.rhymezone.com.

Syllable manipulation. The song "Clap, Clap, Clap Your Hands" can be adapted for language manipulation (Yopp, 1992). The following version of the song encourages blending syllables;

Guided Comprehension in the Primary Grades by Maureen McLaughlin ©2003.
Newark, DE: International Reading Association.

the first two verses are part of the original song, and the last two verses are an adaptation (Yopp & Yopp, 2000).

Clap, clap, clap your hands,
Clap your hands together.
Clap, clap, clap your hands,
Clap your hands together.

Snap, snap, snap your fingers.
Snap your fingers together.
Snap, snap, snap your fingers.
Snap your fingers together.

Say, say, say these parts.
Say these parts together.
Say, say, say these parts,
Say these parts together:

Teacher: *moun* (pause) *tain* (children respond, "mountain!")
Teacher: *love* (pause) *ly* (children respond, "lovely!")
Teacher: *un* (pause) *der* (children respond, "under!")
Teacher: *tea* (pause) *cher* (children respond, "teacher!")

Phoneme manipulation.   Singing traditional songs with lyrics revised to promote phonemic awareness can be used to promote a variety of aspects of phonemic awareness, including sound isolation, sound addition or deletion, and full segmentation. Yopp (1992) suggests the following:

Sound Isolation Activity: Children may be given a word and asked to tell what sound occurs at the beginning, middle, or end of the word. In this activity, students sing new lyrics to the well-known children's song "Old MacDonald Had a Farm." The following lyrics focus on isolating beginning sounds:

What's the sound that starts these words:
Turtle, time, and *teeth?*
/t/ is the sound that starts these words:
Turtle, time, and *teeth.*
With a /t/, /t/ here, and a /t/, /t/ there,
Here a /t/, there a /t/, everywhere a /t/, /t/.
/t/ is the sound that starts these words:
Turtle, time, and *teeth.*
(*Chicken, chin,* and *cheek* would be another option for the song.)

Sound Addition or Deletion Activity: Students may add or substitute sounds in words in familiar songs. In this activity, students sing the traditional verses of the well-known children's song "Row, Row, Row Your Boat," but they sing different beginning sounds in the repeated words in the chorus.

For example, the traditional chorus is "merrily, merrily, merrily, merrily, life is but a dream." In alternate versions of the song designed to promote phonemic awareness, the beginning sound of *merrily* may be replaced by any consonant. It doesn't matter if the word created is a nonsense word. The lyrics to "Row, Row, Row Your Boat" that follow focus on substituting beginning sounds:

Row, row, row your boat
Gently down the stream
Merrily, merrily, merrily, merrily
Life is but a dream
(Berrily, berrily, berrily, berrily)
(Terrily, terrily, terrily, terrily)

Full Segmentation: In full segmentation, the word is segmented or separated into individual sounds. In this activity, students sing new lyrics to the classic children's song "Twinkle, Twinkle, Little Star." The lyrics that follow focus on presenting a word—in this case *face*—and then segmenting or separating the individual sounds that make up the word:

Listen, listen to my word,
Then tell me the sounds you heard: *face*
/f/ is one sound
/a/ is two,
/s/ is the last sound it's true.
Thanks for listening to my words,
And telling me the sounds you heard.

Scavenger Hunt (letters) (Yopp & Yopp, 2000): Children work in teams of three. Each team has a bag. The outside of the bag has a letter and a picture of an object that begins with that letter. For instance, one team receives a bag with letter *M* on it and a picture of a monkey; another team receives a bag with letter *S* on it and a picture of a snake. Next, children set off on a scavenger hunt to find objects in the classroom that begin with their target sound. Provide enough time for the children to be successful and then bring them together to share their target sound and the objects they found.

What can we read to learn more about teaching phonemic awareness?

Ehri, L.C., & Nunes, S.R. (2002). The role of phonemic awareness in learning to read. In A.E. Farstrup & S.J. Samuels (Eds.), *What research has to say about reading instruction* (3rd ed., pp. 110–139). Newark, DE: International Reading Association.

Yopp, H.K. (1992). Developing phonemic awareness in young children. *The Reading Teacher, 45,* 696–703.

Yopp, H.K., & Yopp, R.H. (2000). Supporting phonemic awareness development in the classroom. *The Reading Teacher, 54,* 130–143.

PHONICS

What is it?

Phonics is "a way of teaching reading and spelling that stresses symbol-sound relationships, used especially in beginning instruction" (Harris & Hodges, 1995, p. 186).

What does the research tell us?

Stahl, Duffy-Hester, and Stahl (1998) report that good phonics instruction

- develops the alphabetic principle
- develops phonological awareness
- provides a thorough grounding in the letters
- does not teach rules, need not use worksheets, should not dominate instruction, and does not need to be boring
- provides sufficient practice in reading words
- leads to automatic word recognition
- is one part of reading instruction

Researchers also note that students differ in their needs for phonics instruction and concur with Stahl and colleagues' belief that phonics is just one component of a balanced reading program (Cunningham & Cunningham, 2002; NICHD, 2000). The National Reading Panel (NICHD, 2000) reports that systematic phonics instruction produces significant benefits for students in kindergarten through grade 6 and for children having difficulty learning to read.

What are some practical ideas for teaching phonics?

Cunningham and Cunningham (2002) suggest that children should spend a majority of their time reading and writing and that phonics instruction should be taught through a variety of multilevel activities that emphasize transfer. Numerous teaching ideas support this thinking. *Words Their Way: Word Study for Phonics, Vocabulary, and Spelling* (Bear, Invernizzi, Templeton, & Johnston, 2003) and *Phonics They Use: Words for Reading and Writing* (Cunningham, 2000) are bursting with engaging suggestions. What follows is a sampling of activities that have proven to be effective.

Alphabet Scrapbook. For Alphabet Scrapbook (Bear et al., 2003), prepare a blank dictionary for each child by stapling together sheets of paper. (Seven sheets of paper folded and stapled in the middle is enough for one letter per page.) Children can use this book in a variety of ways.

1. Practice writing uppercase and lowercase forms of the letter on each page.
2. Cut out letters in different fonts or styles from magazines and newspapers and paste them into their scrapbooks.
3. Draw and label pictures and other things that begin with that letter sound.

Guided Comprehension in the Primary Grades by Maureen McLaughlin ©2003.
Newark, DE: International Reading Association.

4. Cut and paste magazine pictures onto the corresponding letter page. These pictures, too, can be labeled.

5. Add sight words as they become known to create a personal dictionary.

Making Words. In Making Words (adapted from Cunningham, 2000), students manipulate a group of letters to create words of varying lengths. They may create the words based on clues or just list as many words as possible. Then they guess the mystery word—the source of the random letters. When creating the words, students may manipulate plastic letters or arrange magnetic letters on a cookie sheet.

Making and Writing Words. In Making and Writing Words (Rasinski, 1999a), students follow the same procedure as in Making Words, but instead of manipulating the letters, they write them. An adaptation is to encourage the students to manipulate the letters and then record them on the Making and Writing Words Chart (see Appendix D, page 291).

Making and Writing Words Using Letter Patterns. In Making and Writing Words Using Letter Patterns (Rasinski, 1999b), students use rimes (word families) and other patterns, as well as individual letters, to write words. Then the students transfer their knowledge to create new words. Finally, they cut up the organizer to create word cards, which they can use to practice the words in games and sorts.

Onset and Rime Word Wall and Portable Word Wall. Use the 37 common rimes and onsets of your choice to create a word wall. Use the word wall as a resource for students' reading and writing.

-ack	-an	-aw	-ick	-ing	-op	
-unk	-ain	-ank	-ay	-ide	-ink	
-or	-ake	-ap	-eat	-ight	-ip	
-ore	-ale	-ash	-ell	-ill	-ir	
-uck	-all	-at	-est	-in	-ock	
-ug	-ame	-ate	-ice	-ine	-oke	-ump

Extend this idea, or any word wall, by having students create Portable Word Walls that they can use in other instructional settings or at home. This is easily accomplished by using manila folders to house the word wall and having students use markers to copy the words onto the inside of the folder.

What can we read to learn more about teaching phonics?

Bear, D.R., Invernizzi, M., Templeton, S., & Johnston, F. (2003). *Words their way: Word study for phonics, vocabulary, and spelling instruction* (2nd ed.). Upper Saddle River, NJ: Prentice Hall.

Cunningham, P.M. (2000). *Phonics they use: Words for reading and writing* (3rd ed.). New York: HarperCollins.

Stahl, S.A., Duffy-Hester, A.M., & Stahl, K.A.D. (1998). Everything you wanted to know about phonics (but were afraid to ask). *Reading Research Quarterly*, 33, 338–355.

FLUENCY

What is it?

Fluency is "(1) the clear, easy, written or spoken expression of ideas; (2) freedom from word-identification problems that might hinder comprehension in silent reading or the expression of ideas in oral reading; automaticity" (Harris & Hodges, 1995, p. 85). The National Reading Panel (NICHD, 2000) notes that fluent readers read orally with speed, accuracy, and expression.

What does the research tell us?

Researchers agree that oral reading fluency contributes to comprehension (Nathan & Stanovich, 1991; NICHD, 2000; Zutell & Rasinski, 1991). The National Reading Panel (NICHD, 2000) reports also that repeated oral reading procedures that include guidance from teachers, peers, or parents have significant and positive impacts on the word recognition, fluency, and comprehension of both good and poor readers.

What are some practical ideas for teaching fluency?

To be fluent readers, students need to have good models, access to text, and time to read. To practice fluency, students engage in techniques such as choral reading and repeated readings. To do this independently, students need to have access to text they can read without teacher assistance. A list of trade books that promote phonemic awareness, phonics, and fluency can be found at the end of this appendix.

Fluent reading models. Providing fluent reading models for students helps them become fluent readers. Teachers, parents, cross-age volunteers, and audio books all can provide good fluency models for students.

Choral reading. In choral reading, the teacher and the students read together. When engaging in choral reading, the pressure is off the individual reader, so there is more of a tendency to focus on the fluent manner in which the poem or text segment is being read. Engaging in choral reading also provides everyone engaged with good fluency models.

Repeated reading. Repeated reading of text helps students read more fluently (Samuels, 1979, 2002). In this process, students work with partners; pairing a strong reader with a less-able reader is preferable. In each pair, students take turns assuming the role of teacher and student. The teacher looks at the words in the text while listening to the student read orally. The passage is read four times, with students changing roles after each reading. This improves comprehension, because as the reading becomes more fluent, less emphasis is placed on decoding and more on constructing meaning.

Readers Theatre. Readers Theatre does not involve producing a class play; it is like a read-through of a script. A narrator often introduces the work, sets the scene, and provides transitional information during the performance. The readers use their voices to create the scene and bring the characters to life. Books that have a lot of dialogue can be used for Readers Theatre. A number of websites also provide scripts for this technique.

Fluency-oriented reading instruction. Fluency-oriented reading instruction (Stahl, Heubach, & Cramond, 1997; Stahl & Kuhn, 2002) helps children become fluent readers so they can focus on text comprehension. To achieve this objective, the program focuses on five goals: (1) to keep the focus of reading lessons on students' comprehension of text, (2) to have students read material on their instructional reading levels, (3) to support students in their reading of instructional level text through repeated readings, (4) to provide opportunities for children to engage in text-based social interactions through partner reading, and (5) to expand the amount of time children spend reading at home and school. To accomplish these goals, students engage in a reading program that has three main components: a redesigned basal lesson, home reading, and a free-choice reading period.

What can we read to learn more about teaching fluency?

Johns, J.L., & Berglund, R.L. (2002). *Fluency: Questions, answers, and evidence-based strategies.* Dubuque, IA: Kendall/Hunt.

Richards, M. (2000). Be a good detective: Solve the case of oral reading fluency. *The Reading Teacher, 53,* 534–539.

Samuels, S.J. (2002). Reading fluency: Its development and assessment. In A.E. Farstrup & S.J. Samuels (Eds.), *What research has to say about reading instruction* (3rd ed., pp.166–183). Newark, DE: International Reading Association.

VOCABULARY

What is it?

Vocabulary development is "(1) the growth of a person's stock of known words and meanings; (2) the teaching-learning principles and practices that lead to such growth, as comparing and classifying word meanings, using context, analyzing root words and affixes, etc." (Harris & Hodges, 1995, p. 275).

What does the research tell us?

Vocabulary instruction leads to gains in comprehension, but the methods must be appropriate to the age and ability of the reader (NICHD, 2000). Baumann and Kameenui (1991) report that direct instruction of vocabulary and learning from context should be balanced. Blachowicz and Fisher

Guided Comprehension in the Primary Grades by Maureen McLaughlin ©2003.
Newark, DE: International Reading Association.

(2000) note that the following four guidelines emerge from existing research about vocabulary instruction:

> Students should be active in developing their understanding of words and ways to learn them; students should personalize word learning; students should be immersed in words; students should build on multiple sources of information to learn words through repeated exposures. (p. 504)

A number of researchers conclude that reading widely is an effective way to promote vocabulary growth (Baumann & Kameenui, 1991; Beck & McKeown, 1991; Hiebert et al., 1998; Snow et al., 1998).

What are some practical ideas for teaching vocabulary?

Descriptions of a variety of ideas for teaching vocabulary and related blackline masters can be found in Appendix C of this book. These include Concept of Definition Maps, Context Clues, List-Group-Label, RIVET, Semantic Feature Analysis, Semantic Maps, Semantic Question Maps, and Text Transformations. In addition, poem forms for cinquains, which work well when teaching synonyms, and diamantes, which work well when teaching antonyms, can be found in Appendix D.

Numerous other ideas for teaching vocabulary can be found in current academic journals and professional books. "Fun With Vocabulary" (Towell, 1997/1998), which is summarized below, is an example of the former; *Classroom Strategies for Interactive Learning* (Buehl, 2001) is an example of the latter.

V Vocabulary Self-Collection Strategy: After locating a new word in their environment, students are asked to share (a) where they found the word, (b) the context, and (c) the importance of the word and why they selected it.

Visual-Auditory-Kinesthetic-Tactile: A multisensory technique in which students trace the target word with a finger while pronouncing each syllable until it can be written from memory.

O Onsets and rimes: The onset is the part of the word before the vowel; the rime includes the vowel and the rest of the letters in the word.

C Color shock: A color shock is a technique originally designed for right-brained learning disabled students to help them remember sight words. Each word is written in a different color beginning with the color green for "go" to designate the beginning of the word.

Clusters: For vocabulary instruction to be meaningful, words should be presented in semantic frameworks through categories or clusters. A cluster is a set of words that relate to a single concept.

A ABC books and anagrams: Students create their own alphabet books and discover words through illustrations on the basis of their prior knowledge or schemata. Anagrams are another fun and interesting way to learn vocabulary or spelling words.

B Book boxes: Boxes for related reading materials.

Boxes for visual configuration: This visual discrimination technique involves drawing around words to emphasize their length and shape.

Word banks: Students should have personal word banks for storing and remembering their self-selected and teacher-selected words, such as spelling words.

U Unusual words: Words created by students are called sniglets and are fun for the intermediate grades and beyond. An example is *baldage*—hair left in the drain after showering.

Unknown words: A strategy for primary grades is beep it, frame it, begin it, split it, and find it in the dictionary.

L List-Group-Label: Working in cooperative groups, students list as many words as possible that begin with a specific letter on a piece of chart paper. Students sort and label the words according to different categories.

Language Experience Approach: A student tells a story, the teacher creates a book using the student's words, and the student reads the book.

A Active involvement: Students must be actively involved in learning and using vocabulary.

R Repetition, rhymes, riddles, roots: Encountering the words they have learned in multiple settings, engaging in word play (books by Fred Gwynne, Marvin Terban), and engaging in structural analysis support vocabulary development.

Y Yarns: Using their vocabulary to spin yarns or tall tales is a fun way for students to use words they have learned. The stories can be shared through storytelling or writing.

What can we read to learn more about teaching vocabulary?

Blachowicz, C.L., & Fisher, P. (2000). Vocabulary instruction. In M.L. Kamil, P.B. Mosenthal, P.D. Pearson, & R. Barr (Eds.), *Handbook of reading research* (Vol. 3, pp. 503–523). Mahwah, NJ: Erlbaum.

Buehl, D. (2001). *Classroom strategies for interactive learning* (2nd ed.). Newark, DE: International Reading Association.

International Reading Association. (2002). *IRA Literacy Study Groups vocabulary module*. Newark, DE: Author.

COMPREHENSION

What is it?

Comprehension is "the construction of the meaning of a written or spoken communication through a reciprocal, holistic interchange of ideas between the interpreter and the message in a particular

---

Guided Comprehension in the Primary Grades by Maureen McLaughlin ©2003.
Newark, DE: International Reading Association.

communicative context. *Note*: The presumption here is that meaning resides in the intentional problem-solving, thinking processes of the interpreter during such an interchange, that the content of meaning is influenced by that person's prior knowledge and experience, and that the message so constructed by the receiver may or may not be congruent with the message sent" (Harris & Hodges, 1995, p. 39).

What does the research tell us?

Much of what we know about comprehension is based on studies of good readers—readers who are actively engaged in the reading process, who have set clear goals, and who constantly monitor the relation between their goals and the text they are reading (Askew & Fountas, 1998; Duke & Pearson, 2002; Keene & Zimmermann, 1997; Pearson, 2001a; Pressley, 2000). Good readers use a repertoire of comprehension strategies to facilitate the construction of meaning (Duke & Pearson, 2002; Keene & Zimmermann, 1997; NICHD, 2000; Palincsar & Brown, 1984; Roehler & Duffy, 1984).

Researchers including Duke and Pearson (2002), Pressley (2001), and Hilden and Pressley (2002) note that reading comprehension strategies can be taught in the primary grades. Pressley (2001) suggests that students begin learning comprehension skills and a few strategies as early as kindergarten.

What are some practical ideas for teaching comprehension?

Comprehension skills and strategies can be taught, and a variety of teaching ideas and related blacklines that support the comprehension strategies can be found in Appendix C of this book. In addition, Reciprocal Teaching, a technique that involves multiple comprehension strategies, is fully delineated in Chapter 4 of this volume and summarized in Appendix C.

What can we read to learn more about teaching comprehension?

Duke, N.K., & Pearson, P.D. (2002). Effective practices for developing comprehension. In A.E. Farstrup & S.J. Samuels (Eds.), *What research has to say about reading instruction* (3rd ed., pp. 205–242). Newark, DE: International Reading Association.

Neuman, S.B., & Dickinson, D.K. (Eds.). (2001). *Handbook of early literacy research*. New York: Guilford.

Pressley, M. (2002). What should comprehension instruction be the instruction of? In M.L. Kamil, P.B. Mosenthal, P.D. Pearson, & R. Barr (Eds.), *Handbook of reading research* (Vol. 3, pp. 545–561). Mahwah, NJ: Erlbaum.

BOOKS TO USE WHEN TEACHING PHONEMIC AWARENESS, PHONICS, AND FLUENCY

Aardema, V. (1983). *Bringing the rain to Kapiti Plain: A Nandi tale*. New York: Penguin.

Adams, P. (1990). *This is the house that Jack built*. New York: Child's Play.

Aliki. (1986). *Jack and Jake*. New York: Greenwillow.

Ashman, L. (2002). *Can you make a piggy giggle?* New York: Dutton.

Axtell, D. (1999). *We're going on a lion hunt*. New York: Scholastic.

Bennett, J. (1987). *Noisy poems*. Hong Kong: Oxford University Press.

Brown, A. (1984). *Willy the wimp*. New York: Knopf.

Brown, M.W. (1993). *Four fur feet*. New York: Doubleday.

Bruss, D. (2001). *Book! Book! Book!* New York: Arthur A. Levine.

Bynum, J. (1999). *Altoona baboona*. New York: Harcourt.

Calmenson, S. (1998). *The teeny tiny teacher*. New York: Scholastic.

Carle, E. (2002). *Does a kangaroo have a mother, too?* New York: HarperCollins.

Carle, E. (2002). *"Slowly, slowly, slowly," said the sloth*. New York: Penguin Putnam.

Christelow, E. (1989). *Five little monkeys jumping on the bed*. New York: Clarion Books.

Christelow, E. (1991). *Five little monkeys sitting in a tree*. New York: Trumpet Club.

Colandro, L. (2002). *There was an old lady who swallowed a bat!* New York: Scholastic.

Cole, B. (1986). *The giant's toe*. New York: Farrar, Straus & Giroux.

Cooney, N. (1987). *Donald says thumbs down*. New York: G.P. Putnam's Sons.

deRegniers, B., Moore, E., White, M., & Carr, J. (1988). *Sing a song of popcorn*. New York: Scholastic.

Deming, A.G. (1994). *Who is tapping at my window?* New York: Penguin.

Dunrea, O. (1985). *Mogwogs on the march!* New York: Holiday House.

Edwards, P. (1995). *Four famished foxes and fosdyke*. New York: Harper Trophy.

Ehlert, L. (1989). *Eating the alphabet: Fruits and vegetables from A to Z*. San Diego: Harcourt Brace Jovanovich.

Fajerman, D. (2002). *How to speak moo!* Hauppauge, NY: Barron's Educational Series.

Freedman, C. (2001). *Where's your smile, crocodile?* Atlanta, GA: Peachtree.

Fuge, C. (2002). *I know a rhino*. New York: Sterling.

Galdone, P. (1968). *Henny Penny*. New York: Scholastic.

Galdone, P. (1979). *The little red hen*. New York: Scholastic.

Gordon, J. (1991). *Six sleepy sheep*. New York: Puffin.

Hague, K. (1984). *Alphabears*. New York: Henry Holt.

Hawkins, C., & Hawkins, J. (1986). *Tog the dog*. New York: G.P. Putnam's Sons.

Hymes, L., & Hymes, J. (1964). *Oodles of noodles*. New York: Young Scott Books.

Jackson, A. (1997). *I know an old lady who swallowed a pie*. New York: Penguin Group.

Keller, H. (1983). *Ten sleepy sheep*. New York: Greenwillow.

Kuskin, K. (1990). *Roar and more*. New York: Harper Trophy.

Lewison, W. (1992). *Buzz said the bee*. New York: Scholastic.

Martin, B. Jr. (1967). *Brown bear, brown bear, what do you see?* New York: Henry Holt.

Guided Comprehension in the Primary Grades by Maureen McLaughlin ©2003.
Newark, DE: International Reading Association.

Martin, B. Jr. (1997). *Polar bear, polar bear, what do you hear?* New York: Henry Holt.

Miranda, A. (1998). *To market to market.* New York: Scholastic.

Numeroff, L. (1999). *Sometimes I wonder if poodles like noodles.* New York: Simon & Schuster.

Obligado, L. (1983). *Faint frogs feeling feverish and other terrifically tantalizing tongue twisters.* New York: Viking.

Ochs, C.P. (1991). *Moose on the loose.* Minneapolis, MN: Carolrhoda Books.

Otto, C. (1991). *Dinosaur chase.* New York: Harper Trophy.

Parry, C. (1991). *Zoomerang-a-boomerang: Poems to make your belly laugh.* New York: Puffin Books.

Patz, N. (1983). *Moses supposes his toeses are roses.* San Diego: Harcourt Brace Jovanovich.

Prelutsky, J. (1982). *The baby uggs are hatching.* New York: Mulberry.

Prelutsky, J. (1986). *Read-aloud rhymes for the very young.* New York: Knopf.

Prelutsky, J. (1989). *Poems of a nonny mouse.* New York: Knopf.

Provenson, A., & Provenson, M. (1977). *Old mother hubbard.* New York: Random House.

Rosen, M. (1997). *We're going on a bear hunt.* New York: Little Simon.

Roth, C. (2002). *The little school bus.* New York: North-South Books.

Rovetch, L. (2001). *Ook the book.* San Francisco: Chronicle.

Segal, L. (1977). *Tell me a Trudy.* New York: Farrar, Straus & Giroux.

Sendak, M. (1990). *Alligators all around: An alphabet.* New York: Harper Trophy.

Seuss, Dr. (1965). *Fox in socks.* New York: Random House.

Seuss, Dr. (1974). *There's a wocket in my pocket.* New York: Random House.

Seuss, Dr. (1976). *One fish, two fish, red fish, blue fish.* New York: Random House.

Seuss, Dr. (1996). *Dr. Seuss's ABC.* New York: Random House.

Seuss, Dr. (1996). *Mr. Brown can moo! Can you? Dr. Seuss's book of wonderful noises.* New York: Random House.

Shaw, N. (1986). *Sheep in a Jeep.* Boston: Houghton Mifflin.

Shaw, N. (1991). *Sheep in a shop.* Boston: Houghton Mifflin.

Shaw, N. (1995). *Sheep out to eat.* Boston: Houghton Mifflin.

Shaw, N. (1997). *Sheep trick or treat.* Boston: Houghton Mifflin.

Shulman, L. (2002). *Old MacDonald had a woodshop.* New York: G.P. Putnam's Sons.

Silverstein, S. (1964). *A giraffe and a half.* New York: Harper Collins.

Slate, J. (1996). *Miss Bindergarten gets ready for kindergarten.* New York: Dutton.

Slate, J. (1998). *Miss Bindergarten celebrates the 100th day.* New York: Puffin.

Slate, J. (2001). *Miss Bindergarten takes a field trip.* New York: Dutton.

Taback, S. (1997). *There was an old lady who swallowed a fly.* New York: Viking.

Tallon, R. (1979). *Zoophabets.* New York: Scholastic.

Weeks, S. (1998). *Mrs. McNosh hangs up her wash.* New York: Harper Trophy.

Wood, A. (1984). *The napping house.* Orlando, FL: Harcourt.

Yolen, J. (1997). *The three bears rhyme book.* San Diego: Harcourt.

Yolen, J. (2000). *Color me a rhyme.* Honesdale, PA: Boyds Mills Press.

Comprehension Skill- and Strategy-Based Teaching Ideas and Blackline Masters

TEACHING IDEAS AT A GLANCE

Teaching Idea	When to Use	Comprehension Strategy	Text
Previewing			
Anticipation/Reaction Guide	Before After	Previewing Monitoring	Narrative Expository
Predict-o-Gram	Before After	Previewing Summarizing	Narrative
Probable Passages	Before	Previewing Making Connections	Narrative
Semantic Map and Semantic Question Map	Before After	Previewing Knowing How Words Work	Narrative Expository
Storybook Introductions	Before	Previewing Knowing How Words Work Making Connections	Narrative Expository
Story Impressions	Before	Previewing Making Connections	Narrative
Self-Questioning			
"I Wonder" Statements	Before During After	Self-Questioning Previewing Making Connections	Narrative Expository
K-W-L and K-W-L-S	Before During After	Self-Questioning Previewing Making Connections	Expository
Paired Questioning	During After	Self-Questioning Making Connections Monitoring	Narrative Expository
Question-Answer Relationship (QAR)	After	Self-Questioning Making Connections Monitoring	Narrative Expository
Thick and Thin Questions	Before During After	Self-Questioning Making Connections	Narrative Expository
Making Connections			
Coding the Text	During	Making Connections	Narrative Expository
Connection Stems	After	Making Connections	Narrative Expository
Double-Entry Journal	Before During After	Making Connections Monitoring Summarizing	Narrative Expository
Drawing Connections	During After	Making Connections Visualizing	Narrative Expository

(continued)

Adapted for the primary grades from *Guided Comprehension: A Teaching Model for Grades 3–8* by Maureen McLaughlin and Mary Beth Allen ©2002. Newark, DE: International Reading Association. May be copied for classroom use.

TEACHING IDEAS AT A GLANCE (continued)

Teaching Idea	When to Use	Comprehension Strategy	Text
Visualizing			
Draw and Label Visualizations	During After	Visualizing Making Connections	Narrative Expository
Graphic Organizers/ Visual Organizers	Before During After	Visualizing Making Connections Summarizing	Narrative Expository
Mind and Alternative Mind Portraits	During After	Visualizing Evaluating	Narrative Expository
Open-Mind Portrait	After	Visualizing Summarizing	Narrative Expository
Sketch to Stretch	After	Visualizing Making Connections	Narrative Expository
Knowing How Words Work			
Concept of Definition Map	Before	Knowing How Words Work	Narrative Expository
Context Clues	During	Knowing How Words Work	Narrative Expository
List-Group-Label	Before After	Knowing How Words Work Previewing Making Connections	Expository
RIVET	Before	Knowing How Words Work Previewing	Expository
Semantic Feature Analysis	Before	Knowing How Words Work Making Connections	Narrative Expository
Text Transformations	After	Knowing How Words Work	Narrative Expository
Monitoring			
Bookmark Technique	During After	Monitoring Knowing How Words Work Making Connections Evaluating	Narrative Expository
Cueing Systems Check	During	Monitoring Making Connections	Narrative Expository
Patterned Partner Reading	During	Monitoring Making Connections Evaluating	Narrative Expository
Say Something	During	Monitoring Making Connections	Narrative Expository
Think-Alouds	Before During After	All	Narrative Expository

(continued)

Adapted for the primary grades from *Guided Comprehension: A Teaching Model for Grades 3–8* by Maureen McLaughlin and Mary Beth Allen ©2002. Newark, DE: International Reading Association. May be copied for classroom use.

TEACHING IDEAS AT A GLANCE (continued)

Teaching Idea	When to Use	Comprehension Strategy	Text
Summarizing			
Bio-Pyramid	After	Summarizing Making Connections Monitoring	Expository
Lyric Retelling and Lyric Summary	After	Summarizing	Narrative Expository
Narrative Pyramid	After	Summarizing Making Connections Monitoring	Narrative
QuIP (Questions Into Paragraphs)	Before During After	Summarizing Self-Questioning	Expository
Retelling	After	Summarizing	Narrative
Story Map	Before After	Summarizing	Narrative
Summary Cube	Before During After	Summarizing	Narrative Expository
Evaluating			
Discussion Web	After	Evaluating Making Connections	Narrative Expository
Evaluative Questioning	During After	Evaluating Self-Questioning	Narrative Expository
Journal Responses	During After	Evaluating Making Connections Summarizing	Narrative Expository
Persuasive Writing	Before During After	Evaluating	Narrative Expository
Comprehension Routines			
Cross-Age Reading Experiences	Before During After	All	Narrative Expository
Directed Reading- Thinking Activity	Before During After	Previewing Making Connections Monitoring	Narrative Expository
Literature Circles	After	All	Narrative Expository
Reciprocal Teaching	Before During After	Previewing Self-Questioning Monitoring Summarizing	Narrative Expository

Adapted for the primary grades from *Guided Comprehension: A Teaching Model for Grades 3–8* by Maureen McLaughlin and Mary Beth Allen ©2002. Newark, DE: International Reading Association. May be copied for classroom use.

TEACHING IDEAS

Anticipation/Reaction Guide

Purposes: To set purposes for reading texts; to activate prior knowledge and help make connections with the text.

Comprehension Strategies: Previewing, Monitoring

Text: Narrative, Expository   **Use:** Before and After Reading

Procedure: (Begin by explaining and modeling Anticipation/Reaction Guides.)

1. Select a text for the students to read.

2. Create three to five general statements for the students to respond to with agree or disagree—as an alternative, yes or no. Create statements that are intuitively sound but may be disconfirmed by reading the text or that appear intuitively incorrect but may be proven true by reading the text. Have students indicate agreement or disagreement by placing a check in the appropriate column.

3. Have students read the text to confirm or disconfirm their original responses.

4. After reading, have students revisit their predictions and modify if necessary.

Example: (*Terrible Tyrannosaurs* [2001] by K.W. Zoehfeld)

Agree   Disagree

_____   _____   1. T-rex ate plants and animals.

_____   _____   2. T-rex was one of the biggest dinosaurs.

_____   _____   3. T-rex could run very fast.

Source: Readence, J.E., Bean, T.W., & Baldwin, R. (2000). *Content area reading: An integrated approach* (7th ed.). Dubuque, IA: Kendall/Hunt.

Predict-o-Gram

(See blackline, page 232.)

Purposes: To make predictions about a story using narrative elements; to introduce vocabulary.

Comprehension Strategies: Previewing, Summarizing

Text: Narrative   **Use:** Before and After Reading (revisit)

Procedure: (Begin by explaining and modeling Predict-o-Grams.)

1. Select vocabulary from the story to stimulate predictions. Vocabulary should represent the story elements: characters, setting, problem, action, and solution.

2. Have students decide which story element the word tells about and write each word on the Predict-o-Gram in the appropriate place.

3. Have students read the story.

4. Revisit the original predictions with students and make changes as necessary. Use the resulting information to summarize or retell the story.

Source: Blachowicz, C.L. (1986). Making connections: Alternatives to the vocabulary notebook. *Journal of Reading, 29,* 643–649.

Adapted for the primary grades from *Guided Comprehension: A Teaching Model for Grades 3–8* by Maureen McLaughlin and Mary Beth Allen ©2002. Newark, DE: International Reading Association. May be copied for classroom use.

Probable Passages

(See blackline, page 233.)

Purposes: To make predictions using story elements; to introduce vocabulary; to use story vocabulary to make connections with story structure.

Comprehension Strategies: Previewing, Making Connections

Text: Narrative   **Use:** Before Reading

Procedure: (Begin by explaining and modeling Probable Passages.)

1. Introduce key vocabulary from the story to students. (Choose vocabulary that represents various elements of the story.)

2. Have students use the key vocabulary to create probable sentences to predict each element in the story. (Providing a story frame/story map facilitates this process.)

3. Encourage students to share their predictions with the class.

4. Read the story to confirm or modify original predictions.

Example: (*Chrysanthemum* [1991] by Kevin Henkes)

Key Vocabulary: *Chrysanthemum, dreadful, school, perfect, Victoria, wilted, bloomed, Mrs. Twinkle, name*

Story Map: Using the words above, create a probable sentence to predict each story element.

Setting:	I think the story takes place in school.
Characters:	The characters' names are Chrysanthemum, Victoria, and Mrs. Twinkle.
Problem:	The flowers were perfect when they bloomed, but then they wilted and looked dreadful.
Solution:	The students decided to buy new flowers for their school.

Source: Adapted from Wood, K. (1984). Probable passages: A writing strategy. *The Reading Teacher, 37,* 496–499.

Semantic Map and Semantic Question Map

Purpose: To activate and organize knowledge about a specific topic.

Comprehension Strategies: Previewing, Knowing How Words Work

Text: Narrative, Expository   **Use:** Before and After Reading

Procedure: (Begin by explaining and modeling Semantic Maps.)

1. Select the main idea or topic of the passage; write it on a chart, overhead, or chalkboard; and put a circle around it.

2. Have students brainstorm subtopics related to the topic. Use lines to connect these to the main topic.

3. Have students brainstorm specific vocabulary or ideas related to each subtopic. Record these ideas beneath each subtopic.

4. Read the text and revise the Semantic Map to reflect new knowledge.

Adaptation: Create a Semantic Question Map (see example lesson in Chapter 9, page 147, and blackline, page 234).

Example:

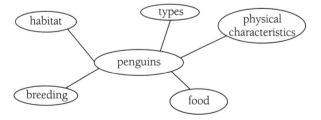

Source: Johnson, D.D., & Pearson, P.D. (1984). *Teaching reading vocabulary* (2nd ed.). New York: Holt, Rinehart and Winston.

Adapted for the primary grades from *Guided Comprehension: A Teaching Model for Grades 3–8* by Maureen McLaughlin and Mary Beth Allen ©2002. Newark, DE: International Reading Association. May be copied for classroom use.

Storybook Introductions

Purposes: To introduce story, characters, vocabulary, and style of a book prior to reading; to promote prediction and anticipation of a story; to make new texts accessible to readers.

Comprehension Strategies: Previewing, Knowing How Words Work, Making Connections

Text: Narrative, Expository   **Use:** Before Reading

Procedure: (Begin by explaining and modeling Storybook Introductions.)

1. Preview the text and prepare the introduction. Focus on those points that will help make the text accessible to students. These may include text structure, specific vocabulary, language patterns, plot, or difficult parts.
2. Introduce the topic, title, and characters.
3. Encourage students to respond to the cover and text illustrations by relating to personal experiences or other texts.
4. While browsing through the illustrations, introduce the plot up to the climax (if possible, not giving the ending away). Throughout this process, encourage students to make connections to personal experiences or other texts, and make predictions about what will happen next.
5. Choose to introduce some literary language, book syntax, specialized vocabulary, or repetitive sentence patterns that will be helpful to the readers.
6. Have students read the text. Then engage in discussion and other activities.

Note: It is important to make decisions about the introduction based on the text and the students' competency and familiarity with the text type.

Adaptation: Use with expository texts, focusing on text elements.

Source: Clay, M.M. (1991). Introducing a new storybook to young readers. *The Reading Teacher, 45,* 264–273.

Story Impressions

(See blackline, page 235.)

Purposes: To provide a framework for narrative writing; to encourage predictions about the story; to make connections between story vocabulary and story structure.

Comprehension Strategies: Previewing, Making Connections

Text: Narrative   **Use:** Before Reading

Procedure: (Begin by explaining and modeling Story Impressions.)

1. Provide students with a list of words that provide clues about the story. Choose words that relate to the narrative elements—characters, setting, problem, events, and solution. Use 8 to 10 clues, each consisting of one to five words.
2. List words in sequential order as they appear in the story. Connect them with downward arrows. Share the list of clues with the students.
3. In small groups, students then create stories using the clues in the order presented.
4. Have students share their stories with the class and discuss them.
5. Read the original story to the class and have students compare and contrast their story with the original.

Example: (*Meteor!* [1978] by Patricia Polacco)

Working in a small group, use the following words in the order they appear here and write a story:

farm
↓
Grandma and Grandpa
↓
meteor
↓
streaked and crashed
↓
front yard
↓
mysterious
↓
telephone conversations
↓
news spread
↓
parade
↓
special magic

Source: McGinley, W., & Denner, P. (1987). Story impressions: A prereading/prewriting activity. *Journal of Reading, 31,* 248–253.

Adapted for the primary grades from *Guided Comprehension: A Teaching Model for Grades 3–8* by Maureen McLaughlin and Mary Beth Allen ©2002. Newark, DE: International Reading Association. May be copied for classroom use.

"I Wonder" Statements

(See blacklines, pages 236–237.)

Purposes: To encourage self-questioning; to provide a model for active thinking during the reading process.

Comprehension Strategies: Self-Questioning, Previewing, Making Connections

Text: Narrative, Expository   **Use:** Before, During, and After Reading

Procedure: (Begin by explaining and modeling "I Wonder" Statements.)

1. Model for the students how to wonder. Do this orally and in writing, beginning your thoughts with "I wonder." Wonder about life experiences or the world, as well as events in stories or facts presented in texts.

2. Guide students to wonder about world or life things, story events, and ideas presented in texts.

3. Provide students with a format for sharing their wonderings orally or in writing. This may include an "I Wonder" book or a Think-Pair-Share session.

4. Share wonders and discuss them with text support, if possible.

5. Encourage students to wonder throughout the reading of a story or content area text. Use students' "I Wonder" Statements to provide structure for further reading or research.

Example Lesson: See Chapter 6, page 77.

Source: Harvey, S., & Goudvis, A. (2000). *Strategies that work: Teaching comprehension to enhance understanding.* York, ME: Stenhouse.

Know–Want to Know–Learn (K-W-L)

(See blacklines, pages 238–239.)

Purposes: To activate students' prior knowledge about a topic; to set purposes for reading; to confirm, revise, or expand original understandings related to a topic.

Comprehension Strategies: Self-Questioning, Previewing, Making Connections

Text: Expository   **Use:** Before, During, and After Reading

Procedure: (Begin by explaining and modeling K-W-L.)

1. Have students brainstorm everything they know, or think they know, about a specific topic. Write or have students write these ideas in the *K* column.

2. Next, have students write or tell some things they want to know about the topic. List these in the *W* column.

3. Have students read the text. (As they read, they can jot down new ideas, facts, or concepts they learn in the *L* column.)

4. List or have students list what they learned in the *L* column.

5. Revisit the *K* column to modify or confirm original understandings.

6. Revisit the *W* column to check if all questions have been answered.

7. Discuss the completed K-W-L.

Source: Ogle, D. (1986). K-W-L: A teaching model that develops active reading of expository text. *The Reading Teacher, 39,* 564–570.

Adaptation: Know–Want to Know–Learned–Still Want to Know (K-W-L-S)

Extend K-W-L by having students list what they still want to know in a fourth column. Develop a plan to help them find answers to these questions.

Example: (*Disasters in Nature: Volcanoes* [2001] by Catherine Chambers)

K (What we think we know)	W (What we want to know)	L (What we learned)	S (What we still want to know)
Volcanoes are dangerous. Volcanoes are hot. They look like fire.	What is a volcano? What is lava? How many volcanoes are there? What countries have volcanoes?	A volcano is an eruption of ash, gases, and molten rock from below the earth's crust. Lava is molten rock that spurts or oozes out of the cracks and faults of the volcano. It is extremely hot. There are about 15,000 active volcanoes. Volcanoes can be found on all continents except Australia.	What causes volcanoes to erupt? When and where was the last eruption? What can we do to stay safe when we are near volcanoes? Did volcanoes play a part in the disappearance of dinosaurs?

Source: Sippola, A.E. (1995). K-W-L-S. *The Reading Teacher, 48,* 542–543.

Adapted for the primary grades from *Guided Comprehension: A Teaching Model for Grades 3–8* by Maureen McLaughlin and Mary Beth Allen ©2002. Newark, DE: International Reading Association. May be copied for classroom use.

Paired Questioning

Purpose: To engage in questioning and active decision making during the reading of a narrative or expository text.

Comprehension Strategies: Self-Questioning, Making Connections, Monitoring

Text: Narrative, Expository   **Use:** During and After Reading

Procedure: (Begin by explaining and modeling Paired Questioning.)

1. In pairs each student reads the title or subtitle of a manageable section of text.

2. Students put the reading materials aside. Each student asks a question that comes to mind related to the title or subtitle. The partner tries to give a reasonable answer to the question.

3. Students silently read a predetermined (by teacher or students) section of text.

4. After reading, the students take turns asking a question about the reading. One student asks a question first; the partner answers, using the text if needed. Then they reverse roles. Students continue this process until the text is finished.

5. After they have completed reading the text, one partner tells what he or she believes to be the important and unimportant ideas in the text and explains why. The partner agrees or disagrees with the choices and offers support for his or her thinking.

Example: (*Habitats: Coral Reef* [1997] by Gary W. Davis)

While reading this text, students engaged in Paired Questioning and developed the following queries and responses:

pp. 1–8:
What are coral polyps?	Tiny sea animals that make up coral colonies.
What are plankton?	Tiny floating plants and animals that polyps and other things eat.

pp. 9–14:
How do colors help sea creatures?	It sends messages like whose territory it is and what is poisonous.
How does camouflage help fish?	It protects them and helps them get food.

pp. 15–19
How do reef animals work together as partners?	Some little fish clean bigger fish and get to eat what they find.
Why is the sea horse so different?	It holds onto the reef with its tail and the male sea horse gives birth.

Source: Vaughn, J., & Estes, T. (1986). *Reading and reasoning beyond the primary grades*. Boston: Allyn & Bacon.

Question-Answer Relationship (QAR)

(See blackline, page 240.)

Purposes: To promote self-questioning; to answer comprehension questions by focusing on the information source needed to answer the question.

Comprehension Strategies: Self-Questioning, Making Connections, Monitoring

Text: Narrative, Expository   **Use:** After Reading

Procedure: (Begin by explaining and modeling QAR.)

1. Introduce the QAR concept and terminology. Explain that there are two kinds of information:

   In the book—The answer is found in the text.

   In my head—The answer requires input from the student's understandings and background knowledge.

   Explain that there are two kinds of QARs for each kind of information:

   In the book:

      Right There—The answer is stated in the passage.

      Think and Search—The answer is derived from more than one sentence or paragraph but is stated in the text.

   In my head:

      On My Own—The answer is contingent on information the reader already possesses in his or her background knowledge.

      Author and Me—The answer is inferred in the text, but the reader must make the connections with his or her own prior knowledge.

2. Use a Think-Aloud to practice using QAR with a text. Model choosing the appropriate QAR, giving the answer from the source, and writing or telling the answer.

3. Introduce a short passage and related questions. Have groups or individuals work through the passages and the questions. Students answer the questions and tell the QAR strategy they used. Any justifiable answer should be accepted.

4. Practice QAR with additional texts.

Principles of Teaching QAR: Give immediate feedback; progress from shorter to longer texts; guide students from group to independent activities; provide transitions from easier to more difficult tasks.

Source: Raphael, T. (1986). Teaching children Question-Answer Relationships, revisited. *The Reading Teacher, 39*, 516–522.

Adapted for the primary grades from *Guided Comprehension: A Teaching Model for Grades 3–8* by Maureen McLaughlin and Mary Beth Allen ©2002. Newark, DE: International Reading Association. May be copied for classroom use.

Thick and Thin Questions

(See blackline, page 241.)

Purposes: To create questions pertaining to a text; to help students discern the depth of the questions they ask and are asked; to use questions to facilitate understanding a text.

Comprehension Strategies: Self-Questioning, Making Connections

Text: Narrative, Expository   **Use:** Before, During, and After Reading

Procedure: (Begin by explaining and modeling Thick and Thin Questions.)

1. Teach the students the difference between thick questions and thin questions. Thick questions deal with the big picture and large concepts. Answers to thick questions are involved, complex, and open-ended. Thin questions deal with specific content or words. Answers to thin questions are short and close-ended.

2. Guide students to create Thick and Thin Questions. Read a portion of text and prompt students with stems, such as "Why…" or "What if…" for thick questions and "How far…" and "When…" for thin questions.

3. Have students create Thick and Thin Questions for the texts they are reading. They can write the questions in their Guided Comprehension Journals or write their thick questions on larger sticky notes and their thin questions on smaller sticky notes.

4. Share questions and answers in small and large groups.

Example Lesson: See Chapter 9, page 153.

Source: Lewin, L. (1998). *Great performances: Creating classroom-based assessment tasks*. Alexandria, VA: Association for Supervision and Curriculum Development.

Coding the Text

Purposes: To make connections while reading; to actively engage in reading.

Comprehension Strategy: Making Connections

Text: Narrative, Expository   **Use:** During Reading

Procedure: (Begin by explaining and modeling Coding the Text.)

1. Using a read-aloud and thinking aloud, model for the students examples of making connections. These may include text-self, text-text, or text-world connections.

2. While reading out loud, demonstrate how to code a section of the text that elicits a connection by using a sticky note, a code (T-S = text-self, T-T = text-text, T-W = text-world), and a few words to describe the connection.

3. Have the students work in small groups to read a short text and code the text. Have them share their ideas with the class.

4. Encourage students to code the text using sticky notes to record their ideas and use these as the basis of small- and large-group discussions.

Example: ("Going to Work" from *Things That Sometimes Happen: Very Short Stories for Little Listeners* [2002] by Avi)

Text-Self	Text-Text	Text-World
This story reminded me of when I go to work with Mom or Dad when they have bring your kid to work day.	The boy being at the office reminded me of Alexander being at his dad's office in *Alexander and the Terrible, Horrible, No Good Very Bad Day*.	This made me think of how parents go to work and kids go to school and how books make everyone feel better.

Source: Harvey, S., & Goudvis, A. (2000). *Strategies that work: Teaching comprehension to enhance understanding*. York, ME: Stenhouse.

Adapted for the primary grades from *Guided Comprehension: A Teaching Model for Grades 3–8* by Maureen McLaughlin and Mary Beth Allen ©2002. Newark, DE: International Reading Association. May be copied for classroom use.

Connection Stems

(See blacklines, pages 242–243.)

Purposes: To provide a structure to make connections while reading; to encourage reflection during reading.

Comprehension Strategy: Making Connections

Text: Narrative, Expository   **Use:** After Reading

Procedure: (Begin by explaining and modeling Connection Stems.)

1. After reading a text aloud, show students a sentence stem and think aloud about the process you use for completing it. Use text support and personal experiences to explain the connection.
2. Read another text aloud and guide the students to complete the stem orally with a partner.
3. Have students read a short text in pairs and work together to complete a stem.
4. Share the completed stems through discussion or journal responses.

   Sentence Stems: • That reminds me of…
                          • I remember when…

                          • I have a connection…

                          • An experience I have had like that…

                          • I felt like that character when…

                          • If I were that character, I would…

Example: (*My Brother Martin: A Sister Remembers Growing Up With the Rev. Dr. Martin Luther King Jr.* [2003] by Christine King Farris)

• This book reminds me that even famous people like Martin Luther King Jr. were children at one time and played practical jokes and did silly things just like we do.

• This book reminded me of *If a Bus Could Talk* because in that book Rosa Parks talked about Dr. King.

• I made connections to the world because the book talks about how the world has changed because of the work of Martin Luther King Jr. and others. Now we can all work and play together.

Example Lesson: See Chapter 7, page 102.

Source: Adapted from Harvey, S., & Goudvis, A. (2000). *Strategies that work: Teaching comprehension to enhance understanding.* York, ME: Stenhouse.

Double-Entry Journal

(See blacklines, pages 244–245.)

Purposes: To provide a structure for reading response; to make decisions about significant aspects of text and reflect on personal connections to the text.

Comprehension Strategies: Making Connections, Monitoring, Summarizing

Text: Narrative, Expository   **Use:** Before, During, and After Reading

Procedure: (Begin by explaining and modeling Double-Entry Journals.)

1. Provide students with a Double-Entry Journal or have them make one.
2. Explain how to use the journal. Model procedure and provide examples of reflective comments. (Encourage text-self, text-text, or text-world connections.)
3. Have students read (or listen to) a text or part of a text.
4. Have students select a key event, idea, word, quote, or concept from the text and write it in the left column of the paper.
5. In the right column, have students write their response or connection to the item in the left column.
6. Use journals as a springboard for discussion of text.

Source: Tompkins, G.E. (2001). *Literacy for the 21st century: A balanced approach* (2nd ed.). Upper Saddle River, NJ: Merrill.

Adapted for the primary grades from *Guided Comprehension: A Teaching Model for Grades 3–8* by Maureen McLaughlin and Mary Beth Allen ©2002. Newark, DE: International Reading Association. May be copied for classroom use.

Drawing Connections

(See blacklines, pages 246–248.)

Purposes: To provide a structure to make connections while reading; to use visual representations to express connections.

Comprehension Strategies: Making Connections, Visualizing

Text: Narrative, Expository   **Use:** During and After Reading

Procedure: (Begin by explaining and modeling Drawing Connections.)

1. Demonstrate how to draw visual representations (pictures, shapes, lines) to communicate connections with text.

2. Read a section of text and think aloud about a connection you can make. Model creating a visual representation of your thoughts. Then think aloud as you write a sentence or paragraph explaining the connection you made.

3. Read another section of text to the students and ask them to create visual representations of their connections to the text. Next, have them write a sentence or paragraph explaining their connection. Finally, have them share their drawings and explain their connections in small groups.

4. Encourage students to create visual representations of texts they are reading on their own and write a sentence or paragraph explaining their connection.

Adaptation: Instead of connections, have students sketch their visualizations.

Example Lesson: See Chapter 6, page 83.

Source: McLaughlin, M., & Allen, M.B. (2002). *Guided Comprehension: A teaching model for grades 3–8*. Newark, DE: International Reading Association.

Draw and Label Visualizations

(See blackline, page 249.)

Purposes: To provide a structure to encourage students to create mental images while reading; to encourage students to use artistic representations to express visualizations.

Comprehension Strategy: Visualizing, Making Connections

Text: Narrative, Expository   **Use:** During and After Reading

Procedure: (Begin by explaining and modeling Draw and Label Visualizations.)

1. Demonstrate how to use visual representations (pictures, shapes, lines) to express the pictures made in your head while reading.

2. Think out loud about the visualization and model, writing a sentence or paragraph about it.

3. Have students listen to a selection and ask them to create an artistic representation of their visualization. Then have them share their drawings in small groups, explaining how their drawings show the pictures they created in their heads.

4. Encourage students to create visual representations of texts they are reading on their own. Have them write sentences or paragraphs explaining their visualizations.

Ideas for Using:

• Use for notes for literature discussions.

• Use as a literacy center activity.

Example Lesson: See Chapter 8, page 123.

Source: McLaughlin, M., & Allen, M.B. (2002). *Guided Comprehension: A teaching model for grades 3–8*. Newark, DE: International Reading Association.

Adapted for the primary grades from *Guided Comprehension: A Teaching Model for Grades 3–8* by Maureen McLaughlin and Mary Beth Allen ©2002. Newark, DE: International Reading Association. May be copied for classroom use.

Graphic Organizers/Visual Organizers

(See blacklines, pages 251–254.)

Purposes: To provide a visual model of the structure of text; to provide a format for organizing information and concepts.

Comprehension Strategies: Visualizing, Making Connections, Summarizing

Text: Narrative, Expository   **Use:** Before, During, and After Reading

Procedure: (Begin by explaining and modeling Graphic Organizers/Visual Organizers.)

1. Introduce the Graphic Organizer to the students. Demonstrate how it works by reading a piece of text and noting key concepts and ideas on the organizer.

2. Have groups of students practice using the Graphic Organizers with ideas from an independently read text. Share ideas with the class.

3. Choose organizers that match text structures and thinking processes.

Examples:

Venn Diagram 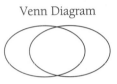   Web 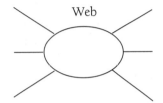   Story Map

Title:

Setting	Characters

Problem

Events

Solution

Mind and Alternative Mind Portraits

(See blackline, page 255.)

Purpose: To examine a topic or issue from two perspectives.

Comprehension Strategy: Visualizing, Evaluating

Text: Narrative, Expository   **Use:** During and After Reading

Procedure: (Begin by explaining and modeling Mind and Alternative Mind Portraits.)

1. Discuss the text and examine which perspective is prevalent. Then contemplate a perspective that is not presented equally or is silenced or missing from the text.

   Mind Portrait: Draw the outline of a head to represent the perspective of one person or character. Label the portrait. Inside the portrait, write, draw, or collage ideas and experiences that delineate that person's perspective.

   Alternative Mind Portrait: Draw the outline of a head that represents a different perspective. Label the portrait. Inside the portrait, write, draw, or collage ideas and experiences that delineate another person's perspective on the same issue.

2. Share and discuss portraits to compare and contrast perspectives.

3. Display completed portraits for others to view.

Adaptations:

   Narratives and Alternative Narratives

   Photographs and Alternative Photographs

   Videos and Alternative Videos

Example Lesson: See Chapter 7, page 107.

Source: McLaughlin, M., & Allen, M.B. (2002). *Guided Comprehension in action: Lessons for grades 3–8.* Newark, DE: International Reading Association.

Adapted for the primary grades from *Guided Comprehension: A Teaching Model for Grades 3–8* by Maureen McLaughlin and Mary Beth Allen ©2002. Newark, DE: International Reading Association. May be copied for classroom use.

Open-Mind Portrait

Purposes: To create and represent personal meanings for a story; to understand a character's perspective or point of view.

Comprehension Strategies: Visualizing, Summarizing

Text: Narrative, Expository   **Use:** After Reading

Procedure: (Begin by explaining and modeling Open-Mind Portraits.)

1. Students draw and color a portrait of a character from a story or a famous person from a biography.

2. Students cut out the portrait and use it to trace on one or several sheets of paper to create one or more blank head shapes.

3. Staple the color portrait and the blank sheets together.

4. On the blank pages, students draw or write about the person's thoughts and feelings throughout the text.

5. Share Open-Mind Portraits in book clubs, Literature Circles, or class meeting time.

Adaptation: Students fold a large sheet of paper (11" × 16") in half. On one half, they draw a portrait of a character from the book. On the other half, they draw the same shape of the portrait but do not fill in facial features. Instead, they fill the head with words and pictures to represent the thoughts and feelings of the character.

Source: Tompkins, G.E. (2001). *Literacy for the 21st century: A balanced approach* (2nd ed.). Upper Saddle River, NJ: Prentice Hall.

Sketch to Stretch

Purposes: To create, represent, and share personal meanings for a narrative or expository text; to summarize understandings through sketches.

Comprehension Strategies: Visualizing, Making Connections

Text: Narrative, Expository   **Use:** After Reading

Procedure: (Begin by explaining and modeling Sketch to Stretch.)

1. After reading or listening to text, have students sketch what the text means to them.

2. Encourage students to experiment and assure them there are many ways to represent personal meanings.

3. Have students gather in groups of three to five.

4. Each person in the group shares his or her sketch. As the sketch is shared, all other group members give their interpretation of the sketch. Once everyone has shared, the artist tells his or her interpretation.

5. Repeat Step 4 until everyone in the group has had a chance to share.

Source: Short, K.G., Harste, J.C., & Burke, C. (1996). *Creating classrooms for authors and inquirers*. Portsmouth, NH: Heinemann.

Adapted for the primary grades from *Guided Comprehension: A Teaching Model for Grades 3–8* by Maureen McLaughlin and Mary Beth Allen ©2002. Newark, DE: International Reading Association. May be copied for classroom use.

Concept of Definition Map

(See blackline, page 256.)

Purposes: To make connections with new words and topics and build personal meanings by connecting the new information with prior knowledge.

Comprehension Strategy: Knowing How Words Work

Text: Narrative, Expository   **Use:** Before Reading

Procedure: (Begin by explaining and modeling a Concept of Definition Map.)

1. Select or have student(s) select a word to be explored and place the word in the center of the map.

2. Ask students to determine a broad category that best describes the word and write it in the *What is it?* section.

3. Have student(s) provide some words that describe the focus word in the *What is it like?* section.

4. Have students provide some specific examples of the word in the *What are some examples?* section.

5. Have students determine a comparison.

6. Discuss the Concept of Definition Map.

7. Read the text. Revisit the map. Make modifications or additions.

Example Lesson: See Chapter 8, page 129.

Source: Schwartz, R., & Raphael, T. (1985). Concept of definition: A key to improving students' vocabulary. *The Reading Teacher, 39,* 198–205.

Context Clues

Purposes: To use semantics and syntax to figure out unknown words; to use a variety of cueing systems to make sense of text.

Comprehension Strategy: Knowing How Words Work

Text: Narrative, Expository   **Use:** During Reading

Procedure: (Begin by modeling how to use Context Clues to figure out word meanings.)

1. Explain to students the eight types of Context Clues and give examples of each:

> Definition—provides a definition that often connects the unknown word to a known word
>
> Example-Illustration—provides an example or illustration to describe the word
>
> Compare-Contrast—provides a comparison or contrast to the word
>
> Logic—provides a connection (such as a simile) to the word
>
> Root Words and Affixes—provides meaningful roots and affixes that the reader uses to determine meaning
>
> Grammar—provides syntactical cues that allow for reader interpretation
>
> Cause and Effect—cause and effect example allows the reader to hypothesize meaning
>
> Mood and Tone—description of mood related to the word allows readers to hypothesize meaning

2. Using a read-aloud and Think-Aloud, demonstrate using one or more of the clues to determine the meaning of a difficult or unfamiliar word in the text. (The Think-Aloud demonstrates the most effective clue based on the context of the sentence.) Readers use several of the clues to figure out unknown words.

3. If the context does not provide enough information, demonstrate other strategies for figuring out the meaning of the word.

Source: Vacca, R.T., & Vacca, J.A. (2002). *Content area reading: Literacy and learning across the curriculum* (7th ed.). New York: Longman.

Adapted for the primary grades from *Guided Comprehension: A Teaching Model for Grades 3–8* by Maureen McLaughlin and Mary Beth Allen ©2002. Newark, DE: International Reading Association. May be copied for classroom use.

Name: _____ Date: _____

CONNECTION STEMS

That reminds me of....

_____

_____

because

_____

That reminds me of…

_____

_____

because

_____

Adapted for the primary grades from *Guided Comprehension: A Teaching Model for Grades 3–8* by Maureen McLaughlin and Mary Beth Allen ©2002. Newark, DE: International Reading Association. May be copied for classroom use.

Name: _____ Date: _____

DOUBLE-ENTRY JOURNAL

Idea	Reflection/Reaction

Adapted for the primary grades from *Guided Comprehension: A Teaching Model for Grades 3–8* by Maureen McLaughlin and Mary Beth Allen ©2002. Newark, DE: International Reading Association. May be copied for classroom use.

Name: _____ Date: _____

DOUBLE-ENTRY JOURNAL

Idea/Text From Story	My Connection

Adapted for the primary grades from *Guided Comprehension: A Teaching Model for Grades 3–8* by Maureen McLaughlin and Mary Beth Allen ©2002. Newark, DE: International Reading Association. May be copied for classroom use.

Name: _____ Date: _____

DRAWING CONNECTIONS

Drawing Connections for _____

I have a connection to this book!

_____

_____

_____

_____

Drawing:

Adapted for the primary grades from *Guided Comprehension: A Teaching Model for Grades 3–8* by Maureen McLaughlin and Mary Beth Allen ©2002. Newark, DE: International Reading Association. May be copied for classroom use.

Name: _____ Date: _____

DRAWING CONNECTIONS

Drawing Connections for _____

I can make a connection between this book and another book!

_____

_____

_____

_____

Drawing:

Adapted for the primary grades from *Guided Comprehension: A Teaching Model for Grades 3–8* by Maureen McLaughlin and Mary Beth Allen ©2002. Newark, DE: International Reading Association. May be copied for classroom use.

Name: _____ Date: _____

DRAWING CONNECTIONS

Drawing Connections for _____

I felt like the character when...

_____

_____

_____

_____

Drawing:

Adapted for the primary grades from *Guided Comprehension: A Teaching Model for Grades 3–8* by Maureen McLaughlin and Mary Beth Allen ©2002. Newark, DE: International Reading Association. May be copied for classroom use.

Name: _____ Date: _____

DRAW AND LABEL VISUALIZATIONS

Drawing:

Label:

Adapted for the primary grades from *Guided Comprehension: A Teaching Model for Grades 3–8* by Maureen McLaughlin and Mary Beth Allen ©2002. Newark, DE: International Reading Association. May be copied for classroom use.

Name: _____

Date: _____

IN MY HEAD...WHAT I READ

In My Head.....	What I Read...

Guided Comprehension in the Primary Grades by Maureen McLaughlin ©2003.
Newark, DE: International Reading Association. May be copied for classroom use.

Name: _____   Date: _____

SEQUENCE CHAIN

Title

| 1 | → | 2 | → | 3 |

| 4 | → | 5 | → | 6 |

Adapted for the primary grades from *Guided Comprehension: A Teaching Model for Grades 3–8* by Maureen McLaughlin and Mary Beth Allen ©2002. Newark, DE: International Reading Association. May be copied for classroom use.

Name: _____   Date: _____

VENN DIAGRAM

Adapted for the primary grades from *Guided Comprehension: A Teaching Model for Grades 3–8* by Maureen McLaughlin and Mary Beth Allen ©2002. Newark, DE: International Reading Association. May be copied for classroom use.

Name: _____ Date: _____

MAIN IDEA TABLE

Main Idea			

Supporting Details

Adapted for the primary grades from *Guided Comprehension: A Teaching Model for Grades 3–8* by Maureen McLaughlin and Mary Beth Allen ©2002. Newark, DE: International Reading Association. May be copied for classroom use.

CONTRAST CHART

Name: _____   Date: _____

1. _____   1. _____

2. _____   2. _____

3. _____   3. _____

4. _____   4. _____

5. _____   5. _____

Adapted for the primary grades from *Guided Comprehension: A Teaching Model for Grades 3–8* by Maureen McLaughlin and Mary Beth Allen ©2002. Newark, DE: International Reading Association. May be copied for classroom use.

Name: _____   Date: _____

MIND AND ALTERNATIVE MIND PORTRAITS

Mind Portrait

Alternative Mind Portrait

Adapted for the primary grades from *Guided Comprehension: A Teaching Model for Grades 3–8* by Maureen McLaughlin and Mary Beth Allen ©2002. Newark, DE: International Reading Association. May be copied for classroom use.

Name: _____   Date: _____

CONCEPT OF DEFINITION MAP

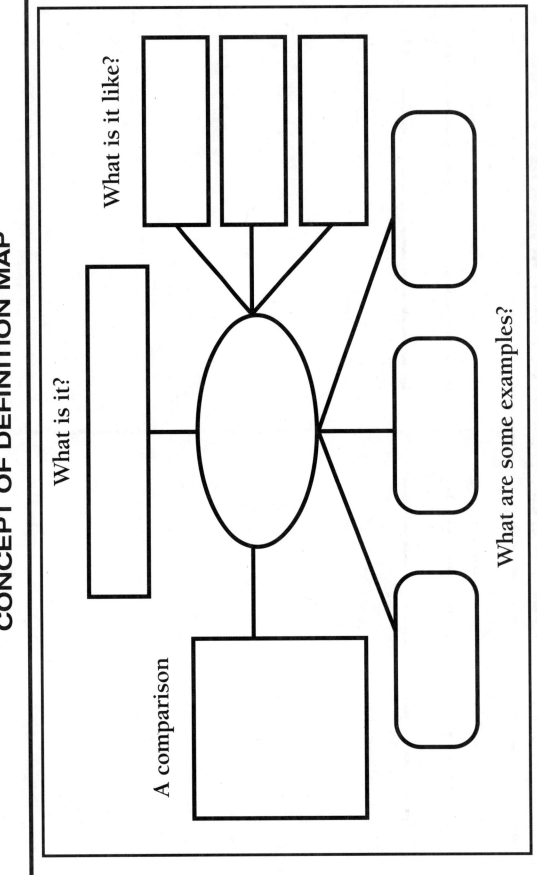

What is it?

What is it like?

A comparison

What are some examples?

Adapted for the primary grades from *Guided Comprehension: A Teaching Model for Grades 3–8* by Maureen McLaughlin and Mary Beth Allen ©2002. Newark, DE: International Reading Association. May be copied for classroom use.

Name: _____ Date: _____

SEMANTIC FEATURE ANALYSIS

	Characteristics								
Categories									

Adapted for the primary grades from *Guided Comprehension: A Teaching Model for Grades 3–8* by Maureen McLaughlin and Mary Beth Allen ©2002. Newark, DE: International Reading Association. May be copied for classroom use.

Name: _____ Date: _____

TEXT TRANSFORMATIONS

Part One: Replace each missing word with a synonym.

Jack and Jill _____ up the hill

To _____ a pail of water.

Jack fell down and broke his _____

And Jill came _____ after.

Part Two: Write a silly rhyme using the same structure.

_____

_____

_____

_____

Adapted for the primary grades from *Guided Comprehension in Action: Lessons for Grades 3–8* by Maureen McLaughlin and Mary Beth Allen ©2002. Newark, DE: International Reading Association. May be copied for classroom use.

BOOKMARK

Name: _____

Date: _____

The most interesting part was...

Page number: _____

BOOKMARK

Name: _____

Date: _____

A word I think the whole class needs to talk about is...

Page number: _____

Adapted for the primary grades from *Guided Comprehension: A Teaching Model for Grades 3–8* by Maureen McLaughlin and Mary Beth Allen ©2002. Newark, DE: International Reading Association. May be copied for classroom use.

BOOKMARK

Name: _____

Date: _____

Something that confused me
was...

Page number: _____

BOOKMARK

Name: _____

Date: _____

My favorite illustration
was...

Page number: _____

Adapted for the primary grades from *Guided Comprehension: A Teaching Model for Grades 3–8* by Maureen McLaughlin
and Mary Beth Allen ©2002. Newark, DE: International Reading Association. May be copied for classroom use.

Name: _____   Date: _____

DRAW SOMETHING

1	2
3	4

Adapted for the primary grades from *Guided Comprehension: A Teaching Model for Grades 3–8* by Maureen McLaughlin and Mary Beth Allen ©2002. Newark, DE: International Reading Association. May be copied for classroom use.

Name: _____   Date: _____

BIO-PYRAMID

1. _____
   Person's name

2. _____
   Two words describing the person

3. _____
   Three words describing the person's childhood

4. _____
   Four words indicating a problem the person had to overcome

5. _____
   Five words stating one of his or her accomplishments

6. _____
   Six words stating a second accomplishment

7. _____
   Seven words stating a third accomplishment

8. _____
   Eight words stating how mankind benefited from his or her accomplishments

Adapted for the primary grades from *Guided Comprehension: A Teaching Model for Grades 3–8* by Maureen McLaughlin and Mary Beth Allen ©2002. Newark, DE: International Reading Association. May be copied for classroom use.

Name: _____ Date: _____

LYRIC RETELLING/LYRIC SUMMARY

Text: _____

Tune: _____

Verse 1:

_____

_____

_____

_____

Verse 2:

_____

_____

_____

_____

Refrain (or Verse 3):

_____

_____

_____

_____

Adapted for the primary grades from *Guided Comprehension: A Teaching Model for Grades 3–8* by Maureen McLaughlin and Mary Beth Allen ©2002. Newark, DE: International Reading Association. May be copied for classroom use.

NARRATIVE PYRAMID

Name: _____   Date: _____

1. _____
   Character's name

2. _____
   Two words describing the character

3. _____
   Three words describing the setting

4. _____
   Four words stating the problem

5. _____
   Five words describing one event

6. _____
   Six words describing another event

7. _____
   Seven words describing a third event

8. _____
   Eight words describing a solution to the problem

Adapted for the primary grades from *Guided Comprehension: A Teaching Model for Grades 3–8* by Maureen McLaughlin and Mary Beth Allen ©2002. Newark, DE: International Reading Association. May be copied for classroom use.

Name: _____ Date: _____

QuIP RESEARCH GRID

Topic: _____

Questions	Answers	
	Source:	Source:
1.		
2.		
3.		

Adapted for the primary grades from *Guided Comprehension: A Teaching Model for Grades 3–8* by Maureen McLaughlin and Mary Beth Allen ©2002. Newark, DE: International Reading Association. May be copied for classroom use.

Name: _____ Date: _____

DRAW AND LABEL RETELLING FOR _____

Who?	Where?
Draw:	Draw:
Label:	Label:

What happened?	How did it end?
Draw:	Draw:
Label:	Label:

Guided Comprehension in the Primary Grades by Maureen McLaughlin ©2003. Newark, DE: International Reading Association. May be copied for classroom use.

Name: _____ Date: _____

STORY MAP

Title/Chapter: _____

Setting		Characters

Problem

Event 1

Event 2

Event 3

Solution

Adapted for the primary grades from *Guided Comprehension: A Teaching Model for Grades 3–8* by Maureen McLaughlin and Mary Beth Allen ©2002. Newark, DE: International Reading Association. May be copied for classroom use.

Name: _____   Date: _____

SUMMARY CUBE

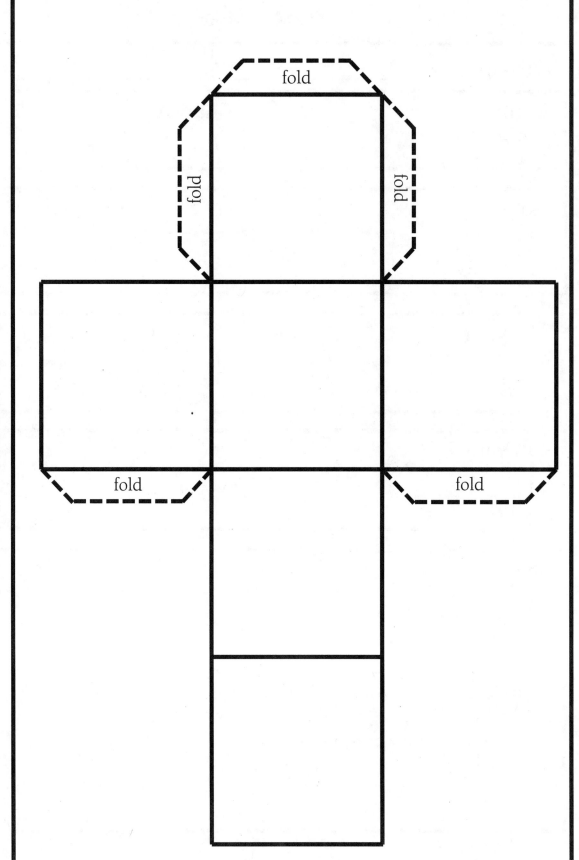

Adapted for the primary grades from *Guided Comprehension: A Teaching Model for Grades 3–8* by Maureen McLaughlin and Mary Beth Allen ©2002. Newark, DE: International Reading Association. May be copied for classroom use.

Name: _____ Date: _____

DISCUSSION WEB

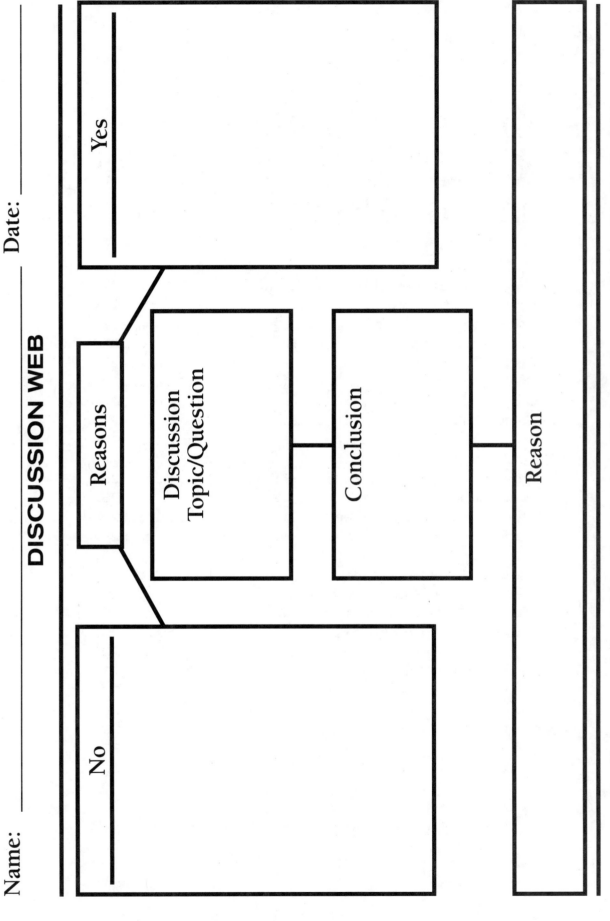

Yes

Reasons

No

Discussion Topic/Question

Conclusion

Reason

Adapted for the primary grades from *Guided Comprehension: A Teaching Model for Grades 3–8* by Maureen McLaughlin and Mary Beth Allen ©2002. Newark, DE: International Reading Association. May be copied for classroom use.

Resources for Organizing and Managing Comprehension Centers and Routines

Name: _____   Date: _____

ABC CENTER
SEQUENTIAL ROUNDTABLE ALPHABET

A		B		C	
D		E		F	
G		H		I	
J		K		L	
M		N		O	
P		Q		R	
S		T		U	
V		W		X	
Y		Z			

Adapted for the primary grades from *Guided Comprehension: A Teaching Model for Grades 3–8* by Maureen McLaughlin and Mary Beth Allen ©2002. Newark, DE: International Reading Association. May be copied for classroom use.

ALPHABET BOOKS

Ada, A.F. (1997). *Gathering the sun: An alphabet in Spanish and English*. New York: HarperCollins.
Azarian, M. (2000). *A gardener's alphabet*. Boston: Houghton Mifflin.
Blackwell, D. (1989). *An ABC bestiary*. New York: Farrar, Straus & Giroux.
Bronson, L. (2001). *The circus alphabet*. New York: Henry Holt.
Browne, P.A. (1995). *African animals ABC*. San Francisco: Sierra Club.
Cheney, L. (2002). *America: A patriotic primer*. New York: Simon & Schuster.
Crane, C. (2000). *S is for sunshine: A Florida alphabet*. Chelsea, MI: Sleeping Bear Press.
Crane, C. (2001). *L is for Lone Star: A Texas alphabet*. Chelsea, MI: Sleeping Bear Press.
Crosby, E.T. (2001). *A is for adopted*. Gilbert, AZ: SWAK PAK.
Demarest, C. (1999). *The cowboy ABC*. New York: Dorling/Kindersley.
Demarest, C. (2000). *Firefighters A to Z*. New York: Scholastic.
Ehlert, L. (1989). *Eating the alphabet: Fruits and vegetables from A to Z*. New York: Harcourt.
Fleming, D. (2002). *Alphabet under construction*. New York: Henry Holt.
Gowan, B. (2002). *G is for Grand Canyon: An Arizona alphabet*. Chelsea, MI: Sleeping Bear Press.
Harley, A. (2001). *Leap into poetry: More ABC's of poetry*. Honesdale, PA: Boyds Mills Press.
Harris, J. (1997). *A is for artist: A Getty Museum alphabet*. Los Angeles: Getty.
Inkpen, M. (2001). *Kipper's A to Z*. New York: Harcourt.
Johnson, S.T. (1995). *Alphabet city*. New York: Penguin.
Jordan, M., & Jordan, T. (1996). *Amazon Alphabet*. New York: Kingfisher.
Kalman, M. (2001). *What Pete ate from A–Z*. New York: Penguin.
Kellogg, S. (1997). *Aster Aardvark's alphabet adventures*. New York: Morrow Junior Books.
Kirk, D. (1998). *Miss Spider's ABC*. New York: Scholastic.
Martin, B. Jr. (2000). *Chicka chicka boom boom*. New York: Aladdin.
McNaught, H., & Mathieu, J. (1998). *ABC and 123: A Sesame Street treasury of words and numbers featuring Jim Henson's Sesame Street Muppets*. New York: Random House.
Merriam, E., & Smith, L. (1987). *Spooky ABC*. New York: Simon & Schuster.
Murphy, C. (1997). *Alphabet magic*. New York: Simon & Schuster Children's Books.
Nathan, C. (1995). *Bugs and beasties ABC*. Boca Raton, FL: Cool Kids Press.
Onyefulu, I. (1993). *A is for Africa*. New York: Puffin.
Pallotta, J. (1989). *The yucky reptile alphabet book*. Watertown, MA: Charlesbridge.
Pallotta, J. (1990). *Dinosaur alphabet book*. Watertown, MA: Charlesbridge.
Pallotta, J. (1990). *The furry animal alphabet book*. Watertown, MA: Charlesbridge.
Pallotta, J. (1990). *The icky bug alphabet book*. Watertown, MA: Charlesbridge.
Pallotta, J. (1991). *The bird alphabet book*. Watertown, MA: Charlesbridge.
Pallotta, J. (1991). *Frog alphabet book*. Watertown, MA: Charlesbridge.
Pallotta, J. (1991). *Ocean alphabet book*. Watertown, MA: Charlesbridge.
Pallotta, J. (1991). *The underwater alphabet book*. Watertown, MA: Charlesbridge.
Pallotta, J. (1992). *Victory garden vegetable alphabet book*. Watertown, MA: Charlesbridge.
Pallotta, J. (1993). *The extinct alphabet book*. Watertown, MA: Charlesbridge.
Pallotta, J. (1994). *The desert alphabet book*. Watertown, MA: Charlesbridge.
Pallotta, J. (1994). *The spice alphabet book: Herbs, spices, & other natural flavors*. Watertown, MA: Charlesbridge.
Pallotta, J. (1995). *The butterfly alphabet book*. Watertown, MA: Charlesbridge.
Pallotta, J. (1996). *The freshwater alphabet book*. Watertown, MA: Charlesbridge.
Pallotta, J. (1997). *The airplane alphabet book*. Minneapolis, MN: Econo-Clad Books.
Pallotta, J. (1997). *The flower alphabet book*. Watertown, MA: Charlesbridge.
Pallotta, J. (1998). *Boat alphabet book*. Watertown, MA: Charlesbridge.
Pallotta, J. (1999). *Jet alphabet book*. Watertown, MA: Charlesbridge.
Pallotta, J. (2002). *The skull alphabet book*. Watertown, MA: Charlesbridge.
Pfister, M. (2002). *Rainbow fish A,B,C*. New York: North-South Books.
Reynolds, C.F. (2001). *H is for Hoosier: An Indiana alphabet*. Chelsea, MI: Sleeping Bear Press.
Reynolds, C.F. (2001). *L is for lobster: A Maine alphabet*. Chelsea, MI: Sleeping Bear Press.
Rose, D.L. (2000). *Into the A, B, sea: An ocean alphabet*. New York: Scholastic.
Schnur, S. (1997). *Autumn: An alphabet acrostic*. New York: Houghton Mifflin.
Schnur, S. (2002). *Winter: An alphabet acrostic*. New York: Houghton Mifflin.
Schonberg, M. (2000). *B is for buckeye: An Ohio alphabet*. Chelsea, MI: Sleeping Bear Press.
Scillian, D. (2001). *A is for America*. Chelsea, MI: Sleeping Bear Press.
Sendak, M. (1999). *Alligators all around: An alphabet*. New York: HarperCollins.
Shahan, S. (2002). *The jazzy alphabet*. New York: Penguin Putnam.
Shoulders, M. (2001). *V is for volunteer: A Tennessee alphabet*. Chelsea, MI: Sleeping Bear Press.
Sierra, J. (1998). *Antarctic antics*. New York: Harcourt Brace.
Slate, J. (1996). *Miss Bindergarten gets ready for kindergarten*. New York: Penguin.
Stutson, C. (1999). *Prairie primer*. New York: Puffin.
Tudor, T. (2001). *A is for Annabelle: A doll's alphabet*. New York: Simon & Schuster.
Ulmer, M. (2001). *M is for maple: A Canadian alphabet*. Chelsea, MI: Sleeping Bear Press.
Walton, R., & Miglio, P. (2002). *So many bunnies: A bedtime ABC and counting book*. New York: Harper Trophy.
Wargin, K. (2000). *L is for Lincoln: An Illinois alphabet*. Chelsea, MI: Sleeping Bear Press.
Wood, A. (2001). *Alphabet adventure*. New York: Scholastic.
Yolen, J. (1997). *All in the woodland early: An ABC book*. Honesdale, PA: Boyds Mills Press.
Young, J. (2001). *S is for show me: A Missouri alphabet*. Chelsea, MI: Sleeping Bear Press.

Name: _____ Date: _____

BOOK MOBILE ORGANIZER

Directions: Write or draw your ideas on the parts of the mobile. Remember to use both sides. Then cut out the six pieces and follow the directions in the folder.

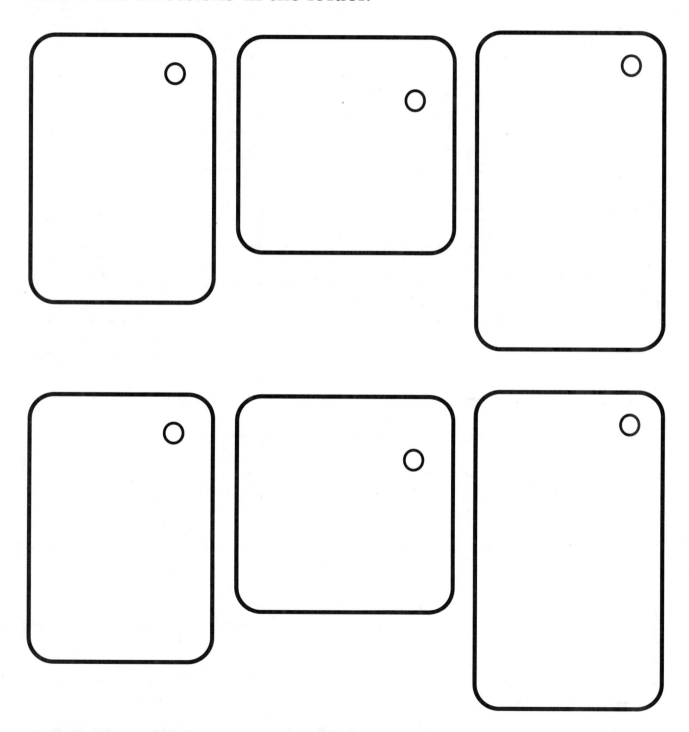

Guided Comprehension in the Primary Grades by Maureen McLaughlin ©2003.
Newark, DE: International Reading Association. May be copied for classroom use.

CENTER CHART FOR STUDENTS

Center: _____ Week: _____

Directions: If you used this center, sign your name and place a check mark underneath the day you visited.

Students	Monday	Tuesday	Wednesday	Thursday	Friday

Adapted for the primary grades from *Guided Comprehension: A Teaching Model for Grades 3–8* by Maureen McLaughlin and Mary Beth Allen ©2002. Newark, DE: International Reading Association. May be copied for classroom use.

CENTER PLANNER

Theme: _____

Center Title: _____

Format: ___Display Board   ___Pizza Box   ___Folder

Schedule: ___Wall Chart   ___Rotation   ___Free Choice

Accountability:
   Assessment: ___Review Strategy Applications
                ___Student Self-Assessments
                ___Other:_____

   Recordkeeping: ___Guided Comprehension Profiles
                ___Center Folders
                ___Other:_____

Materials:
   Texts: _____
       _____

   Suppliers: _____
       _____

Sample Activity: _____
       _____
       _____
       _____

Guided Comprehension in the Primary Grades by Maureen McLaughlin ©2003.
Newark, DE: International Reading Association. May be copied for classroom use.

Name: _____   Date: _____

CENTER REFLECTIONS

Center: _____

While I was working at this center, I was able to

_____

_____

_____

_____

I learned

_____

_____

_____

_____

The next time I plan to

_____

_____

_____

_____

_____

Adapted for the primary grades from *Guided Comprehension: A Teaching Model for Grades 3–8* by Maureen McLaughlin and Mary Beth Allen ©2002. Newark, DE: International Reading Association. May be copied for classroom use.

Name: _____ Date: _____

CENTER RUBRIC

Center: _____

Directions: Think about what you did at the center today. Then use this rubric to describe your performance.

	Minimal	Satisfactory	Good	Excellent
	1	2	3	4
My work is complete.	1	2	3	4
I followed the directions.	1	2	3	4
I made personal interpretations.	1	2	3	4
My presentation is appealing.	1	2	3	4
I made connections that are supported by the text.	1	2	3	4
I used multiple modes of response.	1	2	3	4

Comments:

_____

_____

_____

_____

_____

Adapted for the primary grades from *Guided Comprehension: A Teaching Model for Grades 3–8* by Maureen McLaughlin and Mary Beth Allen ©2002. Newark, DE: International Reading Association. May be copied for classroom use.

Name: _____ Date: _____

CENTER STUDENT SELF-EVALUATION

Center: _____

My goal was

_____

_____

_____

What I did well

_____

_____

_____

I think I achieved my goal because

_____

_____

My new goal is

_____

_____

_____

_____

_____

Adapted for the primary grades from *Guided Comprehension: A Teaching Model for Grades 3–8* by Maureen McLaughlin and Mary Beth Allen ©2002. Newark, DE: International Reading Association. May be copied for classroom use.

Name: _____ Date: _____

CHOOSE YOUR OWN PROJECT

You may work with a partner to do this. Choose a project and follow the directions in the folder.

Write a new ending for the story.

Make a character puppet.

Make a story collage.

Make a picture collage.

Make a character mobile.

Put the characters in a new story.

Create an advertisement for a book.

Create a book jacket.

Write a trifold report.

Interview a classmate.

Survey the class about authors/books.

Write a Lyric Summary and sing it.

Adapted for the primary grades from *Guided Comprehension: A Teaching Model for Grades 3–8* by Maureen McLaughlin and Mary Beth Allen ©2002. Newark, DE: International Reading Association. May be copied for classroom use.

CLASS CENTER CHART FOR TEACHERS

Centers					
Students					

Adapted for the primary grades from *Guided Comprehension: A Teaching Model for Grades 3–8* by Maureen McLaughlin and Mary Beth Allen ©2002. Newark, DE: International Reading Association. May be copied for classroom use.

Name: _____ Date: _____

CROSS-AGE READING EXPERIENCE
SELF-EVALUATION

Text: _____

1. How would you rate your participation in your Cross-Age Reading Experience?

   just right   too much   too little   not at all

2. What is one thing you did to prepare for the Cross-Age Reading Experience that was helpful?

   _____

   _____

   _____

3. What is something you learned in your Cross-Age Reading Experience?

   _____

   _____

   _____

4. How would you rate your Cross-Age Reading Experience?

   lively   average   boring

5. How helpful was today's Cross-Age Reading Experience?

   very helpful   somewhat helpful   not helpful

6. What worked well for you today? What will you do to improve next time?

   _____

   _____

   _____

Guided Comprehension in the Primary Grades by Maureen McLaughlin ©2003.
Newark, DE: International Reading Association. May be copied for classroom use.

DIRECTIONS FOR MAKING BOOKS

Slotted Book

STEP 1

Take at least two pieces of paper and hold them in a landscape (horizontal) position (Fig. 1). You can use more than two pages to create books with more than four pages.

STEP 2—MAKING THE SLOT

Separate one page from the pack of papers. Make sure the fold or SPINE is nice and flat. Measure 1 1/2 inches from the top of the spine and make a mark and the same at the bottom of the page of the spine.

Cut into the spine and carefully cut away the spine between the marks you have made. Only cut into the spine about 1/16 of an inch (Fig. 2). Open your page and you should see a SLOT (Fig. 3).

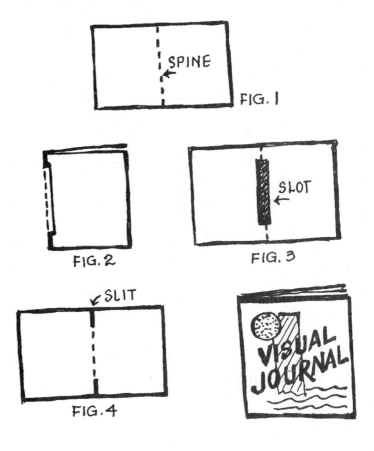

STEP 3—MAKING THE SLITS

Take the other page(s) and make sure the spine is nice and flat. Measure the same 1 1/2 inches from the top and bottom of the spine.

This time cut from the bottom of the page up to the mark to create a SLIT. Repeat the process at the top of the page. You should have a SLIT at the top and bottom of the page (Fig. 4).

STEP 4—SLIPPING THE BOOK TOGETHER

Open the slotted page. Take the other page(s) with slits and bend them in half horizontally. SLIP them through the slot until you have reached the center of the book. Carefully slip the slit and slot together and roll the pages open and fold it like a book.

Source: Pinciotti, P. (2001). *Book arts: The creation of beautiful books*. East Stroudsburg, PA: East Stroudsburg University of Pennsylvania.

Adapted for the primary grades from *Guided Comprehension: A Teaching Model for Grades 3–8* by Maureen McLaughlin and Mary Beth Allen ©2002. Newark, DE: International Reading Association. May be copied for classroom use.

DIRECTIONS FOR MAKING BOOKS

Dos à Dos Dialogue Journals

Dos à dos is a French expression meaning a couch or a carriage that holds two people sitting back to back. When two people sit back to back they see different things or they see the same thing from different points of view. This book is really two books in one (or three or more—you decide). There is room for each person's point of view or story. Dos à dos can be a wonderful way to structure a dialogue journal where you and another person write back and forth to each other. Each person has his or her own book and in turn responds to the others' ideas, questions, and feelings. Turn them around and read each other's response!

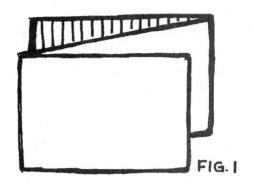

FIG. I

STEP 1

For a two-part dos à dos, take a piece of 11 × 17 paper and cut it lengthwise in half (5½ inches). Take one strip and fold into three equal parts. It should look like a Z (Fig. 1).

STEP 2

Cut all the text pages so they are 8 × 5½ inches. Fold them in half and divide them to create two booklets or signatures with equal pages.

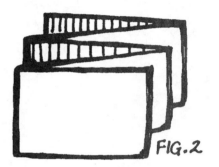

FIG. 2

STEP 3

Slip a signature into the first fold. The crease of the signature or booklet should be nested inside the crease of the cover. You can either staple the signature into the cover or sew the signature into the cover. The simplest way is to staple the booklet in by using a book arm stapler that lets you staple deep into the center of the signature.

STEP 4

Repeat step 3 for other signature nesting it in the other crease.

STEP 5

Fold the book back and forth so that you can open one signature from the front and one from the back.

STEP 6—DECORATE THE COVERS.

Consider these wild variations! As with any book, you can change the shape, size, and materials of this book. Make a dos à dos dialogue journal for three or four people (Fig. 2). Just make an extra long cover or paste together two of them. What an interesting conversation you could have!

Try different types of text pages. If you need some extra long pages, cut some text pages longer than the others, and make fold outs. Cut some pages taller than others and make fold downs. Add some pop-ups.

Source: Pinciotti, P. (2001). *Book arts: The creation of beautiful books*. East Stroudsburg, PA: East Stroudsburg University of Pennsylvania.

Adapted for the primary grades from *Guided Comprehension: A Teaching Model for Grades 3–8* by Maureen McLaughlin and Mary Beth Allen ©2002. Newark, DE: International Reading Association. May be copied for classroom use.

DIRECTIONS FOR MAKING BOOKS

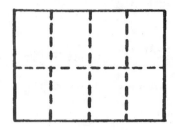

1. Fold an A4 piece of paper into eight equal parts. Lay flat on the landscape position.

2. Fold in half vertically and cut from the folded edge to the center with scissors.

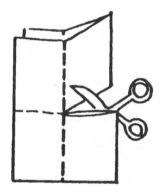

3. Open out then fold horizontally. Push left and right ends to center.

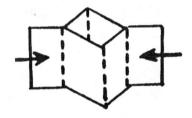

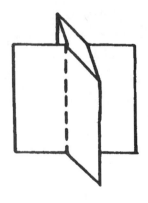

4. Fold around to form a book with six art/writing pages and a front and back cover.

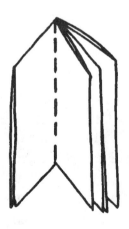

Source: Pinciotti, P. (2001). *Book arts: The creation of beautiful books.* East Stroudsburg, PA: East Stroudsburg University of Pennsylvania.

Adapted for the primary grades from *Guided Comprehension: A Teaching Model for Grades 3–8* by Maureen McLaughlin and Mary Beth Allen ©2002. Newark, DE: International Reading Association. May be copied for classroom use.

Name: _____ Date: _____

GROUP WORK REFLECTION SHEET

Name: _____ Date: _____

How did your group do today?

What did you do to help your group?

What did the others do to help the group?

What will your group do to improve next time?

Adapted for the primary grades from *Guided Comprehension: A Teaching Model for Grades 3–8* by Maureen McLaughlin and Mary Beth Allen ©2002. Newark, DE: International Reading Association. May be copied for classroom use.

GUIDED COMPREHENSION JOURNAL

Adapted for the primary grades from *Guided Comprehension: A Teaching Model for Grades 3–8* by Maureen McLaughlin and Mary Beth Allen ©2002. Newark, DE: International Reading Association. May be copied for classroom use.

"IF I WERE IN CHARGE OF THE WORLD"

If I Were in Charge of _____

by _____

If I were in charge of _____, I'd cancel

_____,

_____,

_____, and also

_____.

If I were in charge of _____,
There'd be_____,

_____, and

_____.

If I were in charge of _____,
You wouldn't have_____
You wouldn't have_____
You wouldn't have_____
Or _____
You wouldn't even have _____

If I were in charge of _____,

_____

_____

And a person_____
And_____
Would still be allowed to be in charge of the world.

Source: Adapted from Viorst, J. (1981). *If I were in charge of the world and other worries*. New York: Atheneum.

Adapted for the primary grades from *Guided Comprehension: A Teaching Model for Grades 3–8* by Maureen McLaughlin and Mary Beth Allen ©2002. Newark, DE: International Reading Association. May be copied for classroom use.

LITERATURE CIRCLE BOOKMARK

Name: _____

Date: _____

I will talk to my group about…

I will ask my group about…

My favorite part was…

Other ideas…

LITERATURE CIRCLE BOOKMARK

Name: _____

Date: _____

I will talk to my group about…

I will ask my group about…

My favorite part was…

Other ideas…

Guided Comprehension in the Primary Grades by Maureen McLaughlin ©2003.
Newark, DE: International Reading Association. May be copied for classroom use.

LITERATURE CIRCLE GROUP EVALUATION

Group Members

_____   _____

_____   _____

_____   _____

4 = Excellent   3 = Good   2 = Fair   1 = Poor

1. My group worked well together. _____

2. My group used its time wisely. _____

3. I worked well and completed all my jobs. _____

4. I think my group deserves a _____

Student Comments:

Teacher Comments:

Adapted for the primary grades from *Guided Comprehension: A Teaching Model for Grades 3–8* by Maureen McLaughlin and Mary Beth Allen ©2002. Newark, DE: International Reading Association. May be copied for classroom use.

Name: _____ Date: _____

LITERATURE CIRCLE SELF-EVALUATION

Text: _____

1. How would you rate your participation in the discussion?

    just right   too much   too little   not at all

2. What did you do to prepare for the Literature Circle that was helpful?

    _____

    _____

    _____

3. What is something you learned in your Literature Circle?

    _____

    _____

    _____

4. How would you rate your group's discussion?
    lively   average   boring

5. How helpful was today's discussion?
    very helpful   somewhat helpful   not helpful

6. What worked well today? What will you do to improve next time?

    _____

    _____

    _____

    _____

Adapted for the primary grades from *Guided Comprehension: A Teaching Model for Grades 3–8* by Maureen McLaughlin and Mary Beth Allen ©2002. Newark, DE: International Reading Association. May be copied for classroom use.

Name: _____ Date: _____

MAKING AND WRITING WORDS

How many words can you make from the word _____?

Two-letter words:

—— ——   —— ——   —— ——   —— ——   —— ——

Three-letter words:

——— ——— ———   ——— ——— ———   ——— ——— ———   ——— ——— ———

——— ——— ———   ——— ——— ———   ——— ——— ———   ——— ——— ———

——— ——— ———   ——— ——— ———   ——— ——— ———   ——— ——— ———

——— ——— ———   ——— ——— ———   ——— ——— ———   ——— ——— ———

Four-letter words:

———— ———— ————   ———— ———— ————   ———— ———— ————

———— ———— ————   ———— ———— ————   ———— ———— ————

———— ———— ————   ———— ———— ————   ———— ———— ————

———— ———— ————   ———— ———— ————   ———— ———— ————

Larger words:

_____   _____

_____   _____

_____   _____

_____   _____

Source: Adapted from Rasinski, T. (1999). Making and writing words using letter patterns. *Reading Online* [Online]. Available: http://www.readingonline.org/articles/words/rasinski_index.html.

Adapted for the primary grades from *Guided Comprehension: A Teaching Model for Grades 3–8* by Maureen McLaughlin and Mary Beth Allen ©2002. Newark, DE: International Reading Association. May be copied for classroom use.

Name: _____ Date: _____

MAKING AND WRITING WORDS

Directions: Use the vowels and consonants provided to make words based on the clues given by the teacher.

Vowels	Consonants

Directions: Listen carefully as your teacher or classmate provides clues to words that you will write in each box.

1	7
2	8
3	9
4	10
5	11
6	12

Source: Adapted from Rasinski, T. (1999). Making and writing words using letter patterns. *Reading Online* [Online]. Available: http://www.readingonline.org/articles/words/rasinski_index.html.

Adapted for the primary grades from *Guided Comprehension: A Teaching Model for Grades 3–8* by Maureen McLaughlin and Mary Beth Allen ©2002. Newark, DE: International Reading Association. May be copied for classroom use.

LITERACY HISTORY PROMPTS

To learn about your students' literacy experiences, you may wish to have them create their literacy histories. The following prompts will facilitate this process. Having the students illustrate their experiences or provide photos related to their experiences enhances their histories. Be sure to demonstrate this activity by sharing this part of your literacy history as a model for the class.

1. What was your favorite book before you came to school?

2. What was your favorite memory of having someone read to you when you were younger?

3. Can you remember a sign you could read at a young age (McDonald's, Burger King, Toys "R" Us, supermarket, etc.)? What do you remember about that experience?

4. Did you ever read to your stuffed animals, dolls, or younger brothers and sisters? What do you remember about those experiences?

5. What was the first thing you ever wrote (crayon scribbles on a wall, writing in a tablet, note to parents, thank-you note, etc.)? What do you remember about that experience?

6. What was the first book that you read? What do you remember about that experience?

7. What was the first thing you wrote that you were really proud of?

8. What book are you reading outside of school now? Why did you choose to read it?

9. What are some things you are writing outside of school now?

10. Do you and your friends talk about what you read? What is something you would tell them about a book you read recently?

11. Do you think you are a good reader now? Do you plan to continue reading as you get older?

12. Do you think you are a good writer now? Do you plan to continue writing as you get older?

Source: Adapted from McLaughlin, M., & Vogt, M.E. (1996). *Portfolios in teacher education.* Newark, DE: International Reading Association.

Guided Comprehension in the Primary Grades by Maureen McLaughlin ©2003.
Newark, DE: International Reading Association. May be copied for classroom use.

MOTIVATION TO READ PROFILE
CONVERSATIONAL INTERVIEW

Student: _____ Date: _____

A. *Emphasis: Narrative text*

Suggested prompt (designed to engage student in a natural conversation): I have been reading a good book...I was talking with...about it last night. I enjoy talking about good stories and books that I've been reading. Today I'd like to hear about what you have been reading.

1. Tell me about the most interesting story or book you have read this week (or even last week). Take a few minutes to think about it. (Wait time.) Now, tell me about the book or story.

Probes: What else can you tell me? Is there anything else? _____

_____

_____

_____

2. How did you know or find out about this story?_____

_____

_____

☐ assigned ☐ in school

☐ chosen ☐ out of school

3. Why was this story interesting to you? _____

_____

_____

_____

(continued)

Source: Gambrell, L.B., Palmer, B.M., Codling, R.M., & Mazzoni, S.A. (1996). Assessing motivation to read. *The Reading Teacher, 49*, 518–533.

Guided Comprehension in the Primary Grades by Maureen McLaughlin ©2003.
Newark, DE: International Reading Association. May be copied for classroom use.

MOTIVATION TO READ PROFILE
CONVERSATIONAL INTERVIEW (continued)

B. Emphasis: Informational text

Suggested prompt (designed to engage student in a natural conversation): Often we read to find out about something or to learn about something. We read for information. For example, I remember a student of mine...who read a lot of books about...to find out as much as he/she could about.... Now, I'd like to hear about some of the informational reading you have been doing.

1. Think about something important that you learned recently, not from your teacher and not from television, but from a book or some other reading material. What did you read about? (Wait time.) Tell me about what you learned.

Probes: What else could you tell me? Is there anything else? _____

_____

_____

_____

2. How did you know or find out about this book/article? _____

_____

_____

☐ assigned ☐ in school

☐ chosen   ☐ out of school

3. Why was this book (or article) important to you?_____

_____

_____

_____

(continued)

Source: Gambrell, L.B., Palmer, B.M., Codling, R.M., & Mazzoni, S.A. (1996). Assessing motivation to read. *The Reading Teacher, 49,* 518–533.

Guided Comprehension in the Primary Grades by Maureen McLaughlin ©2003.
Newark, DE: International Reading Association. May be copied for classroom use.

C. Emphasis: General reading

1. Did you read anything at home yesterday? _____ What?

_____

_____

2. Do you have any books at school (in your desk/storage area/locker/book bag) today that you are reading? _____ Tell me about them.

_____

_____

3. Tell me about your favorite author.

_____

_____

4. What do you think you have to learn to be a better reader?

_____

_____

5. Do you know about any books right now that you'd like to read? Tell me about them.

_____

_____

6. How did you find out about these books?

_____

_____

7. What are some things that get you really excited about reading books?

_____

_____

8. Tell me about…

_____

_____

9. Who gets you really interested and excited about reading books?

_____

_____

10. Tell me more about what they do.

_____

_____

Source: Gambrell, L.B., Palmer, B.M., Codling, R.M., & Mazzoni, S.A. (1996). Assessing motivation to read. *The Reading Teacher, 49,* 518–533.

Guided Comprehension in the Primary Grades by Maureen McLaughlin ©2003.
Newark, DE: International Reading Association. May be copied for classroom use.

CROSS-AGE READING EXPERIENCE OBSERVATION

Student: _____ Date: _____

Directions: Place a check if the behavior is observed.

Observation:

1. Student was prepared for the Cross-Age Reading Experience. _____

2. Student welcomed his or her cross-age reading buddy. _____

3. Student(s) self-selected an appropriate text from the book basket. _____

4. Student focused on the task. _____

5. Student actively engaged in reading. _____

6. Student successfully engaged in strategy application. _____

7. Student engaged in meaningful discussion. _____

8. Student was competent in his or her role. _____

9. Student's contributions demonstrated depth of understanding. _____

10. Student respected ideas of others involved in the experience. _____

Student's self-evaluation indicated _____

_____

_____

_____

Notes:_____

_____

_____

_____

Guided Comprehension in the Primary Grades by Maureen McLaughlin ©2003.
Newark, DE: International Reading Association. May be copied for classroom use.

LITERATURE CIRCLE OBSERVATION

Student: _____ Date: _____

Directions: Place a check if the behavior is observed.

Observation:

1. Student was prepared for the Literature Circle. _____

2. Student was focused on the group task. _____

3. Student engaged in discussion. _____

    Talk focused on the content of the book. _____

    Talk focused on the reading process. _____

    Talk focused on personal connections. _____

    Talk focused on the group process. _____

4. Student was competent in his or her
   discussion role. _____

5. Student's contributions demonstrated
   depth of understanding. _____

6. Student respected ideas of other group
   members. _____

Student's self-evaluation indicated _____

_____

_____

Notes:_____

_____

_____

Guided Comprehension in the Primary Grades by Maureen McLaughlin ©2003.
Newark, DE: International Reading Association. May be copied for classroom use.

RECIPROCAL TEACHING OBSERVATION

Student: _____ Date: _____

Directions: Place a check if the behavior is observed.

Observation:

1. Student was prepared for Reciprocal Teaching.   _____

2. Student was focused on the group task.   _____

3. Student was actively engaged in Reciprocal Teaching.   _____

4. Student successfully engaged in prediction.   _____

5. Student successfully generated meaningful questions.   _____

6. Student successfully clarified meaning.   _____

7. Student successfully summarized text.   _____

8. Student used strategy prompts.   _____

9. Student's contributions demonstrated depth
   of understanding.   _____

10. Student respected ideas of other group members.   _____

Student's self-evaluation indicated _____

_____

_____

_____

_____

Notes:_____

_____

_____

_____

_____

Guided Comprehension in the Primary Grades by Maureen McLaughlin ©2003.
Newark, DE: International Reading Association. May be copied for classroom use.

Name: _____ Date: _____

STUDENT SELF-REFLECTION AND GOAL SETTING

Hobby or Special Interest

This activity is designed to help you reflect on one of your hobbies or special interests. Remember that self-reflection involves thinking about what you did, how well you did it, and what you can do to make it better next time. To begin your reflection, focus on your hobby or special interest. Then think about the last time you did it. How well did it go? What is one thing you can do to improve it next time? What is your new goal?

My hobby or special interest is

Something I learned to do in my hobby or special interest is

The last time I did it

One thing I can do to improve it next time is

My new goal for my hobby or special interest is

Source: Adapted from McLaughlin, M. (1995). *Performance assessment: A practical guide to implementation.* Boston: Houghton Mifflin.

Guided Comprehension in the Primary Grades by Maureen McLaughlin ©2003.
Newark, DE: International Reading Association. May be copied for classroom use.

Name: _____ Date: _____

STUDENT SELF-REFLECTION AND GOAL SETTING IN GUIDED COMPREHENSION

This activity is designed to help you create a self-reflection about your reading. Remember that self-reflection involves thinking about what you did, how well you did it, and what you can do to make it better next time. To begin your reflection, focus on something you have learned during Guided Comprehension. Then think about the last time you did it. How well did it go? What is one thing you can do to improve it next time? What is your new goal?

What I read

What I learned

The last time I did it

One thing I can do to improve it next time is

My new goal is

Source: Adapted from McLaughlin, M. (1995). *Performance assessment: A practical guide to implementation.* Boston: Houghton Mifflin.

Guided Comprehension in the Primary Grades by Maureen McLaughlin ©2003.
Newark, DE: International Reading Association. May be copied for classroom use.

Name: _____ Date: _____

REFLECTION AND GOAL SETTING

Today my goal was

What I did

What I learned

Questions I have

When I reflect on how well I achieved my goal, I think

Tomorrow my goal will be

Guided Comprehension in the Primary Grades by Maureen McLaughlin ©2003.
Newark, DE: International Reading Association. May be copied for classroom use.

TICKETS OUT

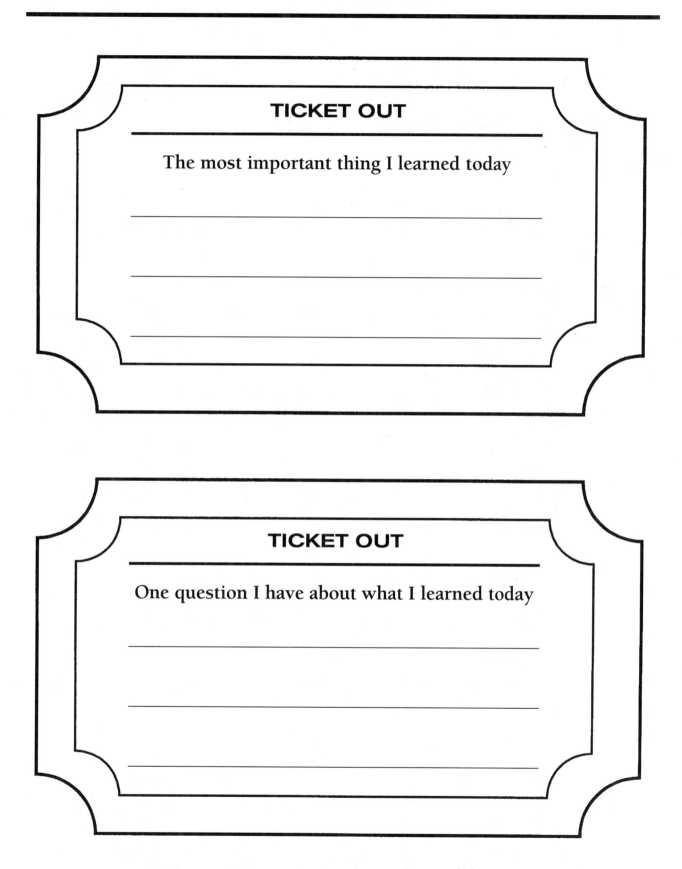

TICKET OUT

The most important thing I learned today

TICKET OUT

One question I have about what I learned today

Guided Comprehension in the Primary Grades by Maureen McLaughlin ©2003.
Newark, DE: International Reading Association. May be copied for classroom use.

Sources of Leveled Narrative and Expository Texts

This appendix features resources for leveled books created by teachers, school districts, and publishers. It is important to remember that all levels are approximate and that students' abilities to read text are influenced by multiple factors, including background knowledge and motivation.

Website Maintained by Individual Teachers

Children's Literature Research Resource Page by Bruce Ellis

Teacher Resource Center
440 Titles Sorted By Reading Level
Reading Level Range: 1.0 to 8.9
www.tamu-commerce.edu/coe/shed/espinoza/s/ellis-b-rdlevl.html

Sample Anchor Books:

Level	Title	Author
1.0	Goodnight Moon	M.W. Brown
1.6	Polar Bear, Polar Bear, What Do You Hear?	B. Martin Jr.
2.0	Freckle Juice	J. Blume
2.6	The Very Hungry Caterpillar	E. Carle
3.0	The Mitten	J. Brett
3.6	The Emperor and the Nightingale	H.C. Anderson
4.0	Dear Mr. Henshaw	B. Cleary
4.6	Fudge-a-mania	J. Blume

Websites Maintained by School Districts

Oster Elementary School, San Jose, California

www.unionsd.org/oster/artestsbylevel.html

Sample Anchor Books:

Level	Title	Author
1.0	Goodnight Moon	M.W. Brown
1.5	Henry and Mudge and the Wild Wind	C. Rylant
2.0	Nate the Great and the Pillowcase	M. Sharmat & R. Weinman
2.5	Two Bad Ants	C. Van Allsburg
3.0	Cam Jansen and the Mystery of the Dinosaur Bones	D. Adler

Guided Comprehension in the Primary Grades by Maureen McLaughlin ©2003.
Newark, DE: International Reading Association. May be copied for classroom use.

3.5	*Encyclopedia Brown Takes the Case*	D. Sobol
4.0	*Dear Mr. Henshaw*	B. Cleary
4.5	*Chocolate Fever*	R. Smith

Portland Public Schools, Portland, Oregon

www.pps.k12.or.us/instruction-c/literacy/leveled_books

Sample Anchor Books:

Level	Title	Author
1.0	*Are You My Mother?*	P.D. Eastman
1.5	*The Carrot Seed*	R. Krauss
2.0	*The Doorbell Rang*	P. Hutchins
2.5	*Madeline's Rescue*	L. Bemelmans
3.0	*Grandfather's Journey*	A. Say
3.5	*Alexander and the Terrible, Horrible, No Good, Very Bad Day*	J. Viorst
4.0	*Ice Magic*	M. Christopher
4.5	*Beezus and Ramona*	B. Cleary

Leveled Materials Available From Publishers

Great Source Education Group

Next Steps: High-interest chapter books for guided instruction

Beginning: Grades K–2

Grades 1–2	*Norma Jean, Jumping Bean*
	Parakeet Girl
	R is for Radish
	Dragon's Scales
	Dinosaur Babies

Intermediate: Grades 2–4

Grade 3	*Brave Maddie Egg*
	Silver
	Little Swan
	Slam Dunk Saturday
	Soccer Mania!
Grade 4	*The Stories Huey Tells*
	Adventure in Alaska
	Harriet's Hare
	Harry's Mad
	Babe: The Gallant Pig

Advanced: Grades 4–6

Grade 5	*The Night Crossing*
	The Secret of the Seal
	Black-Eyed Susan
	Dear Levi
	Toliver's Secret
Grade 6	*Crash*
	Dog Years
	Some Friends
	There's a Boy in the Girl's Bathroom
	Dogs Don't Tell Jokes

Guided Comprehension in the Primary Grades by Maureen McLaughlin ©2003.
Newark, DE: International Reading Association. May be copied for classroom use.

Houghton Mifflin Leveled Readers 2004

www.schooldirect.com

Houghton Mifflin Reading Cumulative Listing of Leveled Books

More than 600 titles, grades K–6

Levels A–B   The books in these first levels are for the emergent reader. This reader is just learning reading behaviors.
Examples: *See What We Can Do*
Nat at Bat
Cat on the Mat
Once Upon a Dig
The Bug Hut

Levels C–G   The books in the second group of levels are for the early reader. These readers range in their abilities and needs. Some are just beginning to decode words, some can read simple sentences, and others can read several lines of text.
Examples: *Curious George Rides a Bike*
Benny's Pennies
One Hundred Hungry Ants
Ira Sleeps Over
Sheep in a Jeep

Levels H–M   The books in the third group are for the transitional reader. These readers have early reading behaviors well under control. They are beginning to be fluent readers.
Examples: *Curious George Flies a Kite*
What Do Authors Do?
The Wednesday Surprise
The Dive
Mufaro's Beautiful Daughters

Levels N–R   The books in the fourth group are for the self-extending reader. These are fluent readers who are able to apply many reading strategies to the task of reading texts. These books are more complex and lengthy.
Examples: *I Am Rosa Parks*
Sarah, Plain and Tall
Jumanji
The Boy Who Loved to Draw
Mark McGwire: Home Run Hero

Levels S–Z   The books in the fifth group are for the advanced reader. The advanced readers have moved well into literacy learning. They are having varied reading experiences and are using literature for many different purposes. Readers at this level see that language has meaning, purpose, and function. They use sophisticated word-solving strategies, read and reread critically and for meaning, and understand and identify nuances in literature. Advanced readers continually build their fluency and the length of text that they can read and understand.

Guided Comprehension in the Primary Grades by Maureen McLaughlin ©2003.
Newark, DE: International Reading Association. May be copied for classroom use.

Examples: *Anastasia at Your Service*
            Pyramid
            Growing Up in Coal Country
            Number the Stars
            Eileen Collins: First Woman Commander in Space

National Geographic School Publishing

www.nationalgeographic.com/education

Windows on Literacy: Nonfiction Readers for Pre-K–3

176 leveled science and social studies titles designed to meet the needs of beginning through fluent readers

Sample Science Titles:

A Dog's Life
Who Lives at the Zoo?
What Can a Diver See?
Sea and Land Animals
On Safari
Plants in the Park
When the Rain Comes
Seeds Grow Into Plants
Cactuses
The Rain Forest

Sample Social Studies Titles:

What's My Job?
Signs on the Way
Loading the Airplane
The Car Wash
Going Up the Mountain
Wheels
Up the Amazon
Our Town
What's on Ships?
The Great Pyramid

Guided Comprehension in the Primary Grades by Maureen McLaughlin ©2003.
Newark, DE: International Reading Association. May be copied for classroom use.

Home-School Connections

Creating and maintaining positive relationships with students' families is a valued component of the educational process. A variety of ideas for facilitating such relationships in the primary grades are presented in this appendix.

Alphabetize Environmentally

Foster the child's knowledge of the alphabet by providing environmental print (labels, advertisements, store bags, street names) to alphabetize. (Rule, 2001)

Billboards, Street Signs, and Labels

Parents or older siblings walk with the student throughout the community, pointing out different types of environmental print. Students can notice street signs in their neighborhood and see billboard advertisements. If a stop is made at a local market or if a snack is served after the walk, the student can also make connections between the foods and their labels.

Book Backpacks

Fill a backpack with reading and writing materials and send it home with a student for a weekend. Have the family members use the materials together to read stories, write stories, or create illustrations for stories. You also can include a list of creative ways to respond to literature, and the families can choose what they would like to do. When the backpack is returned to school, the child shares how the family engaged in literacy.

It Happened Just This Way

After reading aloud to a child or having the child read to you, have the child retell the story orally, through drawings, through dramatization, or by writing.

Library Buddies

Send a list of popular book titles home to parents. Have a parent or older sibling become the student's library buddy. The buddies can check out the latest in children's literature, listen to an audio book, or attend a story hour together. When they return home, they can talk about their experience, draw pictures about it, or write about it in a special journal.

Read the Pictures

Take photographs during favorite family moments at home, on vacations, or in the community and use them as the basis of storytelling. (Spielman, 2001)

Reading Time Just for You and Me

Parents should read aloud to their child every day in a special place and at a special time. As the child grows, he or she can read to the parents.

Storypals

Students practice reading storybooks with classmates or cross-age partners in school. They explore the narrative structure of stories and write retellings of familiar storybooks. Children read these same storybooks to younger siblings, cousins, and neighborhood children at home.

Guided Comprehension in the Primary Grades by Maureen McLaughlin ©2003.
Newark, DE: International Reading Association. May be copied for classroom use.

READING = SUCCESS...

...when parents or caregivers

R — Read aloud every day. Read old favorites and new books. Read different kinds of books. Talk when reading with the children. Ask them what pictures they liked or to tell what they think might happen next.

E — Ensure that the environment is literacy-rich, filled with books, magazines, and newspapers for reading as well as papers, cards, pens, and pencils for writing.

A — Allow children to see reading and writing for different purposes every day. Having positive role models will encourage children to read and write.

D — Develop an excitement and enthusiasm about reading when the teacher sends home the classroom's "reading suitcase." It is filled with books that can be shared with everyone in the family.

I — Invite children to talk, read, and write about their favorite experiences. They may even make a family book to which all members can contribute.

N — Nurture children's love of books by taking them to the library on a regular basis and allowing them to buy books that interest them.

G — Guide children's comprehension of a story through responding. You and the children can sketch or dramatize the events of the story.

S — Share stories with predictable texts that will encourage children to read along.

U — Use the Internet as a resource for ideas and materials. Some websites that are helpful include www.famlit.org, www.rif.org, www.ed.gov/pubs/SimpleThings.

C — Create opportunities that foster literacy development. Have the children act out television commercials or put new words to familiar songs.

C — Collect recipes together and make something special with the children. Cooking and eating is a shared bonding experience as well as a learning one.

E — Encourage the children to take risks when they attempt reading and writing. Praise them for their efforts. Leave notes in their lunchboxes.

S — Support the children's learning by reading the "book in the bag" sent home that day. This gives the children opportunities to practice, build confidence, and gain fluency.

S — Stay in regular contact with the children's teachers.

Source: Romano, S. (2002). *Reading = Success: Literacy activities that promote home-school connections* [Emergent Literacy Course Syllabus]. East Stroudsburg University of Pennsylvania.

Guided Comprehension in the Primary Grades by Maureen McLaughlin ©2003.
Newark, DE: International Reading Association. May be copied for classroom use.

Books About Families and Communities: A List to Share!

Families

Beaton, C. (1997). *Family*. Hauppauge, NY: Barron's Educational Series.

Bridwell, N. (1990). *Clifford's family*. New York: Scholastic.

Brown, M. (1995). *Arthur's family vacation* (Arthur adventures series). New York: Little, Brown.

Bunting, E. (1989). *The Wednesday surprise*. New York: Clarion.

Carlson, N.S. (1989). *The family under the bridge*. New York: HarperCollins.

Chall, M.W. (2000). *Happy birthday, America!* Ft. Atkinson, WI: Highsmith Press.

Cleary, B. (1992). *Ramona Quimby, age 8*. New York: William Morrow.

Cole, J. (1997). *I'm a big sister*. New York: William Morrow.

Cosgrove, S. (2001). *Hucklebug*. New York: Penguin Putnam.

Evans, D. (2001). *The elevator family*. New York: Bantam Doubleday Dell.

Garza, C.L. (2000). *In my family*. Chicago: Children's Book Press.

Harris, R.H., & Emberley, M. (2002). *It's so amazing! A book about eggs, sperm, birth, babies, and families*. Cambridge, MA: Candlewick.

Hoberman, M.A. (2001). *Fathers, mother, sisters, brothers: A collection of family poems*. New York: Little, Brown.

Jarrell, R. (1995). *The animal family*. New York: HarperCollins.

Kalman, B.D. (1995). *A child's day*. New York: Crabtree.

Mayer, G., & Mayer, M. (1992). *This is my family*. New York: Golden Books.

McBratney, S. (1999). *Guess how much I love you*. Cambridge, MA: Candlewick.

Moss, M. (2000). *Amelia's family ties*. Middleton, WI: Pleasant Company.

Munsch, R. (1988). *Love you forever*. Willowdale, ON: Firefly Books.

Munsch, R. (1991). *Good families don't*. New York: Bantam Doubleday Dell.

Murkoff, H.E. (2000). *What to expect when mommy's having a baby*. New York: HarperCollins.

Parish, P. (1997). *Amelia Bedelia's family album*. New York: HarperCollins.

Pellegrini, N. (1991). *Families are different*. New York: Holiday House.

Polacco, P. (1994). *My rotten redheaded older brother*. New York: Simon & Schuster.

Rylant, C. (1998). *Henry and Mudge in the family trees: The fifteenth book of their adventures*. New York: Simon & Schuster.

Sandburg, C. (1999). *The Huckabuck family: And how they raised popcorn in Nebraska and quit and came back*. New York: Farrar, Straus & Giroux.

Say, A. (1993). *Grandfather's journey*. Boston: Houghton Mifflin.

Skutch, R. (1998). *Who's in a family?* Berkeley, CA: Tricycle Press.

Sweeney, J. (2000). *Me and my family tree*. New York: Random House.

Taylor, S. (1976). *All-of-a-kind family*. New York: Bantam Doubleday Dell.

Viorst, J. (1976). *Alexander and the terrible, horrible, no good, very bad day*. New York: Simon & Schuster.

White, E.B. (1974). *Stuart Little*. New York: HarperCollins.

Wild, M., & Argent, K. (2000). *Nighty night*. Atlanta, GA: Peachtree.

Wilder, L.I. (1976). *Little house in the big woods*. New York: HarperCollins.

Wyss, J. (1999). *The Swiss family Robinson*. New York: Random House.

Guided Comprehension in the Primary Grades by Maureen McLaughlin ©2003.
Newark, DE: International Reading Association. May be copied for classroom use.

Communities

Bauer, J. (2002). *Hope was here*. New York: Penguin Putnam.

Bunting, E. (1994). *Smoky night*. New York: Harcourt.

Caseley, J. (2002). *On the town: A community adventure*. New York: HarperCollins.

Flanagan, A.K. (2000). *Mr. Paul and Mr. Lueke build communities*. New York: Scholastic.

Greenfield, E. (1996). *Night on a neighborhood street*. New York: Penguin.

Hayward, L. (2001). *Day in the life of a police officer*. New York: Dorling/Kindersley.

Kalman, B.D. (1995). *Visiting a village*. New York: Crabtree.

Kalman, B.D. (1999). *What is a community? A to Z*. New York: Crabtree.

Kalman, B.D., & Walker, N. (1997). *Community helpers from A to Z*. New York: Crabtree.

Kottke, J. (2000). *A day with police officers*. New York: Scholastic.

Maass, R. (2002). *Fire fighters*. New York: Scholastic.

Mecca, J.T. (1999). *Multicultural plays: A many-splendored tapestry honoring our global community*. Nashville, TN: Incentive Publications.

Parish, H.S. (2001). *Amelia Bedelia 4 mayor* (Vol. 36). New York: HarperCollins.

Pellegrino, M.W. (1999). *My grandma's the mayor: A story for children about community spirit and pride*. Washington, DC: American Psychological Association.

Polacco, P. (1998). *Thank-you, Mr. Falker*. New York: Philomel.

Rael, E.O. (2000). *What Zeesie saw on Delancey Street*. New York: Aladdin.

Rey, M. (1985). *Curious George at the fire station*. Boston: Houghton Mifflin.

Rey, M. (1998). *Curious George goes to a movie*. Boston: Houghton Mifflin.

Rey, M., & Rey, H.A. (1966). *Curious George goes to the hospital*. Boston: Houghton Mifflin.

Rathmann, P. (1995). *Officer Buckle and Gloria*. New York: Putnam.

Salvo-Ryan, D.D. (1994). *City Green*. New York: William Morrow.

Saunders-Smith, G. (1997). *Communities*. Mankato, MN: Capstone.

Schecter, E. (1996). *The big idea* (Vol. 1). New York: Hyperion.

Sommer, C. (2001). *Mayor for a day*. Houston, TX: Advance.

Soto, G. (1992). *Neighborhood ODEs*. New York: Harcourt.

Steiner, S.F., & Ada, A.F. (2001). *Promoting a global community through multicultural children's literature*. Westport, CT: Libraries Unlimited.

Wawrychuk, C., & McSweeney, C. (1998). *The post office: Active learning about community workers*. Palo Alto, CA: Monday Morning Books.

REFERENCES

Allen, M.B. (2002). *Reciprocal teaching: A Guided Comprehension routine*. Paper presented at the 47th Annual Convention of the International Reading Association, San Francisco, CA.

Almasi, J.F. (1996). A new view of discussion. In L.B. Gambrell & J.F. Almasi (Eds.), *Lively discussions! Fostering engaged reading* (pp. 2–24). Newark, DE: International Reading Association.

Alvermann, D. (1991). The discussion web: A graphic aid for learning across the curriculum. *The Reading Teacher, 45*, 92–99.

Anderson, R.C. (1994). Role of the reader's schema in comprehension, learning, and memory. In R.B. Ruddell, M.R. Ruddell, & H. Singer (Eds.), *Theoretical models and processes of reading* (4th ed., pp. 469–482). Newark, DE: International Reading Association.

Anderson, R.C., & Pearson, P.D. (1984). A schema-theoretic view of basic processes in reading comprehension. In P.D. Pearson, R. Barr, M.L. Kamil, & P. Mosenthal (Eds.), *Handbook of reading research* (pp. 225–253). New York: Longman.

Askew, B.J., & Fountas, I.C. (1998). Building an early reading process: Active from the start! *The Reading Teacher, 52*, 126–134.

Au, K.H., Carroll, J.H., & Scheu, J.A. (1997). *Balanced literacy instruction: A teacher's resource book*. Norwood, MA: Christopher-Gordon.

Au, K.H., & Raphael, T.E. (1998). Curriculum and teaching in literature-based programs. In T.E. Raphael & K.H. Au (Eds.), *Literature-based instruction: Reshaping the curriculum* (pp. 123–148). Norwood, MA: Christopher-Gordon.

Baker, L., Afflerbach, P., & Reinking, D. (1996). Developing engaged readers in school and home communities: An overview. In L. Baker, P. Afflerbach, & D. Reinking (Eds.), *Developing engaged readers in school and home communities* (pp. xiii–xxvii). Hillsdale, NJ: Erlbaum.

Baker, L., & Wigfield, A. (1999). Dimensions of children's motivation for reading and their relations to reading activity and reading achievement. *Reading Research Quarterly, 34*, 452–481.

Ball, E., & Blachman, B. (1991). Does phoneme awareness training in kindergarten make a difference in early word recognition and developmental spelling? *Reading Research Quarterly, 26*, 49–66.

Baumann, J.F., & Kameenui, E.J. (1991). Research on vocabulary instruction: Ode to Voltaire. In J. Flood, J.M. Jensen, D. Lapp, & J.R. Squire (Eds.), *Handbook on teaching the English language arts* (pp. 604–632). New York: Macmillan.

Bean, T.W. (2000). Music in the content areas. In M. McLaughlin & M.E. Vogt (Eds.), *Creativity, innovation, and content area teaching* (pp. 91–103). Norwood, MA: Christopher-Gordon.

Bear, D.R., Invernizzi, M., Templeton, S., & Johnston, F. (2003). *Words their way: Word study for phonics, vocabulary, and spelling instruction* (2nd ed.). Upper Saddle River, NJ: Prentice Hall. (*Words Their Way* videotape available from Prentice Hall, ISBN 013022183X)

Beck, I., & McKeown, M. (1991). Conditions of vocabulary acquisition. In R. Barr, M.L. Kamil, P.B. Mosenthal, & P.D. Pearson (Eds.), *Handbook of reading research* (Vol. 2, pp. 789–814). White Plains, NY: Longman.

Blachowicz, C.L.Z. (1986). Making connections: Alternatives to the vocabulary notebook. *Journal of Reading, 29*, 643–649.

Blachowicz, C.L.Z., & Fisher, P. (2000). Vocabulary instruction. In M.L. Kamil, P.B. Mosenthal, P.D. Pearson, & R. Barr (Eds.), *Handbook of reading research* (Vol. 3, pp. 503–523). Mahwah, NJ: Erlbaum.

Blachowicz, C.L.Z., & Lee, J.J. (1991). Vocabulary development in the whole literacy classroom. *The Reading Teacher, 45*, 188–195.

Brabham, E.G., & Villaume, S.K. (2000). Continuing conversations about literature circles. *The Reading Teacher, 54*, 278–280.

Brooks, J.G., & Brooks, M.G. (1993). *In search of understanding: The case for constructivist classrooms*. Alexandria, VA: Association for Supervision and Curriculum Development.

Brown, K.J. (1999/2000). What kind of text—for whom and when? Textual scaffolding for beginning readers. *The Reading Teacher, 53*, 292–307.

Brown, L.A. (1993). Story collages: Help for reluctant writers. *Learning, 22*(4), 22–25.

Buehl, D. (2001). *Classroom strategies for interactive learning* (2nd ed.). Newark, DE: International Reading Association.

Busching, B.A., & Slesinger, B.A. (1995). Authentic questions: What do they look like? Where do they lead? *Language Arts, 72*(5), 341–351.

Cambourne, B. (2002). Holistic, integrated approaches to reading and language arts instruction: The constructivist framework of an instructional theory. In A.E. Farstrup & S.J. Samuels (Eds.), *What research has to say about reading instruction* (3rd ed., pp. 25–47). Newark, DE: International Reading Association.

Ciardiello, A.V. (1998). Did you ask a good question today? Alternative cognitive and metacognitive strategies. *Journal of Adolescent & Adult Literacy, 42,* 210–219.

Clay, M.M. (1985). *The early detection of reading difficulties: A diagnostic survey with recovery procedures* (3rd ed.). Portsmouth, NH: Heinemann.

Clay, M.M. (1991). Introducing a new storybook to young readers. *The Reading Teacher, 45,* 264–273.

Clay, M.M. (1993a). *An observation survey of early literacy achievement.* Portsmouth, NH: Heinemann.

Clay, M.M. (1993b). *Reading Recovery: A guidebook for teachers in training.* Portsmouth, NH: Heinemann.

Clemmons, J., Laase, L., Cooper, D., Areglado, N., & Dill, M. (1993). *Portfolios in the classroom.* Jefferson City, MO: Scholastic.

Cooper, J.D. (2003). *Comprehension: Helping students construct meaning.* Boston: Houghton Mifflin.

Cooper, J.D., & Kiger, N.D. (2001). *Literacy assessment: Helping teachers plan instruction.* Boston: Houghton Mifflin.

Cunningham, P.M. (2000). *Phonics they use: Words for reading and writing* (3rd ed.). New York: HarperCollins.

Cunningham, P.M., & Allington, R.L. (1999). *Classrooms that work: They can all read and write* (2nd ed.). New York: Addison-Wesley.

Cunningham, P.M., & Cunningham, J.W. (2002). What we know about how to teach phonics. In A.E. Farstrup & S.J. Samuels (Eds.), *What research has to say about reading instruction* (3rd ed., pp. 87–109). Newark, DE: International Reading Association.

Dahl, K.L., & Farnan, N. (1998). *Children's writing: Perspectives from research.* Newark, DE: International Reading Association.

Daniels, H. (1994). *Literature circles: Voice and choice in the student-centered classroom.* York, ME: Stenhouse.

Darling-Hammond, L.D., Ancess, J., & Falk, B. (1995). *Authentic assessment in action: Studies of schools and students at work.* New York: Teachers College Press.

Davey, B. (1983). Think-aloud—Modeling the cognitive processes of reading comprehension. *Journal of Reading, 27,* 44–47.

Dewey, J. (1933). *How we think: A restatement of reflective thinking to the educative process.* Lexington, MA: D.C. Heath.

Dixon-Krauss, L. (1996). *Vygotsky in the classroom: Mediated literacy instruction and assessment.* White Plains, NY: Longman.

Duffy, G.G. (2001, December). *The case for direct explanation of strategies.* Paper presented at the 51st annual meeting of the National Reading Conference, San Antonio, TX.

Duffy, G.G., Roehler, L.R., Sivan, E., Rackville, G., Meloth, M., Vavrus, L.G., et al. (1987). Effects of explaining the reasoning associated with using reading strategies. *Reading Research Quarterly, 22,* 347–368.

Duke, N.K. (2001, December). *A new generation of researchers looks at comprehension.* Paper presented at the 51st annual meeting of the National Reading Conference, San Antonio, TX.

Duke, N.K., & Pearson, P.D. (2002). Effective practices for developing reading comprehension. In A.E. Farstrup & S.J. Samuels (Eds.), *What research has to say about reading instruction* (3rd ed., pp. 205–242). Newark, DE: International Reading Association.

Durkin, D. (1978/1979). What classroom observations reveal about reading comprehension instruction. *Reading Research Quarterly, 14,* 481–533.

Ehri, L.C., & Nunes, S.R. (2002). The role of phonemic awareness in learning to read. In A.E. Farstrup & S.J. Samuels (Eds.), *What research has to say about reading instruction* (3rd ed., pp.110–139). Newark, DE: International Reading Association.

Fielding, L.G., & Pearson, P.D. (1994). Reading comprehension: What works. *Educational Leadership, 51*(5), 62–68.

Ford, M.P., & Opitz, M.F. (2002). Using centers to engage children during guided reading time: Intensifying learning experiences away from the teacher. *The Reading Teacher, 55,* 710–717.

Forman, E.A., & Cazden, C.B. (1994). Exploring Vygotskian perspectives in education: The cognitive value of peer interaction. In R.B. Ruddell, M.R. Ruddell, & H. Singer (Eds.), *Theoretical models and processes of reading* (4th ed., pp. 155–178). Newark, DE: International Reading Association.

Fountas, I.C., & Pinnell, G.S. (1996). *Guided reading: Good first teaching for all children.* Portsmouth, NH: Heinemann.

Fountas, I.C., & Pinnell, G.S. (1999). *Matching books to readers: Using leveled books in guided reading, K–3*. Portsmouth, NH: Heinemann.

Gambrell, L.B. (1996a). Creating classroom cultures that foster reading motivation. *The Reading Teacher, 50*, 14–25.

Gambrell, L.B. (1996b). What research reveals about discussion. In L.B. Gambrell & J.F. Almasi (Eds.), *Lively discussions! Fostering engaged reading* (pp. 25–38). Newark, DE: International Reading Association.

Gambrell, L.B. (2001). *It's not either/or but more: Balancing narrative and informational text to improve reading comprehension*. Paper presented at the 46th annual convention of the International Reading Association, New Orleans, LA.

Gambrell, L.B., Palmer, B.M., Codling, R.M., Mazzoni, S.A. (1996). Assessing motivation to read. *The Reading Teacher, 49*, 518–533.

Gilles, C. (1998). Collaborative literacy strategies: "We don't need a circle to have a group." In K.G. Short & K.M. Pierce (Eds.), *Talking about books: Literature discussion groups in K–8 classrooms* (pp. 55–68). Portsmouth, NH: Heinemann.

Goldman, S.R., & Rakestraw, J.A. (2000). Structural aspects of constructing meaning from text. In M.L. Kamil, P.B. Mosenthal, P.D. Pearson, & R. Barr (Eds.), *Handbook of reading research* (Vol. 3, pp. 311–335). Mahwah, NJ: Erlbaum.

Goodman, Y.M. (1997). Reading diagnosis—Qualitative or quantitiative? *The Reading Teacher, 50*, 534–538.

Goodman, Y.M., Watson, D.J., & Burke, C. (1987). *Reading miscue inventory*. Katonah, NY: Richard C. Owen.

Gunning, T.G. (1998). *Best books for beginning readers*. Boston: Allyn & Bacon.

Guthrie, J.T., & Alvermann, D. (Eds.). (1999). *Engagement in reading: Processes, practices, and policy implications*. New York: Teachers College Press.

Guthrie, J.T., & Wigfield, A. (1997). *Reading engagement: Motivating readers through integrated instruction*. Newark, DE: International Reading Association.

Hansen, J. (1998). *When learners evaluate*. Portsmouth, NH: Heinemann.

Harris, T.L., & Hodges, R.E. (Eds.). (1995). *The literacy dictionary: The vocabulary of reading and writing*. Newark, DE: International Reading Association.

Harvey, S. (1998). *Nonfiction matters: Reading, writing, and research in grades 3–8*. Portland, ME: Stenhouse.

Harvey, S., & Goudvis, A. (2000). *Strategies that work: Teaching comprehension to enhance understanding*. York, ME: Stenhouse.

Hiebert, E.H. (1994). Becoming literate through authentic tasks: Evidence and adaptations. In R.B. Ruddell, M.R. Ruddell, & H. Singer (Eds.), *Theoretical models and processes of reading* (4th ed., pp. 391–413). Newark, DE: International Reading Association.

Hiebert, E.H., Pearson, P.D., Taylor, B.M., Richardson, V., & Paris, S.G. (1998). *Every child a reader*. Ann Arbor, MI: Center for the Improvement of Early Reading Achievement.

Hilden, K., & Pressley, M. (2002, December). *Can teachers become comprehension strategies teachers given a small amount of training?* Paper presented at the 52nd annual meeting of the National Reading Conference, Miami, FL.

Hill, B.C., & Ruptic, C.A. (1994). *Practical aspects of authentic asessment: Putting the pieces together*. Norwood, MA: Christopher-Gordon.

Houghton Mifflin. (2001). *Leveled reading passages assessment kit*. Boston: Author.

Hoyt, L., & Ames, C. (1997). Letting the learner lead the way. *Primary Voices, 5*, 16–29.

Hunt, L.C. (1996/1997). The effect of self-selection, interest, and motivation upon independent, instructional, and frustration levels. *The Reading Teacher, 50*, 278–282.

International Reading Association. (1998). *Phonemic awareness and the teaching of reading: A position statement of the International Reading Association*. Newark, DE: Author.

International Reading Association. (1999). *Using multiple methods of beginning reading instruction: A position statement of the International Reading Association*. Newark, DE: Author.

International Reading Association. (2000). *Excellent reading teachers: A position statement of the International Reading Association*. Newark, DE: Author.

International Reading Association. (2002). *IRA Literacy Study Groups vocabulary module*. Newark, DE: Author.

International Reading Association & National Association for the Education of Young Children. (1998). Learning to read and write: Developmentally appropriate practices for young children. *The Reading Teacher, 52*, 193–216.

Johns, J.L., & Berglund, R.L. (2002). *Fluency: Questions, answers, and evidence-based strategies*. Dubuque, IA: Kendall-Hunt.

Johnson, D.D., & Pearson, P.D. (1984). *Teaching reading vocabulary* (2nd ed.). New York: Holt, Rinehart and Winston.

Johnston, P.H. (2000). *Running records: A self-tutoring guide*. Portland, ME: Stenhouse.

Keene, E., & Zimmermann, S. (1997). *Mosaic of thought: Teaching comprehension in a reader's workshop*. Portsmouth, NH: Heinemann.

Klein, A. (1995). Sparking a love for reading: Literature circles with intermediate students. In B.C. Hill, N.J. Johnson, & K.L. Noe (Eds.), *Literature circles and response*. Norwood, MA: Christopher-Gordon.

Leslie, L., & Caldwell, J.A. (2000). *Qualitative Reading Inventory–3*. New York: Longman.

Lewin, L. (1998). *Great performances: Creating classroom-based assessment tasks*. Alexandria, VA: Association for Supervision and Curriculum Development.

Lipson, M.Y. (2001). *A fresh look at comprehension*. Paper presented at the Reading/Language Arts Symposium, Chicago, IL.

Lipson, M.Y., & Wixson, K. (2003). *Assessment and instruction of reading and writing disability: An interactive approach* (3rd ed.). New York: Longman.

Macon, J.M. (1991). *Literature response*. A paper presented at the Annual Literacy Workshop, Anaheim, CA.

Maring, G., Furman, G., & Blum-Anderson, J. (1985). Five cooperative learning strategies for mainstreamed youngsters in content area classrooms. *The Reading Teacher, 39*, 310–313.

McGinley, W., & Denner, P. (1987). Story impressions: A prereading/prewriting activity. *Journal of Reading, 31*, 248–253.

McLaughlin, E.M. (1987). QuIP: A writing strategy to improve comprehension of expository structure. *The Reading Teacher, 40*, 650–654.

McLaughlin, M. (1995). *Performance assessment: A practical guide to implementation*. Boston: Houghton Mifflin.

McLaughlin, M. (2000a). Assessment for the 21st century: Performance, portfolios, and profiles. In M. McLaughlin & M.E. Vogt (Eds.), *Creativity and innovation in content area teaching* (pp. 301–327). Norwood, MA: Christopher-Gordon.

McLaughlin, M. (2000b). Inquiry: Key to critical and creative thinking in the content areas. In M. McLaughlin & M.E. Vogt (Eds.), *Creativity and innovation in content area teaching* (pp. 31–54). Norwood, MA: Christopher-Gordon.

McLaughlin, M. (2002). Dynamic assessment. In B. Guzzetti (Ed.), *Literacy in America: An encyclopedia*. Santa Barbara, CA: ABC.

McLaughlin, M., & Allen, M.B. (2002a). *Guided Comprehension: A teaching model for grades 3–8*. Newark, DE: International Reading Association.

McLaughlin, M., & Allen, M.B. (2002b). *Guided Comprehension in action: Lessons for grades 3–8*. Newark, DE: International Reading Association.

McLaughlin, M., Corbett, R., & Stevenson, C. (2000). Celebrating mathematics: Innovative, student-centered approaches for teaching and learning. In M. McLaughlin & M.E. Vogt (Eds.), *Creativity and innovation in content area teaching* (pp. 157–182). Norwood, MA: Christopher Gordon.

McLaughlin, M., & Vogt, M.E. (1996). *Portfolios in teacher education*. Newark, DE: International Reading Association.

McMillan, J.H. (1997). *Classroom assessment: Principles and practice for effective instruction*. Needham Heights, MA: Allyn & Bacon.

McTighe, J., & Lyman, F.T. (1988). Cueing thinking in the classroom: The promise of theory-embedded tools. *Educational Leadership, 45*(7), 18–24.

Minick, N. (1987). Implications of Vygotsky's theory for dynamic assessment. In C.S. Lidz (Ed.), *Dynamic assessment: An interactional approach for evaluating learning potential* (pp. 116–140). New York: Guilford.

Morrow, L.M. (1985). Retelling stories: A strategy for improving children's comprehension, concept of story, and oral language complexity. *The Elementary School Journal, 85*(5), 647–661.

Mowery, S. (1995). *Reading and writing comprehension strategies*. Harrisburg, PA: Instructional Support Teams Publications.

Nathan, R.G., & Stanovich, K.E. (1991). The causes and consequences of differences in reading fluency. *Theory Into Practice, 30*, 176–184.

National Commission on Teaching and America's Future. (1997). *Doing what matters most: Investing in quality teaching*. Available: http://www.tc.columbia.edu/-teachingcomm

National Institute of Child Health and Human Development (NICHD). (2000). *Report of the National Reading Panel. Teaching children to read: An evidence-based assessment of the scientific research literature on reading and its implications for reading instruction* (NIH Publication No. 00-4769). Washington, DC: U.S. Government Printing Office.

Neuman, S.B., & Dickinson, D.K. (Eds.). (2001). *Handbook of early literacy research*. New York: Guilford.

Newmann, F.M., & Wehlage, G.G. (1993). Five standards for authentic instruction. *Educational Leadership, 50*, 8–12.

Noe, K.L.S., & Johnson, N.J. (1999). *Getting started with literature circles*. Norwood, MA: Christopher-Gordon.

Page, S. (2001). *Tips and strategies for independent routines*. Muncie, IN: Page Consulting.

Palincsar, A.S., & Brown, A.L. (1984). Reciprocal teaching of comprehension-fostering and monitoring activities. *Cognition and Instruction, 1*, 117–175.

Palincsar, A.S., & Brown, A.L. (1986). Interactive teaching to promote independent learning from text. *The Reading Teacher, 39*, 771–777.

Partnership for Educational Excellence Network. (2001). *Early childhood learning continuum indicators*. Harrisburg, PA: Pennsylvania Department of Education. Available: http://www.pde.state.pa.us/nclb/lib/nclb/earlychildhood continuum.pdf

Partnership for Reading. (2001). *Put reading first: The research building blocks for teaching children to read*. Jessup, MD: National Institute for Literacy.

Pearson, P.D. (2001a). *Comprehension strategy instruction: An idea whose time has come again*. Paper presented at the annual meeting of the Colorado Council of the International Reading Association, Denver, CO.

Pearson, P.D. (2001b, December). *What we have learned in 30 years*. Paper presented at the 51st annual meeting of the National Reading Conference, San Antonio, TX.

Peterson, R., & Eeds, M. (1990). *Grand conversations: Literature groups in action*. New York: Scholastic.

Pinciotti, P. (2001). *Book arts: The creation of beautiful books*. East Stroudsburg, PA: East Stroudsburg University of Pennsylvania.

Pressley, M. (2000). What should comprehension instruction be the instruction of? In M.L. Kamil, P.B. Mosenthal, P.D. Pearson, & R. Barr (Eds.), *Handbook of reading research* (Vol. 3, pp. 545–561). Mahwah, NJ: Erlbaum.

Pressley, M. (2001, December). *Comprehension strategies instruction: A turn of the century status report*. Paper presented at the 51st annual meeting of the National Reading Conference, San Antonio, TX.

Raphael, T. (1986). Teaching children Question-Answer Relationships, revisited. *The Reading Teacher, 39*, 516–522.

Rasinski, T. (1999a). Making and writing words. *Reading Online*. Available: http://www.readingonline.org/articles/words/rasinski.index.html.

Rasinski, T. (1999b). Making and writing words using letter patterns. *Reading Online*. Available: http://www.reading online.org/articles/words/rasinski_index.html

Readence, J.E., Bean, T.W., & Baldwin, R. (2000). *Content area reading: An integrated approach* (7th ed.). Dubuque, IA: Kendall/Hunt.

Rhodes, L.K., Shanklin, N.L., & Valencia, S.W. (1990). Miscue analysis in the classroom. *The Reading Teacher, 44*, 252–254.

Richards, M. (2000). Be a good detective: Solve the case of oral reading fluency. *The Reading Teacher, 53*, 534–539.

Rigby. (2001). *PM benchmark introduction kit*. Crystal Lake, IL: Author.

Roehler, L.R., & Duffy, G.G. (1984). Direct explanation of comprehension processes. In G.G. Duffy, L.R. Roehler, & J. Mason (Eds.), *Comprehension instruction: Perspectives and suggestions* (pp. 265–280). New York: Longman.

Roehler, L.R., & Duffy, G.G. (1991). Teachers' instructional actions. In R. Barr, M.L. Kamil, P.B. Mosenthal, & P.D. Pearson (Eds.), *Handbook of reading research* (Vol. 2, pp. 861–883). White Plains, NY: Longman.

Romano, S. (2002). *Reading = Success: Literacy activities that promote home-school connections* [Emergent Literacy Course Syllabus]. East Stroudsburg University of Pennsylvania.

Rosenblatt, L.M. (1978). *The reader, the text, and the poem: The transactional theory of the literary work*. Carbondale, IL: Southern Illinois University Press.

Rosenblatt, L.M. (1980). What facts does this poem teach you? *Language Arts, 57*(4), 386–394.

Rosenblatt, L.M. (2002, December). *A pragmatist theoretician looks at research: Implications and questions calling for answers*. Paper presented at the 52nd annual meeting of the National Reading Conference, Miami, FL.

Ruddell, R.B. (1995). Those influential reading teachers: Meaning negotiators and motivation builders. *The Reading Teacher, 48*, 454–463.

Rule, A.C. (2001). Alphabetizing with environmental print. *The Reading Teacher, 54*, 558–562.

Samuels, S.J. (1979). The method of repeated readings. *The Reading Teacher, 32*, 403–408.

Samuels, S.J. (2002). Reading fluency: Its development and assessment. In A.E. Farstrup & S.J. Samuels (Eds.), *What research has to say about reading instruction* (3rd ed., pp.166–183). Newark, DE: International Reading Association.

Samway, K.D., & Wang, G. (1996). *Literature study circles in a multicultural classroom*. York, ME: Stenhouse.

Schon, D. (1987). *Educating the reflective practitioner*. San Francisco: Jossey-Bass.

Schwartz, R., & Raphael, T. (1985). Concept of definition: A key to improving students' vocabulary. *The Reading Teacher, 39*, 198–205.

Short, K.G., & Burke, C. (1996). Examining our beliefs and practices through inquiry. *Language Arts, 73*, 97–103.

Short, K.G., Harste, J.C., & Burke, C. (1996). *Creating classrooms for authors and inquirers.* Portsmouth, NH: Heinemann.

Sippola, A.E. (1995). K-W-L-S. *The Reading Teacher, 48,* 542–543.

Snow, C.E., Burns, M.S., & Griffin, P.G. (Eds.). (1998). *Preventing reading difficulties in young children.* Washington, DC: National Academy Press.

Spielman, J. (2001). The family photography project: "We will just read what the pictures tell us." *The Reading Teacher, 54,* 762–770.

Stahl, S.A. (1992). Saying the "p" word: Nine guidelines for exemplary phonics instruction. *The Reading Teacher, 45,* 618–625.

Stahl, S.A., Duffy-Hester, A.M., & Stahl, K.A.D. (1998). Theory and research in practice: Everything you wanted to know about phonics (but were afraid to ask). *Reading Research Quarterly, 33,* 338–355.

Stahl, S.A., & Kuhn, M.R. (2002, December). *Developing fluency in classrooms.* Paper presented at the 52nd annual meeting of the National Reading Conference, Miami, FL.

Stahl, S.A., Heubach, K., & Cramond, B. (1997). *Fluency-oriented reading instruction* (Reading Research Report No. 97). Athens, GA: National Reading Research Center.

Stauffer, R. (1975). *Directing the reading-thinking process.* New York: Harper & Row.

Szymusiak, K., & Sibberson, F. (2001). Beyond leveled books. Portland, ME: Stenhouse.

Tierney, R.J. (1998). Literacy assessment reform: Shifting beliefs, principled possibilities and emerging practices. *The Reading Teacher, 51,* 374–390.

Tierney, R.J. (1990). Redefining reading comprehension. *Educational Leadership, 47*(6), 37–42.

Tierney, R.J., & Pearson, P.D. (1994). A revisionist perspective on "learning to learn from text: A framework for improving classroom practice." In R.B. Ruddell, M.R. Ruddell, & H. Singer (Eds.), *Theoretical models and processes of reading* (4th ed., pp. 514–519). Newark, DE: International Reading Association.

Tompkins, G.E. (2001). *Literacy for the 21st century: A balanced approach* (2nd ed.). Upper Saddle River, NJ: Merrill.

Towell, J. (1997/1998). Fun with vocabulary. *The Reading Teacher, 51,* 356–360.

Vacca, R.T., & Vacca, J.A. (2002). *Content area reading: Literacy and learning across the curriculum* (7th ed.). New York: Longman.

Vaughn, J., & Estes, T. (1986). *Reading and reasoning beyond the primary grades.* Boston: Allyn & Bacon.

Vygotsky, L. (1978). *Mind in society: The development of higher psychological processes* (M. Cole, V. John-Steiner, S. Scribner, & E. Souberman, Eds. & Trans.). Cambridge, MA: Harvard University Press. (Original work published 1934)

Waldo, B. (1991). Story pyramid. In J.M. Macon, D. Bewell, & M.E. Vogt (Eds.), *Responses to literature: Grades K–8* (pp. 23–24). Newark: DE: International Reading Association.

Weaver, B.M. (2000). *Leveling books K–6: Matching readers to text.* Newark, DE: International Reading Association.

Wiggins, G., & McTighe, J. (1998). *Understanding by design.* Alexandria, VA: Association for Supervision and Curriculum Development.

Wood, K. (1984). Probable passages: A writing strategy. *The Reading Teacher, 37,* 496–499.

Yopp, H.K. (1992). Developing phonemic awareness in young children. *The Reading Teacher, 45,* 696–703.

Yopp, H.K. (1995). Read-aloud books for developing phonemic awareness. *The Reading Teacher, 48,* 538–542.

Yopp, H.K., & Yopp, R.H. (2000). Supporting phonemic awareness development in the classroom. *The Reading Teacher, 54,* 130–143.

Zutell, J., & Rasinski, T. (1991). Training teachers to attend to their students' oral reading fluency. *Theory Into Practice, 30,* 211–217.

Children's Literature Cited

Avi. (2002). *Things that sometimes happen: Very short stories for little listeners.* New York: Atheneum.

Barner, B. (2001). *Dinosaur bones.* San Francisco: Chronicle Books.

Base, G. (1996). *Animalia.* New York: Puffin.

Benton, M. (2000). *The encyclopedia of awesome dinosaurs.* Brookfield, CT: Copper Beech Books.

Berger, M., & Berger, G. (1998). *Did dinosaurs live in your backyard?* New York: Scholastic.

Berger, M., & Berger, G. (2000). *Do penguins get frostbite? Questions and answers about polar animals.* New York: Scholastic.

Brown, M. (1986). *Arthur's nose.* Boston: Little, Brown.

Brown, M. (1990). *Arthur's baby*. Boston: Little, Brown.

Brown, M. (1990). *Arthur's pet business*. Boston: Little Brown.

Brown, M. (1993). *Arthur's family vacation*. Boston: Little, Brown.

Brown, M. (1994). *Arthur's first sleepover*. New York: Little Brown.

Brown, M. (1995). *Arthur goes to school*. New York: Random House.

Brown, M. (1996). *Arthur writes a story*. New York: Little, Brown.

Brown, M. (1997). *Arthur's computer disaster*. New York: Little, Brown.

Brown, M. (2000). *Arthur's lost puppy*. New York: Random House.

Brown, M.W. (1990). *The important book*. New York: Harper Trophy.

Cannon, J. (1993). *Stellaluna*. New York: Scholastic.

Carle, E. (1988). *Do you want to be my friend?* New York: Putnam.

Carle, E. (1989). *Eric Carle's animals, animals*. New York: Philomel.

Carle, E. (1991). *Pancakes, pancakes!* New York: Simon & Schuster.

Carle, E. (1991). *Papa, please get the moon for me*. New York: Simon & Schuster.

Carle, E. (1994). *The very hungry caterpillar*. New York: Philomel.

Carle, E. (1995). *My apron: A story from my childhood*. New York: Putnam.

Carle, E. (1997). *Flora and Tiger: 19 very short stories from my life*. New York: Philomel.

Carle, E. (1997). *The secret birthday message*. New York: HarperCollins.

Carle, E. (1997). *The very quiet cricket*. New York: Penguin.

Carle, E. (1998). *The mixed-up chameleon*. New York: HarperCollins.

Carle, E. (1998). *Walter the baker*. New York: Simon & Schuster.

Carle, E. (1999). *The grouchy ladybug*. New York: HarperCollins.

Carle, E. (1999). *The very lonely firefly*. New York: Philomel.

Carle, E. (2000). *Dream snow*. New York: Philomel.

Carle, E. (2002). *Does a kangaroo have a mother, too?* New York: HarperCollins.

Carle, E. (2002). *"Slowly, slowly, slowly," said the sloth*. New York: Penguin Putnam.

Chambers, C. (2001). *Disasters in nature: Volcanoes*. Chicago: Heinemann Library.

Charlip, R. (1993). *Fortunately*. New York: Aladdin.

Cronin, D. (2000). *Click, clack, moo: Cows that type*. New York: Simon & Schuster.

Day, A. (1995). *Carl goes to daycare*. New York: Farrar Straus & Giroux.

Davis, G.W. (1997). *Habitats: Coral reef*. New York: Children's Press.

Dowswell, P., Malam, J., Mason, P., & Parker, S. (2002). *The ultimate book of dinosaurs: Everything you always wanted to know about dinosaurs—but were too terrified to ask*. London: Parragon.

Farris, C.K. (2003). *My brother Martin: A sister remembers growing up with the Rev. Dr. Martin Luther King Jr.* New York: Simon & Schuster.

Galdone, P. (1979). *The little red hen*. Boston: Houghton Mifflin.

Gibbons, G. (1987). *Dinosaurs*. New York: Scholastic.

Gibbons, G. (1998). *Sea turtles*. New York: Holiday House.

Gibbons, G. (2000). *Bats*. New York: Holiday House.

Harris, J. (1999). *The three little dinosaurs*. Gretna, LA: Pelican.

Henkes, K. (1991). *Chrysanthemum*. NewYork: Greenwillow.

Henkes, K. (1995). *Julius: The baby of the world*. New York: Mulberry.

Lester, H. (1996). *Author: A true story*. Boston: Houghton Mifflin.

Levitt, P. (1990). *The weighty word book*. Boulder, CO: Manuscripts Ltd.

Martin, B. Jr. (1967). *Brown bear, brown bear, what do you see?* New York: Henry Holt.

Martin, B. Jr. (1997). *Polar bear, polar bear, what do you hear?* New York: Henry Holt.

McGough, K. (2001). *Fossils*. Washington, DC: National Geographic Society.

McVeigh, L. (2003). *Miss Hen's feast*. Boston: Houghton Mifflin.

Polacco, P. (1978). *Meteor!* New York: Putnam.

Polacco, P. (1998). *Thank you, Mr. Falker*. New York: Philomel.

Prelutsky, J. (1986). *Read-aloud rhymes for the very young*. New York: Knopf.

Prelutsky, J. (1992). *Tyrannosaurus was a beast: Dinosaur poems*. New York: William Morrow.

Rey, H.A. (1998). *Curious George makes pancakes*. Boston: Houghton Mifflin.

Rosen, M. (1997). *We're going on a bear hunt*. New York: Little Simon.

Scieszka, J. (1996). *The true story of the 3 little pigs!* New York: Puffin.

Shaw, N.E. (1986). *Sheep in a Jeep*. Boston: Houghton Mifflin.

Shaw, N.E. (1991). *Sheep in a shop*. Boston: Houghton Mifflin.

Shaw, N.E. (1995). *Sheep out to eat*. Boston: Houghton Mifflin.

Shaw, N.E. (1997). *Sheep trick or treat*. Boston: Houghton Mifflin.

Simon, S. (1993). *Wolves*. New York: Scholastic.

Stevens, J., & Crummel, S.S. (1999). *Cook-a-doodle-doo!* New York: Harcourt Brace.

Sturges, P. (1999). *The little red hen makes a pizza*. New York: Dutton.

Vail, R. (2001). *Mama Rex & T: Homework trouble*. New York: Scholastic.

Viorst, J. (1981). *If I were in charge of the world and other worries*. New York: Atheneum.

Wiesner, D. (1991). *Tuesday*. New York: Clarion.

Wiesner, D. (1999). *Sector 7*. New York: Clarion.

Wiesner, D. (2001). *The three pigs*. New York: Clarion.

Yolen, J. (1990). *Dinosaur dances*. New York: Putnam.

Zoehfeld, K.W. (2001). *Terrible tyrannosaurs*. New York: Harper Trophy.

INDEX

Note: Page numbers followed by *f* indicate figures.

E–F

G–H

T

V

W

Y–Z